THE STORY OF ILLINOIS

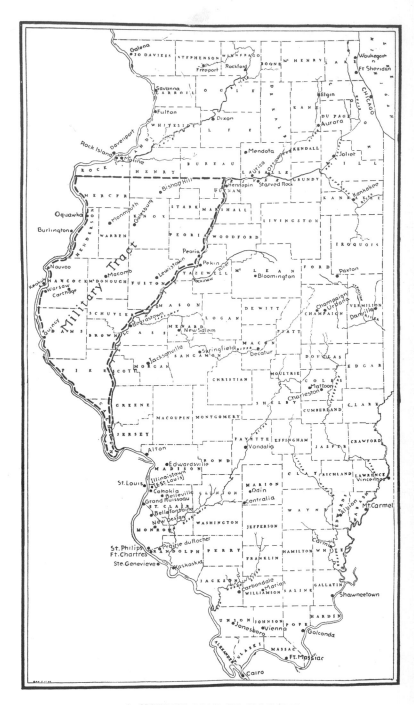

A SKETCH MAP OF ILLINOIS

THEODORE CALVIN PEASE

THE STORY OF
ILLINOIS

THIRD EDITION
REVISED BY
MARGUERITE JENISON PEASE

THE UNIVERSITY OF CHICAGO PRESS
CHICAGO AND LONDON

Library of Congress Catalog Card Number: 65-17299

THE UNIVERSITY OF CHICAGO PRESS, CHICAGO & LONDON
The University of Toronto Press, Toronto 5, Canada

*Copyright 1925 by A. C. McClurg and Co. Copyright
1949, 1965 by The University of Chicago. All rights
reserved. Published 1925. Second Edition 1949. Third
Edition 1965. Composed and printed by* THE UNI-
VERSITY OF CHICAGO PRESS, *Chicago, Illinois, U.S.A.*

The second edition of *The Story of Illinois* was published in 1949 as the Fiftieth Anniversary Publication
of the Illinois State Historical Society

Preface to the 1949 Edition

WHEN plans were being made to observe the golden anniversary of the founding of the Illinois State Historical Society with some special publications, Theodore Calvin Pease, for many years a director of the Society, agreed to revise *The Story of Illinois* for a new edition and volunteered terms of publication which amounted to a material contribution to the occasion. At the time of his death on August 11, 1948, he had revised the text, making substantial additions particularly in the field of his researches in British and French diplomacy as related to the Illinois Country, and had made a draft of the final chapter. The preparation of the manuscript was completed by his wife, Marguerite Jenison Pease, who had worked with him on the revision.

Preface to the 1925 Edition

THIS volume is an attempt to present a short, readable history of the state of Illinois, embodying the results of the latest research. Naturally, it is based to a considerable extent on the five-volume *Centennial History of Illinois*, but for most of the period covered by the volume the body of source material has been carefully examined. Still, my indebtedness to the other authors of the *Centennial History*, especially to Professor Clarence W. Alvord, will be apparent to anyone who is acquainted with their work. I have also to express my gratitude to Dr. Otto L. Schmidt for encouragement and kindly criticism.

THEODORE CALVIN PEASE

v

Introduction

THE Illinois of the present may be understood only as the product of the past. On the basis of a physical environment made by past geological ages, the state has arisen, an edifice of political, industrial, and social organization, to be comprehended only through a study of the plans and methods by which the successive generations have built it tier by tier. In York Cathedral in England, beneath the present fabric illustrating the successive Gothic styles of four centuries, are shown the crypt of an earlier Norman church and the foundations of a still earlier Saxon one. Similarly, the story of Illinois necessarily includes as well the failure of both France and England to solve the problem of empire in the heart of the Mississippi Valley as the final success in the task of the United States.

Nor can our study be confined too closely within the geographical limits of present-day Illinois. State boundaries are at best but artificial lines drawn at a late day. Frenchman and Englishman, pursuing their imperial ambitions in the Great Valley, did not parcel out their visions according to the limits of our present states. When between 1783 and 1815 England and the United States struggled for the possession of the Northwest, the fate of Illinois was decided by events a thousand miles distant from her borders. The westward movement of population that created the present commonwealth, once the United States had won the prize, cannot be isolated for study in a single state. In the later period, if we ignore the ways in which citizens of Illinois thought and acted like people elsewhere in the United States and record only the state's peculiarities, our narrative will be distorted and misleading. If we confine ourselves to a description of the workings of the state government, our story will be mechanically dull. A true understanding of the history of Illinois must be as broad as the imperial visions of the men who first foresaw the destiny of her prairies and as broad as the pioneer flood that in the first half of the nineteenth century swept over the whole West.

Not that Illinois by virtue of her geographical character and the idiosyncrasies of the individuals and groups that sought homes in her did not speedily develop a strongly marked character and a part all her own to play in the Union. Geographically located at the heart of the great interior river system of the continent, spanning the divide between the St. Lawrence and the Mississippi system at the point where men can pass it most easily, lying athwart the easiest paths which man may travel from east to west, she and her great market at Chicago stand at the crossroads of world trade such as those which in earlier ages made Vienna, Constantinople, and Damascus. Shaped like a rivet interlocked at the head with the commonwealths of the North, her point drives deep into the states of the upper South. In earlier days Tennessean and New Yorker, Virginian and New Englander, Kentuckian and Pennsylvanian, here stood face to face and learned by political combat each to know and to respect the other. In later days immigrants of all the races of Europe have met in her borders and have been set to learn the hard lessons of toleration and mutual respect. Amid tumult, disorder, and violence, Illinois has pressed on her way in the performance of her political mission in the United States; physically and intellectually in the days of the Civil War and in the days of the first and second World War alike, a bond of union among sections and races.

The geological story of the making of Illinois of today is not for a historian to tell in detail. Sometimes covered with tropical forest, sometimes the bed of a great inland sea, sometimes partly overlain with glacial icecaps, until recently the trough by which the Great Lakes flowed to the Mississippi, Illinois at length became what she was when the white man first looked on her landscape—a land in places level as the bed of a prehistoric lake, elsewhere gently rolling or even hilly, trenched from northeast to southwest by the valley of the Illinois River, crossed in the extreme south by the Ozark Hills but with only a difference of a few hundred feet elevation between her highest and lowest points. Over her surface in places stretched the prairies, their fertile soils throwing up grass as high as a horseman's waist, bordered with woods along the watercourses; in other places were the hills, more or less fertile, covered by hardwood forest or scrub oak. Beneath her surface lay deposits of lead and other nonprecious metals and vast beds of bituminous coal. On the northeast, west, south, and east she touched navigable waters, and across her flowed many rivers—the Kaskaskia, the Illinois, the Sangamon, the Embarrass, the Rock, and the Des Plaines— that in their day served as highways of trade. These are the facts of the physical Illinois that especially concern the student of her history.

Of the races that lived in Illinois before the white man came, the archeologists have produced a wealth of knowledge in the past fifty years. From their researches we learn that, as soon as the glacial ice melted along the Mississippi bluffs, hunters appeared to spear the mastodon and other game. Later, they turned to farming and communal living, and from the artifacts of camp-sites, villages, and temples have been determined the existence of a succession of cultures more than ten thousand years before the white man arrived to begin a written record.

We need not linger over the Indian inhabitants found by the white man in the Illinois country nor consider them save as the hapless tools and victims of the superior races that marked the region for their own. Of the Indians in general it may be said that they had attained a primitive culture that included agriculture, weaving, the making of pottery, and the fashioning of weapons, utensils, clothing, and ornaments from materials at hand.

So soon after the coming of the whites were the Indian and his political and social life debased that it is not easy to describe him accurately as he was at that moment. In his villages were chiefs whose prestige came from their prowess in arms, medicine men whose influence flowed from their reputed control of the supernatural, and civil chiefs whose authority arose from their ability or descent. In the villages the chiefs exercised little real control over the warriors, who lawlessly broke many a solemnly made treaty. Custom was law and was invoked by individuals, penalties being enforced by the injured man or his kindred with the support of public opinion. Parents exercised little control over their children. After the white man had come, at least, immorality, polygamy, and divorce were frequent. Few children were born, and only the hardiest survived the starvation of the hard winter. The Indian population at best was but stationary in a land of plenty where pioneers of the white race were prolific. And by war, by the white men's disease, and, above all, by the white men's ardent spirits, the God of the white men day by day removed their red opponents from before their faces.

Much has been written about the belief of the Indians in a Great Spirit and in a monotheistic religion; but the error has doubtless arisen from the confusion inevitable when one attempts to seek abstract thoughts in a language that has almost no words for them. The Indian appears to have lived in a spiritual anarchy comparable to the political anarchy of his villages; the tree, the rock, the waterfall, the animal he hunted, even the weapon with which he stalked it, had each its manito or presiding spirit to be appeased by rites and offerings. The notion of one overruling Great Spirit, or Manito, he perhaps borrowed at an early date from the Roman Catholic missionary who threaded the forest to bring him the sacraments of the church for salvation, or from the gentle Moravian who sought to teach him the

Christian practice of humility, gentleness, and nonresistance.

The enumeration of the Indian tribes of the Illinois is not a matter of importance; those tribes generation by generation changed their habitat. Father Marquette found on the Mississippi and Illinois rivers the confederated tribes of the Cahokia, Tamaroa, Michigamea, Kaskaskia, Peoria, and others, the group that called themselves the "Illinois," or *the men*. Later explorers found the Sauk and the Foxes in northwestern Illinois, the Potawatomi around the foot of Lake Michigan, the Kickapoo in the central prairies, the Shawnee in the southeast. War and famine, the pressure of the dreaded Iroquois, and the influence of French commanders anxious to group the Indians for military use made incessant changes in the hunting grounds of the tribes. The reader will forgive the omission of details that would only weary him.

Table of Contents

List of Illustrations

CHAPTER I

The French Regime

THE coming of white men to the Northwest and to Illinois turns on a succession of motives: the search for a route to the western sea, the fur trade, the Christianization of the Indians, the founding of commercial and military empires, the search for homes. All of these in their order influenced the French and English as in the seventeenth and eighteenth centuries they approached the Illinois country.

The appearance of the first Frenchman in the West is but a phase of the age-long search for trade routes from Europe to the riches of the Far East. That trade was old at the beginning of the Christian Era, when bales of Chinese silks intended to be worn by Roman ladies were lost in the great deserts of Central Asia, to be preserved in the sands and recovered in our own day. In the fifteenth century it was the aspiration of the European nations that fronted the Atlantic to find a route for that trade by sea which perhaps sent Columbus on the famous voyage to the west, and certainly sent Vasco da Gama around the Cape of Good Hope.

Early in the sixteenth century men finally recognized the fact that to the south the New World barred the way to Cathay; and after 1540 the Spaniards knew well enough the span of the North American continent. But the search for a Northwest Passage, a way to China through the Arctic regions, was to drive men to repeated expeditions doomed to failure until Roald Amundsen in 1905 crossed from east to west. In our own day our anxious attention to the polar regions over which a third world war may be fought has led to an achievement only imagined by Jules Verne—a submarine crossing the North Pole under a polar icecap. In the early seventeenth century it was the dream of a sea-to-sea route which set Captain John Smith to exploring the upper reaches of the Virginia rivers for a way to China. In 1634 it sent Jean Nicolet, dispatched by Champlain from the struggling little French colony on the rock of Quebec, to the shores of Green Bay dressed in "a grand robe of China damask, all strewn with flowers and birds of many colors"—perhaps that he might make with due éclat his entry into the capital of the Great Khan.[1]

"If he had voyaged three days more on a great river which issues from this lake, he would have reached the sea."[2] Such was Nicolet's later report of his achievement, based on information obtained in the partially understood language of the savages among whom he was living. Its ambiguity is provoking. The sea may be the "Big Water" of the Indians, the Mississippi; Nicolet may have failed to understand his hosts as saying that three days off was a stream that would lead to it. But, at all events, the phrase shows how present in men's thoughts was the western sea.

Nicolet's discoveries were not followed up for twenty years. The scourge of the Iroquois fell heavily upon the struggling colony of New France. Their confederation, in which the fraternal clans of the same totem throughout the five tribes linked the whole in close alliance, was famous for prowess and savagery in war. The Jesuits, strong in unquestioning military obedience to superiors, in the education, the devotion, and the intelligence of their fathers, had aspired to do in New France what they had done in Paraguay: to gather round Jesuit priests villages of Indians to be instructed in the faith and to be made adept and obedient pupils of their spiritual guides alike in the concerns of war and peace. Their work had begun among the Hurons, when in 1648 and 1649 the Iroquois fell upon their villages and amid

1. Thwaites, *Jesuit Relations*, XXIII, 279.   2. *Ibid.*, XVIII, 236.

their slaughtered converts Jesuit fathers gained the crown of martyrdom. The remnant of the Hurons fled from the eastern shore of their lake to the forests beyond Superior, and here the Jesuits were to follow them. First at La Pointe on Lake Superior and then at Green Bay, Jesuit missionaries established themselves in the West.

Even before the Jesuit the fur trader had penetrated to the West. In the northern parts of America the white pioneers sought in vain for the pearls and precious metals that enriched the Spaniards to the south; but early in the seventeenth century they had discovered a source of wealth in the fur-bearing animals. The trade in furs, though small if judged by present-day standards, speedily became one of the important branches of international trade. Amsterdam became a great fur market, supplying western Europe and distant Russia. Most important in the trade was the pelt of the beaver or castor, as the French called him. Both his names came to be English cant synonyms for hat, and the manufacture developed in both France and England. In America the demands of the trade forced the Indians to become the white man's hunters, abandoning the practice of their primitive domestic arts in order to purchase with furs the white man's blankets, textiles, kettles, guns, ornaments, and, above all, his "fire water," whether Dutch gin, English rum, French brandy, or American whiskey. At various times after 1654 Groseilliers and his kinsman, Radisson, had journeyed far into the Northwest, even if not to the Mississippi River, in search of furs. Their presence antedated even that of the Jesuit.

Jesuit and fur trader found each his place in the new imperialism developing in France with the accession to power in 1661 of Louis XIV. Colbert, Louis' great minister of finance, had imbibed the mercantilist idea of the value of colonies in making the mother-country strong and self-sufficing, and his policy looked to strengthening the colony of Canada and to extending its bounds and trade. The exponents of his policy in Canada were the intendant, Jean Talon, and after 1672 the gov-

ernor, Louis de Buade, Comte de Frontenac. Troops were sent
to Canada in sufficient force to inspire the Iroquois with respect
and produce a peace in 1667. In a great military ceremony at
Sault Ste Marie in 1671, St. Lusson took possession of the West
in the name of Louis XIV. Where Jesuit and trader had come
before by sufferance of the Indian, the imperialist followed,
secure in armed might.

In extension of this policy, Louis Joliet, already explorer of
Lake Erie, was sent in 1673, accompanied by the Jesuit Father
Jacques Marquette, to search out the Mississippi River. Reaching it by the Fox-Wisconsin portage, they floated down as far
as the Arkansas country. Having determined that the river must
flow into the Gulf of Mexico, and fearing capture by the
Spaniards if they kept on, they turned back. They passed up the
Illinois on their return, where Joliet, wiser than many a man of
later day, noted the richness of the prairie soil and the fact that
no trees barred access to it; they passed the portage to the
Chicago River, where Joliet again anticipated later ages by
pointing out the possibility and advantage of a canal.[3]

The life of Father Marquette as it emerges from contemporary records is almost the epic of Catholic Christianity in
America. The moving impulse of his existence was his devotion
to the Virgin and a desire to bring the knowledge of her inter-
cession to men who lived in darkness. For this he had become a
missionary, for this he had embarked on the voyage, and for this
he promised the confederation of the Illinois that he would
come back and establish a mission among them. Returning in the
late autumn of 1674 in spite of the fact that death had already
marked him, he spent the winter in a hut near the Chicago portage, racked by illness, ministered to by his two companions, by
neighboring fur traders, and by the Indians. In the spring, rally-

3. Joliet's journal was lost when his canoe was overset near Montreal.
Our main source for the expeditions, long known as the journal of Father
Marquette, is now considered by scholars to have been the compilation
by Father Claude Dablon, superior of all the Canadian missions, from
records of Marquette, Joliet, and others.

STATUE OF MARQUETTE BY GAETANO TRENTANOVE
IN THE HALL OF FAME, WASHINGTON, D.C.

THE PIASA BIRD, PAINTED BY HENRY LEWIS IN 1846

The pictograph of the Piasa Bird which appeared on the Mississippi River bluffs above Alton, Illinois, was first seen by Maring his last strength, he proceeded down the Illinois as far as the villages of his friends to preach the gospel to them and found his mission.

Above all he preached to them Jesus Christ on the very eve (of that great day) that He died upon the cross for them as well as for all the rest of mankind; then he said holy mass. Three days later on Easter Sunday things being prepared in the same manner as on the Thursday, he celebrated the holy mysteries for the second time. And by these two sacrifices—the first ever offered thus to God, he took possession of that land in the name of Jesus Christ, and gave to that mission the name of the Immaculate Conception of the Blessed Virgin.[4]

His mission thus founded, he regarded his life's work as accomplished. He set out on his return to the mission at Mackinac, growing weaker day by day until finally at the Marquette River he died the death of a saint, "dying as the apostle of the Indians in a wretched cabin on the shore of lake Illinois, forsaken by all the world."[5]

As lonely in his life as was Marquette in his death, but differing from him in all else, was his successor in the story of Illinois, the imperialist Robert Cavelier, Sieur de la Salle. Born in 1643, he had been in youth the pupil of the Jesuits; but La Salle's was not the metal to be tempered in that forge, and to the end he hated his old masters. He had come to New France in 1666, obtaining near Montreal a grant of land, soon called, probably in derision of him because he was always dreaming of a route to the Far East, "La Chine"—China. In 1674 with the favor of Governor Frontenac he had acquired Fort Frontenac on Lake Ontario and an opportunity of growing rich from the fur trade. But the paradox of fate had made this man who could not keep accounts a dreamer of vast empires based on trade in the western wilderness, had destined a reserved, haughty man capable of winning the loyalty only of the finest characters among his followers to a great task of exploration and colonization. A will of

4. See Thwaites, *op. cit.*, LIX, 188, 190.
5. *Ibid.*, p. 206.

tempered steel drove him on at his task in spite of foreclosures by his creditors, the sinking of his ships, repeated mutinies and desertions, and, above all, that brute, inert, cruel opponent—the American wilderness, terrible in its forests and morasses, its treacherous lakes and rivers, and its winter snows. Counting three failures for every success, by the day in 1687 when he fell by the hands of mutinous followers, he had done his work: he had laid in the Illinois the foundations of a French colony.

Briefly stated, his project was that of establishing posts to the south of the Great Lakes to link the fur trade of the region to Fort Frontenac and to hold the Mississippi River as a second great trade outlet from the interior to the ocean. Late in 1679 by way of Lake Michigan and the St. Joseph River, where he built a fort, he found his way to the Illinois country. In January, 1680, he built Fort Crèvecoeur at the Lake of Peoria among the Illinois tribes. The loss of his vessel, the "Griffon," on the Great Lakes, and the attachment of his property in Canada by his creditors compelled him to return, leaving in command his trusted lieutenant, Henri de Tonty. In La Salle's absence happened one of the great tragedies of primitive Indian history.

The Iroquois were sufficiently advanced in the arts of trade to recognize the advantage of acting as middlemen in the fur trade between the western Indians and the Dutch and the English at Albany. The likelihood of that trade being diverted elsewhere by La Salle they did not like; and in the summer of 1680 their war parties appeared before the great Illinois village on the river of that name, probably where the little hamlet of Utica stands today. Tonty, already deserted by most of La Salle's followers, used every means that his dauntless spirit could devise to overawe the Iroquois by fear of the French and save the Illinois from their tomahawks. The fears of the Iroquois, however, served only to save the lives of Tonty and his few men. The Iroquois dogged the Illinois on their flight down the river and, when the Tamaroa did not follow the other tribes across the

Mississippi, drove off their warriors and slew their women and children by torture. Once more an essential part of La Salle's great edifice had collapsed; but again he took up the task of replacing it.

In the winter of 1681–82 he returned to the Illinois with new resources and early in the spring descended the Mississippi to its mouth, on April 9, 1682, formally taking possession of the river and all the territory it drained in the name of Louis XIV. Returning to the Illinois River, he began a new fort at Starved Rock (Crèvecoeur had been burned by the mutineers of 1680), calling it Fort St. Louis. Around it he gathered the Indian tribes for mutual protection until he had nearly four thousand warriors, too large a force for any Iroquois war party to overcome. In March, 1684, under Tonty, the fort beat off an Iroquois attack.

Once more La Salle's project was threatened with destruction, this time at the hands of the new governor of Canada, La Barre. Desirous of undoing the work of his predecessors, Frontenac and La Salle, La Barre took over La Salle's posts, including Fort St. Louis. In a vain search for justice in Canada, La Salle left the Illinois forever. Passing on to France, he secured the favor of Louis XIV, obtaining not merely the return of his posts but also royal aid in the establishment of a colony at the mouth of the Mississippi. His expedition missed the mouth of the river and was landed four hundred miles to the west, at Matagorda Bay. Setting out in 1687 overland to the Illinois in a desperate attempt to reach Tonty and bring reinforcements for his colony, he was murdered by mutinous followers. Some of his men made their way to the Illinois, and the Indians forestalled the Spaniards in accounting for the rest of his colony.

But if La Salle was gone, Tonty and his colony in Illinois were left. On hearing of La Salle's death a year after it occurred, he descended the Mississippi in a vain attempt to rescue the Texas colony. In 1690 he with La Forest, another of La Salle's followers, was granted all La Salle's rights in the Illinois. Fort St.

Louis was moved to the neighborhood of Lake Peoria once more, and subsidiary posts appeared at Maramec on the Fox River and at Chicago.

The Jesuit influence now turned the scale against the imperialists. La Salle had always hated the Jesuits, believing that they had carried their opposition to him even to the point of stirring up the Iroquois against him. The Jesuits on their part disliked the whole imperial scheme of La Salle. Their enemies maintained that they wished to keep traders out of the West in order themselves to enjoy a monopoly of trade; but such a motive is not necessary to explain why men engaged in Christianizing the Indians should oppose the introduction of brandy into their villages; for, perhaps because they lacked the white man's partial immunity gained by hereditary use, strong waters literally turned the Indians to beasts. The Montreal traders who suspected that, in spite of royal prohibitions, La Salle's establishments in the West bought furs that otherwise would have come to Montreal added their complaints to those of the Jesuits. The Jesuit influence through the pious Mme de Maintenon, privately married to Louis XIV, prevailed on the king. Partly on the ground of the preservation of the Indians, partly on the ground that the fur trade of the West was not worth the wars and military preparations it cost, in 1696 an edict was issued barring all traders from the West. Henceforth the Indians were to bring their furs to Montreal to trade under supervision of the authorities. Tonty and La Forest might retain their post but must not trade in beaver.

In spite of this prohibition the Illinois posts survived. Tonty was removed by death at Mobile in 1704; after that year La Forest was not in the Illinois.[6] But the missions were developing.

6. The terms "the Illinois" and "the Illinois country" are used here and hereafter in the loose sense which they retained until the nineteenth century, referring to settlements scattered from the banks of the Mississippi and the Lower Ohio to the Great Lakes. In using the terms, men ordinarily did not think of any exact boundaries.

Father Claude Allouez had carried on the work of Marquette until his death in 1689. Father Jacques Gravier succeeded him, laboring until 1705. For a few years after 1696 the mission station of the Guardian Angel stood at Chicago. In 1699 the Seminary for Foreign Missions established a mission to the Tamaroa at Cahokia in the American Bottom. After a controversy with the Jesuits it was decided finally that the Seminary was to retain its station and the Jesuits were to control the rest of the Illinois field. In 1703 they had moved Marquette's Mission of the Immaculate Conception to Kaskaskia. Settlement in the Illinois was shifting toward the place at which it was to rest for a century and more—the rich bottom lands of the east side of the Mississippi below the mouth of the Missouri—the American Bottom of later pioneer parlance. This result was due to the fact that La Salle's plan for the occupation of the mouth of the Mississippi had at last been accomplished. In 1699 the Sieur d'Iberville had founded Biloxi; and he looked for a reorganization of trade around the new colony and proposed a regrouping of Indian tribes in the upper country for defense. Accordingly, he brought the Illinois tribes to the Mississippi to link them closer to Louisiana. In 1702 he projected a post near the mouth of the Tennessee to shut out the English. One was established near the present site of Cairo; it lasted but a year or two.

For the Illinois settlement thus relocated for strategic and commercial purposes there followed years of slow growth, transmuting trading posts into frontier villages. *Coureurs de bois* married squaws and became domestic; families of settlers found their way out. In one way or another Illinois held its own during the critical years of the War of the Spanish Succession (1701–13). The trading restrictions had always been hard to enforce on the lawless men of the wilderness. The Indians had never liked the requirement that they carry furs to Montreal or the prohibition of the trade in brandy; and in the stress of war, to keep them away from English influence, violations of the edict on the part of the French traders had been winked at. With 1714 the policy was practically abandoned. Then a Scotch adventurer, John Law, of Lauriston, came to Paris with the project of an imperial speculation: a great bank in Paris rejuvenating the finances with paper money and a vast trading and colonizing enterprise in the Mississippi Valley to give that paper money validity.[7] Even the early eighteenth century knew something of advertising, and Law's glowing prospectuses of squaws weaving silks, of a land flowing with milk and honey, out of whose hills might be dug, if not brass, at least gold and silver, drew men's attention to the Great Valley, even drew colonists into it. When the scheme crashed in 1720, the awakened interest of France in the Illinois and her enlarged settlements were intangible assets with real value.

With the year 1721 came a reorganization of French dominions in America. Louisiana was laid off into districts; two of them, Arkansas and Illinois, were united in the commandery of Illinois. In it a court was established in 1722. In 1720 Philippe Renault had come to Illinois in search of mines. That same year Fort de Chartres was begun; rebuilt in 1753 as the Louisbourg of the West, it was continued on a site which the English later condemned as dictated by the pecuniary interests of its builders rather than its command of the Mississippi River. The interminable succession of battles and campaigns dragged on from 1712 in the Fox war, a struggle between the Foxes and the French and their Indian allies. Outlying settlements grew up: Ouiatenon near the present site of Lafayette, Indiana, in 1720; Vincennes in 1731. In that year the control of the Company of the Indies, the successor of Law's enterprise, came to an end; and throughout the remainder of the French regime Illinois was governed by the king.

The history of the Illinois until 1765 must thenceforth be a

7. Crozat's trading charter of 1712 did not cover Illinois. It included only Louisiana, but at that date the boundary of Louisiana was the Ohio River.

recital of the names of the intendants and commandants who ruled in the Illinois and of the Jesuits and Seminary priests who labored there. One romantic name stands out, that of Pierre Dartaguiette, the brave young commandant in the Illinois from 1733 to 1736. His end was tragic. In 1736 he led an expedition down the Mississippi to co-operate with the governor of Louisiana in an attack on the Indians of the Southwest, who, under the influence of English traders among them, attacked the French convoys on the river. The conjunction of the French forces was never made, the Indians, under the guidance of the English, defeating both expeditions in detail. Dartaguiette was captured at the defeat of the Chickasaw Bluffs, and he perished at the stake, singing his death song undaunted by the flames.

The settlement in the Illinois country was never very large. It numbered perhaps two thousand French and Negroes at the most, scattered mainly in the little villages of Kaskaskia, Prairie du Rocher, St. Philips, Fort de Chartres, and Cahokia. Yet in the fertile lands of the American Bottom this little population raised grain that supplied not merely the later posts on the Ohio but Louisiana and New Orleans as well. Where wealth such as this existed commerce flourished. The fur trade was mainly carried on by way of the Missouri River, furs being shipped out through Canada. In the government of the colony the French authorities applied their favorite principle of check and govern: against the authority of the commandant they balanced that of the civil and criminal judge or intendant, representative of the finance department. Lesser figures were the storekeeper and the notary, an official whose records included legal instruments, deeds, agreements, marriage contracts, and wills. A degree of self-government in village concerns devolved upon the inhabitants of the villages, who elected officials to attend to local affairs. The villages had their common fields administered in common; otherwise land was held by various tenures, some of them feudal but none of them oppressive. As in Canada, the holdings took the form of ribbons of land running back from a narrow river frontage.

Externally an Illinois village of the French regime represented various classes and standards of life. There was a sprinkling of nobles and bourgeois, the officials and well-to-do traders, living as close to the fashions of Versailles as three thousand miles of sea and one thousand of wilderness would let them, their houses garnished with good furniture and plate. There were the habitants, illiterate, simple, lighthearted folk ready always for dance or frolic, taking not too much thought for the morrow, and not cleaning their homes too carefully. "For clothing, the cotton plant furnished its fibre, and the warm Mackinaw blanket the indispensable *capot,* with a blue cloth hood for 'winter wear,' and skins of the deer dressed in the Indian manner for trousers and moccasins. Thus appareled, and with a short clay pipe burnt to an ebony color by constant use, wending his way to gossip with his neighbor, or by his own ingle, you have a picture of a colonial subject of the 'Grand Monarque.' "[8] The lawless *coureur de bois* is always in the background—and the Negro. One man in 1765 owned no less than eighty Negro slaves. Around the settlements was a fringe of Indians, half-civilized and half-Christianized by the Jesuit fathers, and wholly decadent.

With the middle of the eighteenth century came the crisis of the struggle between Great Britain and France for the control of the Ohio Valley. The part of the English in western exploration, not so well known as that of the French, is equally daring. At point after point French and English came into rivalry from the beginning.

Soon after they had explored the North for France, Radisson and Groseilliers went over to the English service and taught their new masters of the rich fur trade that could be made tributary to Hudson Bay. English ships could enter it and, tied up to wharves in its harbors, exchange goods for furs far cheaper than

8. Breese, *Early History of Illinois,* p. 198.

could the French, obliged to carry their merchandise over a thousand miles of lakes, rivers, and portages. The French seized the Hudson Bay posts in 1686 and maintained partial possession for almost thirty years, but the Hudson's Bay Company by the Treaty of Utrecht in 1713 was restored to its rights.

Barely had St. Lusson raised the lilies of France at Sault Ste Marie on the western edge of the Great Lakes Basin, when Batts and Fallam, adventurous Virginia explorers, passed the heights of the Blue Ridge and on the New River reached westward-flowing waters, finding by their way evidence that other and unknown Englishmen had preceded them. By the latter part of the seventeenth century, Virginia pack trains were seeking the fur trade of the interior with the southern Indians by way of the defiles of the French Broad and the Little Tennessee and around the southern end of the Appalachian barrier in the present state of Georgia. A letter left by Father Marquette in 1673 on the Lower Mississippi to be delivered to some Spanish priest to the south found its way ultimately to William Byrd of Virginia—how we can only conjecture. By the beginning of the eighteenth century the English had passed down the Tennessee to its mouth and had crossed the Mississippi to the Arkansas country. They were only months behind the French in reaching to seize the mouth of the Mississippi. Fifteen years before under the protection of the Iroquois their traders had ventured on the Great Lakes from Albany as far as Mackinac. The French in the West felt themselves beset; at all events, they strove to make the home government think that they were.

The pressure of the English and the hostility of Indian tribes had caused the French to pay but little attention to the Upper Ohio country before the forties. Their fur trade had lain across the Mississippi; they were concerned more immediately in making sure of their communication with New Orleans by way of the Mississippi and with Canada by way of the Upper Wabash and Maumee and by the Chicago and St. Joseph Portages to Lake Michigan. Accordingly, about 1740 English trading posts began to spring up in the present state of Ohio; and the French feared in King George's War (1744–48) that the influence of English traders on the Indians might rouse them to a general massacre in the Illinois. The French occupation in 1753 and 1754 of the portages from Lake Erie to the Forks of the Ohio was a desperate attempt to block off the English from the Great Valley. Their clash with the Ohio Company of Virginia, land speculators with official backing, George Washington's campaign of Fort Necessity, and the outbreak in 1754 of the French and Indian War are a part of the nation's history.

In that war Illinois had but a minor part to play. From the wheat fields of the American Bottom it supplied the French garrisons with food. It sent military contingents to the Forks of the Ohio that participated in the actions of 1754–59. It saw a fort, often incorrectly called Fort Gage,[9] erected at Kaskaskia in 1759, and Fort Massac built opposite the mouth of the Tennessee two years earlier. Its garrisons took part in one or two later campaigns in the main seats of war; but there the story ends. The military decisions in the war of 1756–63 were to come in fields remote from Illinois, at Louisbourg, at the Forks of the Ohio, on the Plains of Abraham; and when the Treaty of Paris in 1763 ceded to England all France had claimed east of the Mississippi save New Orleans, for two years the French garrisons held the Illinois until Pontiac's rebellion had subsided and the English troops could make their way to Fort Chartres and take possession.

So passed the French regime in Illinois. It had begun in the dreams of imperial trade expansion and the conversion of the Indians, and it had failed. France, unlike England, had resolved to exclude from her colony religious dissent; and the Huguenot elements that might have raised her an empire over-

9. This fort was on the bluffs above the town. Fort Gage was the name given to the Jesuits' house in Kaskaskia when used as a fort by the British.

STATUE OF LA SALLE, LINCOLN PARK, CHICAGO

HENRI DE TONTY
From bas-relief in Marquette Building, Chicago

seas built one for England instead. Her policy of restriction and regulation had allured but a handful of docile Frenchmen to filter into the West to hold it against the onward rush of the English thousands. The few hundreds of French inhabitants remained clinging to their old customs and speech until submerged in the vast tide of emigration that brought men of other European races to Illinois by the hundred thousand and the million. Of material results of the French regime it is vain to inquire: a few oddly shaped landholdings, a few peculiar titles to be fitted into a world of township surveys and Anglo-Saxon land laws, a few names of places. In spiritual results the contribution is far richer: it has thrown a gleam of the romance and chivalry of old France across the page of Illinois history in the engaging figures of Dartaguiette and the loyal Tonty; above all, it has left to all time the two ideal figures of the missionary and the explorer, the saintly Marquette and the heroic La Salle.

CHAPTER II

The Day of the Briton

TO THE French regime in Illinois succeeded the English. From the year 1763, when the English acquired title to the French territory east of the Mississippi, to the outbreak of the American Revolution, Great Britain faced the problem of organizing the Illinois country and her other American acquisitions and of co-ordinating them in the empire which the war of 1754–63 had thrust upon her hands. For the British Empire did not begin with a far-flung plan of imperial dominion; it was a casual growth. English traders had traded in India, and the exigencies of trade forced them to govern the people with whom they traded. English colonies had grown up on the Atlantic seaboard largely through the salutary neglect of the mother-country and had committed England to an American war in which France was driven from the continent. The problem of forming an imperial system out of these accidental beginnings in 1763 was indeed a great one. To enlarge a little island's government, gnarled and twisted with centuries of constitutional quibbles and compromises until it might serve also as the government of some three million Englishmen, Scotchmen, Irishmen, Germans, and French on the Atlantic seaboard; to regulate through it the inevitable displacement of the Indian by the expansion of the whites; to extend it over a trading corporation such as the East India Company, fast acquiring dominions in India, larger, more populous, perhaps more wealthy than England herself, and insure that the corporation should not itself corrupt English politics; to extend an imperial order alike over the primitive barbarism of the American Indian and the ancient civilization of the Hindu; in short, to unite the North American wilderness, the seaboard colonies, the Sugar Islands, the African Slave Coast, and India into an empire in which all should contribute justly to the common defense—here was the problem of England in 1763. Her attempts to solve it are written in many places: in the projects of legislation for the East India Company, in the parliamentary independence for a time bestowed on Ireland, in the measures of taxation that produced the American Revolution, and lastly in the abortive attempts from 1763 to 1774 to evolve a policy for the West.

The failure of England to solve her problem is to be traced to the character of the English government of the eighteenth century. The revolution of the seventeenth century, ostensibly transferring control from the crown to the parliament, had really transferred it from the king to the great landholders. Representation in the House of Commons was in no sense equally proportioned. Great cities had no representatives or at best but two or four, while medieval towns that had long since turned to sheep walks or sunk beneath the North Sea had their members duly nominated by some local landholder; and in many a little village the ownership of a few houses or a few acres of land conferred on the holder the right to name two members in the most august legislative assembly in the world. From the time when the rising importance of the House of Commons became apparent, great nobles and great landholders had been consolidating their control of the boroughs that sent members to Parliament. Cliques based on family relationship or political alliances pooled their holdings in the House of Commons and made or unmade ministries by giving or withholding the support of their votes in the House. Party government, as we understand it, was nonexistent; the art of constituting a ministry lay in gaining the support of a sufficient number of aristocratic factions to secure majorities in

Lords and Commons. The policies of ministries so constituted, on the West as on every other subject, were in continual fluctuation.

After 1760 a new king, George III, who could say of himself, "Born and educated in this country, I glory in the name of Briton," who, unlike his German predecessors, could speak English intelligibly and therefore need fear nothing from the plots of the decaying Stuart pretenders, was able, by use of the great patronage of the throne, to make himself a political boss and consolidate his following in both Lords and Commons. He added confusion to a government already rendered ineffective by the quarrels of the factions on which it was based.

It was formerly the fashion to trace the differences of political factions intent on promoting or hindering the development of the West to the positions which their leaders had taken on the question, whether at the Peace of 1763 England should exact from France Canada or the Sugar Island of Guadeloupe in the West Indies. Now it seems that this question, while the subject of a pamphlet war from 1759 onward, actually was of little concern to the responsible heads of the government. After 1759 the government was consistent in demanding of France extensive cessions on the North American continent. Finally, it secured Canada and the territory east of the Mississippi River as far south as New Orleans, where France retained and ultimately ceded to Spain the banks of the Mississippi at its outlet.

Many interests awaited with impatience the decisions the ministry must make as to the disposal of the new domain. Land speculation had been a mania in Virginia for a century and a quarter. Virginia gentlemen of influence had secured larger and larger grants until the good lands of Virginia were spent, and they looked with longing eyes to the rich country beyond the mountains. Already in 1748 the Ohio Company had received a grant on the Upper Ohio; but the French and Indian War had hindered its exploitation. Pennsylvania speculators were as acute and as determined to forestall their Virginia rivals; it was a saying that every great fortune made in the province within fifty years had been made in land. The sea-to-sea charter claims of Connecticut and Massachusetts cut belts across the new West. On every side were men eager that the government permit them to go up and possess it; on every side, even highly placed in England, were men who owned land elsewhere, in Ireland, on the Atlantic seaboard, in Florida, which they feared would be depopulated or settled slowly were the new lands opened to settlement. Beneath the aristocratic speculators fretted the mass of frontiersmen, eager to sweep over the new paradise in spite of the Indians. In deciding on its policy of settlement in the West and in pursuing it, the British ministry had need of firmness.

The problem of trade offered as much difficulty. It was estimated that the fur trade formerly tributary to Montreal was worth £135,000 each year. The English traders in the back country, men who could not be controlled, whose cheating and abuse of the Indians often foiled the best endeavors of the Indian agents to keep them loyal to the British, might lick their lips at the thought of this prize. Other fur-trading interests at home, such as the Hudson's Bay Company, powerful in backstairs influence in politics, had no desire to see English rivals master this trade. In later years a group of Scotch merchants took over the Montreal trade and found kindly Scots at home to defeat measures that threatened their control of it. As many economic interests were arrayed on either side of the trade question as on that of the land.

The expansionist groups were in control of the ministry at the treaty of peace; and the young Earl of Shelburne, president of the Board of Trade, began to develop a colonial policy. Already it had been decided to maintain a force of twenty battalions of regular troops in the colonies, to garrison the interior, and to draw a line between the possessions of the whites and the Indians beyond which purchases were to be made only by imperial authority, when in the late summer of 1763 the news of Pontiac's insurrection reached London. Pontiac, an Ottawa chief, dismayed at seeing the French replaced by the English in the west and outraged by the rapacity of the lawless English traders and the encroachments of the white settlers, had formed a confederacy of Indian tribes and lifted the tomahawk. The Indian agents were powerless to check the uprising. Every British garrison in the West save Detroit, Niagara, and Fort Pitt fell into the hands of the Indians, and a long and costly Indian war seemed the only alternative to a speedy reassurement and conciliation of the Indians by imperial authority.

To bring this about, the famous Proclamation of October 7, 1763, was issued. "A very silly proclamation it was," exclaimed one of the men responsible for it, in a moment of candor years later.[1] Before its preparation was completed, Shelburne, owing to a factional upheaval, had left office; it passed through the hands of his successor, the Earl of Hillsborough, accumulating divers blunders on its way. Intentionally it set the crest of the mountains as the limit of settlement, thereby for the time being shutting off the older colonies from the newer West. In enumerating other colonies, East and West Florida, Nova Scotia, and Quebec, to which population was to be invited to flow, it specified among their advantages English law and English government, thereby at a stroke of the pen depriving the French inhabitants of Canada of the law by which their lands and lives were secured and imposing on them a representative government from which religious tests barred them. Eleven years passed before this injustice was undone.

A second step of imperial policy taken under the new British ministry, made up of an alliance of the Grenville and Bedford political factions, was the organization of an Indian Department. Since 1755 there had been Indian superintendencies North and

1. Lord Chancellor Northington (C. W. Alvord, *Mississippi Valley in British Politics*, I, 264).

South, the first under the famous Sir William Johnson, supervising more or less under the control of the military department all dealings with the Indians, issuing presents to them, and otherwise working to conciliate them. The organization was now enlarged and elaborated. Representatives of the superintendencies were lodged with every tribe, and all trade with the Indians was to take place at fixed posts, under licenses issued by the superintendents. To carry out the new Indian policy and to provide military support for it, money was necessary; and the Stamp Act was passed to secure from the colonies their share of it. Their vociferous protest at being obliged to pay for an imperial policy that they had not approved and at being committed to subordination to the imperial authority of the British Parliament in taxation coincided with the fall of the Grenville-Bedford ministry.

The Duke of Bedford since the 1750's had been in favor of bringing the colonies to heel; he had had misgivings lest relief from the French menace in Canada might lead the colonies to declare their independence of England. He had, therefore, collaborated with George Grenville in promoting an imperialist policy toward the colonies in the West. The succeeding ministry, the Old Whigs, had a tradition of easygoing treatment of the colonies. They were great favorers of vested and corporate interests and thus inclined to sympathize with the outcry of the colonies as corporations against encroachment on their privileges by the Stamp Act; hence this ministry repealed it. The Old Whigs went out of office in 1766 before they had time to formulate a western policy; but it is not improbable that they would have withdrawn Indian superintendents, traders, and soldiers alike and, shutting the door on westward expansion, have sought to preserve the West for all time as an Indian reservation.

The most promising attempt was now to be made to reach a real solution of the western problem. William Pitt, the war minister who in the Seven Years' War had won England her imperial rank, whose greatness in English politics depended on force of character rather than the number of his henchmen in Parliament, by the king's command sought to gather a ministry undominated by factions that would seek to solve in terms of the public good the problem of the West, the problem of the East India Company, and the problem of governmental reorganization. To formulate a broad western policy, he summoned to the office of secretary of state for the southern department the Earl of Shelburne.

The three years that had passed since 1763 had given an opportunity for the testing by actual facts of the theories of the earlier period. The unhappy plight in which the Proclamation of 1763 had put the French-Canadians was long since apparent. The Indian Department had duly gone into operation; it was submitting most astounding bills for presents made to the Indians. Especially generous were those which Commissary Edward Cole was sending from the Illinois, where at last the English had arrived. George Croghan, ablest of Indian diplomatists and the trusted assistant of Sir William Johnson, in the summer of 1765 had completed the pacification of the Indians of the Wabash country; and on October 9, 1765, Captain Thomas Stirling with one hundred men of the Black Watch or Forty-second Highlanders, who had descended the Ohio from Fort Pitt, relieved the French garrison at Fort de Chartres.

Almost immediately it became apparent that the fur trade of the West was a negligible asset to British merchants. The news of the cession of Illinois to the English had been followed by a migration of many of the wealthier French inhabitants across the river to the new villages of Ste Genevieve and St. Louis, the latter founded by Pierre Laclede in 1764. "He appears," wrote Captain Gordon in 1766, "to be sensible, clever, & has been very well educated; is very active, and will give us some Trouble before we get the Parts of this Trade that belong to us out of His

Hands."[2] From its beginning St. Louis dominated southern Illinois. French traders roamed at large on the British side of the Mississippi where no British trader dared set his foot outside the protection of the posts, even though he chafed at the regulation of the Indian Department that confined him to them. Under Laclede's guidance the fur trade flowed down the Mississippi to Spanish New Orleans, whose control of the river from the east bank men were repeatedly to bewail in later years. Was the limited trade in the West worth the amount it cost to regulate it?

Further, Shelburne was made aware of the existence of numerous colonizing projects based on purchases, grants, or hoped-for grants in the Ohio and Mississippi valleys. Virginia projectors, Pennsylvania projectors, and Connecticut projectors crowded in, each with his map and his smoothly written prospectus, each pointing out that his western colony would enable the forts to be cheaply rationed and would serve as a bulwark to hold the country for England. These projects, many of them dating from before the treaty of peace, had been checked temporarily by the Proclamation of 1763, but now they took on new vigor.

The real motives of the Earl of Shelburne are hard to penetrate beneath the ostensible professions with which he deliberately misled his fellow-politicians. We can only imagine that, as he studied in every possible detail the complex problem before him, he tended toward certain conclusions derived in a large part from the laissez faire economics he might have learned from his friend, Dr. Adam Smith, later author of the *Wealth of Nations*. If he believed with Smith that human legislation could not permanently alter the trend of economic events, he doubtless regarded it as a vain endeavor to seek to chain the Indian trade

2. C. W. Alvord and C. E. Carter, *The New Regime, 1765–67* ("Illinois Historical Collections," Vol. XI [Springfield, Ill.: Illinois Historical Library]), p. 300.

by the regulations of a distant imperial organization or to dam up the inevitable flow of settlement over the West. In that event the only possible course would be to return the Indian trade to the colonies for such regulation as it was to have; the westward movement might be rendered as little harmful to the Indians as possible by establishing new colonies in the West under imperial auspices, but with almost complete democratic self-government, their expenses to be paid by quitrents exacted on all grants of land by the British government. The very policy of expansion that, formulated by the United States in the Northwest Ordinance, was to cover the wilderness with sovereign states on an equality with the original thirteen was already hovering in Shelburne's mind.

Only the preliminaries of his plan were worked out. The illness of the great William Pitt, now Earl of Chatham, had fatally weakened his ministry; the nominal second in command, the Duke of Grafton, was an easygoing nobleman not too fond of Shelburne: "The duke of Grafton," so Junius pilloried him to eternity, "has always some excellent reason for deserting his friends."[3] Grafton sought factional support for his ministry; and the incoming representatives of the Bedford faction made their bargain for the removal of colonial matters from Shelburne's hands. Once more the jest of fate had made Hillsborough his successor, and once more his work went for naught.

Meanwhile events had moved fast in the Illinois. Garrison followed garrison and commandant replaced commandant. Stirling was succeeded by Major Robert Farmar, Farmar by Lieutenant Colonel John Reed in 1766, Reed by Captain Hugh Forbes in 1768, and Forbes by Lieutenant Colonel John Wilkins until 1771. Some of them, such as Stirling and Forbes, seem kindly and honest men; others, like Reed and Wilkins, were tyrannical and corrupt, charging fees for administering oaths of

3. *Letters of Junius* (1806 ed.), I, 163.

allegiance to the inhabitants and making their profit in the purchase of rations for the garrison.

The religious problem was serious. Before England took possession of the Illinois, France had decreed the banishment of the Jesuits from all her domains; the possessions of the Society in the Illinois were confiscated and its fathers expelled. One of the Seminary priests, presumably fearing the heretic English would not respect the possessions of a Catholic mission, sold without due authority for much less than its value the property of the Seminary at Cahokia and left a community of devout Catholics scattered from the Wabash to the Mississippi without any spiritual guidance whatever. As English law still prohibited the Catholic hierarchy, no organization existed to supply the want until Monseigneur Jean Olivier Briand, with the title of superintendent, was allowed to function as bishop of Quebec in 1766.

Meanwhile, one of the banished Jesuits, Father Meurin, gained permission to return to the care of his flock. His story would be a pitiful one were it not illuminated by his saintliness and resignation. Old and feeble of body, he labored heavily at his task. The Spaniards drove him from the western side of the river when he accepted from Briand the powers of apostolic vicar. Despite the threat of being sent in chains to New Orleans, he returned secretly when he was needed. The Jesuits in the day of their power had made themselves hated by continually setting on the civil power to punish; and now many men withheld their confessions from Meurin as a Jesuit and accused him of avarice. He toiled to the limit of his feeble physical powers, uncomplaining, vaunting not himself, asking of his superior only that laborers be sent into the harvest to relieve him.

In answer to his prayer there came a young priest, Pierre Gibault. Aggressive, with an excellent opinion of himself, with all the arts of popularity, he soon gained the affections of the people and pushed his way to Vincennes to be received there with the deepest feeling of delight by Catholics, who feared damnation for their lack of the ordinances of the church. Gibault was fond of Meurin but regarded him with pity as feeble in mind as well as body. There was little of the saint about Gibault. He petitioned Briand to be allowed to bear arms to defend himself against the savages. Ingenuously he confessed his love of liberty was such that a rebuke from his superior put him at death's door. The spirit of a younger generation unused to obedience and resignation spoke in him.

As early as 1766 Illinois had begun a trade connection with the seaboard English colonies. In 1765 the shifty Samuel Wharton, of the Philadelphia firm of Baynton, Wharton, and Morgan, had listened to private representations from George Croghan that he would take a secret partnership with them and buy their goods at high prices to be given in the king's name as presents to the western Indians whom he was undertaking to pacify as he descended the Ohio. The firm dreamed of 200 per cent profits. Wharton tumbled all the firm's unsalable stock in dry goods, fine groceries, and other commodities, whether suited to the Indian trade or not, into wagons and sent them off by back roads to Pittsburgh. Although attempts were made to conceal the transaction, rival firms which were still barred from the Indian trade as a military measure clamorously protested to the British commander-in-chief, Major General Thomas Gage. Despite protestations of innocence from Wharton and Croghan, Gage made no attempt to conceal his opinion that both were lying.

Meanwhile unsupervised wagoners had forded rivers with loads of chocolate and tea and had liberally helped themselves to the goods in their charge. The lawless "Paxton Boys" of backwoods Pennsylvania, whose axiom was that there was no good Indian but a dead Indian, and who deduced the corollary that any goods destined for an Indian belonged to any white man who had a use for them, had plundered what the wagoners had spared. Finally, a much reduced stock of damaged goods unsuited to the Indian trade had reached Pittsburgh too late and was wasted on fair and frail ladies by the rascally agents of the firm.

In 1766 Croghan was again to descend the Ohio to treat with the western Indians. Samuel Wharton hoped to recoup his losses by sending a second consignment of goods. He persuaded his young partner, George Morgan, to accompany them. Once en route Croghan withdrew from his partnership in the firm and bought little from it. Morgan found himself at length in the Illinois country with a poorly assorted lot of goods in competition with skilled French merchants who were in debt to New Orleans firms and therefore bound to deal with them. The commandant, Lieutenant Colonel John Reed, had his favorites among the French traders and fiercely resented Wharton's attempt to secure the contract for rationing his regiment by proffering a bribe to Shelburne's secretary. The firm of Baynton, Wharton, and Morgan fell into difficulties and had to carry on its business under the supervision of its creditors.

The ever optimistic Wharton hoped for better things in 1768 when a general regimental relief took place among the British garrisons in America. Lieutenant Colonel John Wilkins and the Eighteenth Royal Irish Regiment were on their way out to relieve Reed in the Illinois country. Before Wilkins left New York, Wharton entered into a formally signed and sealed contract with him: in return for 5 per cent of the firm's profits, Wilkins was to favor its business and discourage its competitors in every way.

Wilkins, as occasionally happens to field officers who have long exercised despotic command, was somewhat impaired in judgment. On his first arrival in the Illinois, without any authorization he set up a court of civil justice. Something of the sort was needed; but the court's membership was selected from Morgan's associates and clerks and was manifestly designed to assist him in collecting his debts from French merchants. For Wilkins' own financial benefit members of the court sold what were in effect *lettres de cachet*—writs of imprisonment signed and sealed by Wilkins with blank spaces for names. For twenty dollars one could purchase a writ and, filling in an enemy's name, consign him to the guardhouse for an indefinite term. At last for a time the firm of Baynton, Wharton and Morgan prospered. James Rumsey on its account successfully brought out a cargo of Negro slaves which had a ready sale among the Illinois French. Morgan dispatched his Virginia hunters to Kentucky to kill and salt buffalo beef for the garrison. They reported the game badly thinned by French interlopers from across the Mississippi, years before the crack of Daniel Boone's rifle was ever heard within the bounds of the Commonwealth.

But once again Mr. Samuel Wharton overreached himself. He and Morgan persuaded themselves that it was unethical to pay Colonel Wilkins a percentage for doing what, after all, was no more than his duty. When payments stopped, Wilkins began a series of clumsy retaliations to induce their renewal. He replaced Morgan's satellites in the court of justice by Frenchmen. He gave it criminal jurisdiction on March 4, 1770, and then discontinued it on June 6. He refused to sign Morgan's vouchers for supplies to the garrison. Morgan, an earnest horticulturalist, had established a farm stocked with choicer field seeds, fruit trees and livestock; when he quarreled with his farmer, Wilkins endeavored to countenance the farmer. He encouraged Morgan to buy a distillery to distil his produce and then put him under £20,000 bond to distil no spiritous liquors. He placed him in the guardhouse and then invited him to Christmas dinner. Finally, Morgan abandoned the firm's property and escaped to the seaboard to press civil and criminal suits against Wilkins. Morgan's friends among the officers of the Eighteenth redoubled their charges against their colonel, who was equally vociferous in his countercharges.

General Gage acidly concluded that everyone had behaved ill. Daniel Blouin, representing the French inhabitants of the

Illinois, complained of oppression on the part of both Wilkins and Morgan. But when he proposed that the Illinois French be erected into an autonomous self-governing colony like Connecticut, Gage listened no further. Repulsed by the commander-in-chief, the Frenchman published at Philadelphia a most interesting pamphlet, *Invitation sérieuse aux habitants des Illinois*. It called on the Illinois French to accept the English regime and to make themselves a part of it, exploiting the economic resources of their country and teaching their children English. The restless American spirit and love of liberty had already fired the docile French of the Illinois.

In these same years the English ministry had been little by little reaching a decision of pure negation. There was a period of hesitancy. To the eye of the ministry the real situation of the distant West lay as obscure as though veiled in the morning mists that rise from the bosom of its great river. Now reports would come to them with a note of optimism. Strong garrisons and forts at the mouths of the Wabash and the Illinois would shut out the French traders. Western colonies of British subjects would supply the garrisons with cheap food and support them in time of war. A little patience, above all, a little more expenditure, and the prize of trade and possession would be in their grasp.

Then alternated pessimism. The trade was bound to follow the course of the Mississippi to New Orleans; the endeavor to divert it through British territory by cutting a canal outlet to the sea from the Mississippi to the Iberville was fruitless. The expense of the garrisons was very great, they would be useless in time of war, their walls were falling in decay, and there was no British fur trade left for them to protect. Colonies would only inspire the Indians with resentment and cause a new war. Month by month the reports foreboded an Indian war in spite of all efforts to avert it, especially after April, 1769, when the great Pontiac had fallen at Cahokia under the tomahawk of an

Illinois bribed by the English. To these latter voices Hillsborough came more and more to listen; and General Gage, a political soldier, tuned his reports to fit the mood of the secretary. Hillsborough therefore adopted Shelburne's plan of dropping imperial regulation of Indian trade; he dropped also the project of colonies. Finally, he decided to abandon most of the western posts. Fort de Chartres was demolished in 1772 as a military post, though its stoneworks still survive in part as a memento of French Illinois. A little garrison was kept in the Illinois, however, at Fort Gage at Kaskaskia. The ministry had drifted under the control of Bedfords and Grenvilles; but its policy was now centered on the exertion and display of the imperial authority over the contumacious inhabitants of the seaboard. It had no inclination for the imperial exploitation of the West.

After 1772 a reduced garrison of two companies of the Eighteenth Royal Irish occupied as a fort the Jesuits' house in the village of Kaskaskia. Their commander, the upright Captain Hugh Lord, got on well with the inhabitants save when under the orders of his superiors he tried to persuade them to petition for the establishment over them of a simple autocratic government. The high command had always regarded the French inhabitants as a nuisance. At one time Gage had tried to evacuate the inhabitants of Vincennes to the seaboard colonies, learning to his surprise that they had land titles and vested interests. He was still hoping to group the inhabitants into concentrated communities watched by small British garrisons. A trade connection continued with Pennsylvania through the firms of Gratz and Company and Franks and Company, which enjoyed the ration contract for Lord's garrison. Its Illinois representative was a certain William Murray, formerly a captain in the Black Watch in garrison at Pittsburgh. In 1773 he begins a new era in western land speculation which is essentially the last act of British domination in the West. His speculation is based on a forgery that is a historical enigma, the so-called "Yorke-Camden Opinion."

In 1757 Charles Yorke and Charles Pratt, later Earl Camden, as law advisers of the British crown had given an opinion justifying the East India Company in acquiring lands from the rulers of India without specific permission of the British crown. This opinion was as follows:

> In respect to such places, as have been or shall be acquired by treaty or grant from the grand Mogul or any of the Indian princes or governments, your Majesties letters patents are not necessary the property of the soil vesting in the grantee by the Indian grants, subject only to your Majesties right of sovereignty over the settlements as English settlements: and over the inhabitants, as English subjects, who carry with them your Majesties laws wherever they form colonies, and receive your Majesties protection, by virtue of your royal charters.

After the two men had become successively lord chancellors of Great Britain, some shifty pettifogger had dropped out the words "the grand Mogul or" and pretended that two lord chancellors had approved the right of any British subject to buy land of any Indian who would sell it to him. William Murray used this opinion in 1773 to buy most of southern Illinois for an Illinois land company which was based on the firm of Gratz and Company. Obtaining the support of Lord Dunmore, the land-speculating governor of Virginia, he allowed the governor to participate in a second purchase in 1775 of lands on the Wabash.

Murray's defiance of the will of the British crown as set forth in the Proclamation of 1763 was only symptomatic. With imperial forces opposing instead of guiding the westward movement, government officials and private men alike were exploiting the West for themselves. At the actual running of the Indian boundary line tentatively laid down in the Proclamation, the complacency of John Stuart, the southern Indian superintendent, and strange mistakes on the part of surveyors pushed it as far west as the Kentucky River. At the treaty of Fort Stanwix in 1768 Sir William Johnson accepted of the Iroquois a similar cession of the greater part of Kentucky. The lawless white frontiersmen began to swarm over the mountains; even before them came the surveyors and agents of the land speculators, choosing the choicest tracts far down the Ohio. In 1774 Richard Henderson of North Carolina scented a revolution on the way that would throw the West open to American settlement and projected his Transylvania colony in central Kentucky.

The British government found that, if it would not adopt a decisive policy, its subjects would. Ever since 1769 it had been coquetting with a scheme for a colony on the upper course of the Ohio—Vandalia—for which the astute Samuel Wharton of Baynton, Wharton, and Morgan had adroitly secured plenty of the best social and political backing; Hillsborough had been driven from office on the pretext that he opposed it. But the news of the Boston Tea Party of December, 1773, ruined Vandalia's chances. Baffled by the impudent forgery of the Yorke-Camden Opinion and the unpleasant fact that its principle was said to have the approval of Lord Camden and was probably consonant to English common law, the British ministry pressed through the Quebec Act of 1774. Originally designed to restore to the French of Canada their law, the full exercise of their religion, and relief from a representative government exercised among them by a handful of Englishmen, it sought to deal with the problem of the Illinois by extending the bounds of Quebec to take in the whole Northwest. Not only would this allow the little French settlements at Detroit, Ouiatenon, Vincennes, and the Illinois to be governed economically by representatives of the governor at Quebec; but the presence of French law might keep out English settlers and land speculators, invalidate the Yorke-Camden Opinion, check lawless land purchases, and tie the trade to Montreal and its Scotch merchants.

On this note of negation ends the eleven years of British opportunity in the Illinois. The British government had shown itself as incapable of projecting the orderly settlement of the West as it had of incorporating the Atlantic seaboard colonies in an imperial system. It had hoped to maintain the status quo indefinitely in the West by means of the Quebec Act. The inevitable taking possession of the interior by the new American people might have been regulated as Shelburne had wished to do; but it was to be checked neither by paper proclamations nor by the terms of acts of Parliament. France had failed in the Illinois because she had no materials there for building a strong colony. England had failed because by her regulations she defied great human forces. As the imperial opportunity offered her in 1763 fades out in the Quebec Act of 1774, certain facts remain. The squatter and the land speculator, familiar figures of the frontier for a century before and a century and a quarter to follow, have passed the edge of the Great Valley. The French in Illinois have become restive and are dreaming of a state of things in which they may work out their destiny independent of St. James's Palace and Versailles alike. Most important of all, Pennsylvania trader and Virginia hunter have found the path to the Illinois. If the opportunity invites thither, they may tread it again.

CHAPTER III

The American Conquest

I N MANY respects the American Revolution was a frontier movement. In colony after colony the dwellers in the up-country were the deciding weight in the scale of revolt against British rule. Many of them were non-British in race and chafed at the British policy of barring the West to them. Compared with the tidewater colonists, their sense of the social prestige that reflected from London and their respect for British military and naval power were of the slightest. Almost coincident in point of time with the Revolution was the first great rush of settlement in the Ohio Valley, and the need of protecting the new settlements against the tomahawks of British Indians led to projected attacks on Detroit and the conquest of the French villages in the Illinois by George Rogers Clark. Ultimately this last contributed to the diplomatic situation that in the treaty of 1783 gave the United States title to Illinois and the Northwest.

The story of the conquest of the Illinois is, then, interwoven with the story of the Revolution in the West; and that story begins with Dunmore's War, in the summer of 1774, when, goaded by continual encroachment from squatter and surveyor in the Ohio Valley, the Indians raised the hatchet. Lord Dunmore, last royal governor of Virginia, himself foremost among the land speculators, proclaimed a crusade against the redskins in which backwoodsman and speculator joined. "The Oppertunty we hav So long wished for, is now before us," wrote Colonel William Preston of the frontier Virginia county of Fincastle.[1] The Indians were defeated near the site of Charleston, West Virginia, at the Battle of Point Pleasant; but before the day in 1775 which was to see the definitive treaty, Dunmore was a refugee on a British ship of war; and some of his former associates in the war, securing possession of Fort Pitt, negotiated the final treaty in the name and interests of the Continental Congress.

Not all of Dunmore's associates joined the Revolution. Refugees among the British like the Girtys and Alexander McKee, hated from one end of the frontier to the other, were to marshal the Indians in the British interest against Kentucky. To Dr. John Connelly, for thirty years the stormy petrel of the northwest frontier, occurred the project of leading a British and Indian expedition from Detroit to seize Fort Pitt, break the rebellion in the back country, and ultimately establish communication with the British fleet. The American attack on Canada of 1775 frustrated the scheme. No forces could be spared from the defense of essential points like Quebec and Montreal; and Connelly's plans in the hands of Lieutenant-Governor Henry Hamilton of Detroit degenerated into a series of Indian raids on the new Kentucky settlements in 1777. The Indians, it is true, were urged to take prisoners, but they usually took scalps. In 1776 George Morgan, formerly trader in the Illinois, took station at Fort Pitt as Indian commissioner for Congress in the middle district, seeking to keep the Indians friendly to the United States; but murders by lawless whites and the constant encroachment of new settlers made his task supremely difficult. From end to end the frontier was harried by bands, often led by renegades like the Girtys.

The Americans, however, had soon discovered that down the Mississippi lay needed military stores and supplies presided over by a Spanish governor whose neutrality toward the United

1. R. G. Thwaites and Louise Phelps Kellogg (eds.), *Documentary History of Dunmore's War, 1774* (Madison, Wis., 1905), p. 93.

States was most benevolent. In 1776–77 powder was run up the river from New Orleans to Wheeling, probably with the assistance of some men in the Illinois country. In 1778 Captain George Willing set out on a grand expedition of plunder against the hapless British settlements in West Florida. It served as a feint to distract attention from Clark's blow at the Illinois in that very year.

Men's minds were turned not only to the Southwest. It was becoming clearer and clearer that Detroit was the strategic point in the British position in the West. Its loss would confine them to Lakes Ontario and Erie, and the upper lake region and the Mississippi would slip from their grasp. In 1776 both Morgan and General Arthur St. Clair had urged a blow from Fort Pitt at Detroit, and in 1777 and 1778 expeditions under Continental generals were actually projected. In the latter year George Rogers Clark carried out his project of seizing the Illinois country both as a link with the Spaniards across the Mississippi and at New Orleans and as a base for an attack on Detroit.

It is necessary to glance back at the situation in the Illinois villages. In 1772, after the dismantling of Fort de Chartres, Captain Hugh Lord had gathered the little English garrison at Kaskaskia. His relations with the French inhabitants were pleasant. The Quebec Act designated Vincennes, Detroit, and the Illinois as districts each to be governed by a lieutenant-governor and judges; but the lieutenant-governor for the Illinois had never repaired to his post. In 1776 Captain Lord and his garrison were withdrawn for duty farther east; and Lord deputed his authority to Philippe de Rocheblave, last of the British commandants in the Illinois.

De Rocheblave's record had not been very prepossessing. He had begun his career in the French regime, acquiring speedily a reputation for intrigue, and had governed at Ste Genevieve for the Spaniards but had left his post under a cloud. In 1776 he was available for chance employment and accordingly, without subordinates, troops, or funds, was left to exert in the Illinois such authority as the inhabitants would allow him. Under the circumstances he accomplished as much perhaps as anyone could have done. He had the support of Cerré and Viviat, two of the most substantial Frenchmen of the villages, and of the lesser inhabitants; but such resident Englishmen as Thomas Bentley, William Murray, and others who had come for trade were outspoken in their opposition. Rocheblave dispatched long reports to his superiors, begging for support, but he wrote and implored in vain. Through his letters runs the note of foreseen disaster impending: The Spanish commandant across the river has told the Indians that when the corn is so high he will have something to tell them. Bentley is a traitor he dares not have arrested until he is lured away to Mackinac. Some of the inhabitants have supplied boats bringing munitions to the Americans from New Orleans. He is surrounded by spies, traitors, and enemies. The last of these letters he penned July 4, 1778, the day George Rogers Clark broke in on him.

The figure of Clark is one of the stateliest and most pathetic in American history. In 1778 he was twenty-six years old. At twenty he had first come to the Ohio country; at twenty-two he had served in Dunmore's War. He had been instrumental in securing the absorption of Henderson's colony of Transylvania into the Virginia county of Kentucky. As major of militia in the new county he decided to protect his charge by capturing the British bases for the Indian raids. Never successful so far, to the end of the Revolution, with inadequate resources in men and means, he kept the grip on the region of the Ohio that helped to secure it for the United States in 1783. His later years, beset by poverty and drink, in which he intrigued with Spaniard and Frenchman, are pitiful. He prided himself much on his strong resemblance to George Washington in form and feature; like him also in courage, resource, and resolution, he fell short of that perfect balance in character, that wisdom in public and private concerns alike, that makes Washington nearer the ideal citizen of the Greek philosophers than any other man who has arisen in the twenty-odd centuries since they first framed it. Washington could render his country supreme service and at the same time lay the foundations of a great estate. Clark conquered for Virginia an abiding place for twenty millions of his countrymen but lived to see himself a poverty-stricken stranger in it.

It was in December, 1777, that Clark obtained the consent of Governor Patrick Henry of Virginia to his scheme; the next spring he set out, collecting his meager forces at the Falls of the Ohio, near the present site of Louisville. With a little band thinned by desertion to a hundred and seventy-five rifles, he floated down the Ohio to the site of Fort Massac, whence he struck out overland for Kaskaskia rather than stem the current of the Mississippi with his boats. He arrived at Kaskaskia on the evening of July 4, 1778. Rocheblave could not muster the French militia against him. Clark won over Cerré and Father Gibault, the busy young priest sent out by Briand ten years before; and the French inhabitants joyfully embraced the cause of American liberty. Gibault hastened off to Vincennes and persuaded the inhabitants to accept the American cause and, transferring their allegiance, to sign the famous Oath of Vincennes. Clark made treaties with the Indian tribes of the Northwest. He supported his little army by supplies purchased from the inhabitants with drafts on New Orleans drawn on Oliver Pollock, the loyal financial agent of Virginia who, in keeping Clark supplied, was to ruin himself.

On hearing of Clark's success, the Virginia assembly on December 9, 1778, created the County of Illinois as a county of Virginia. Three days later John Todd was appointed county lieutenant. On his arrival in the Illinois he laid off in his county, as large as an empire, three districts, Kaskaskia, Cahokia, Vincennes; in each of these a court of justice was elected by the inhabitants. The Illinois country was now a part of the Old Dominion.

STATUE OF GEORGE ROGERS CLARK BY CHARLES J.
MULLIGAN AT QUINCY, ILLINOIS

CAHOKIA, ILLINOIS

From J. C. Wild *The Valley of the Mississippi* (1841)

Clark's work of conquest was by no means complete. In the early winter of 1778–79 Governor Hamilton of Detroit launched an expedition—English, French, and Indian—against Vincennes. The fickle French, unwilling to fight against their countrymen, deserted their leader, Captain Helm, who surrendered to Hamilton. The "Hair-buyer" now only awaited settled weather in the spring to recapture Kaskaskia and Cahokia in the same way.

Clark saw that the situation demanded desperate measures. With what was left of his Virginia forces and with the French of the Illinois, he set out for Vincennes across the swollen rivers and flooded bottom lands of an Illinois February. The story of that journey, of weary men wading for miles in water reaching to the waist or the neck, crossing one by one the swollen tributaries of the Wabash without place to rest for days together, spurred on by the indomitable will of their leader, is one of the stirring episodes of Illinois history. Arrived at Vincennes, Clark, by the art of bluffing he understood so well, separated the inhabitants of the town from the "Hair-buyer," Hamilton, besieged him in Fort Sackville, and took him and his forces prisoner.

With the recapture of Vincennes and the taking of Hamilton, Clark stood at the zenith of his achievements. All that seemed left to be done was to complete his original plan by the capture of Detroit, which would bar the British once and for all from the upper lakes and the Upper Mississippi. Clark failed to take Detroit in 1779 because three hundred Kentuckians under Colonel John Bowman, instead of co-operating with him, went on a futile Indian raid. In the fall of that year Clark disposed his forces in the Illinois villages and at Vincennes, himself taking post at Fort Jefferson at the Iron Banks on the Mississippi a few miles below the mouth of the Ohio. He hoped to take Detroit in the spring of 1780. But the French were tired of supplying his troops for pay in paper money, and the commander at Pittsburg failed to co-operate. Instead of taking the offensive, Clark planned to withdraw his forces to Fort Jefferson, and there from a position in readiness prevent the British from reoccupying the Illinois.

It was well that Clark was based for defense. In 1780 the English from Detroit and Mackinac launched an expedition, proceeding by various routes designed to reconquer the Illinois and Spanish St. Louis and then to slip down the Mississippi and combine with the English in West Florida to seize New Orleans and the mouth of the river. Clark successfully defended Cahokia from the English assault; a few weeks later the Spanish at St. Louis beat off a British-Indian attack, and Clark dispatched Colonel John Montgomery to pursue the retreating English to Lake Michigan and to burn the Sac and Fox villages at Rock Island, a service that is termed the westernmost battle of the Revolution. Later in the same year a French officer, La Balme, came to the Illinois, under what auspices and for what purpose is not clear. He led an ill-considered expedition of Illinois French against Detroit but was defeated and killed on the way. In revenge, under the auspices of the Spanish commandant at St. Louis, the French captured the British post of St. Joseph, at present Niles, Michigan, hoisted the Spanish flag over it on January 1, 1781, and then retreated as they had come.

The Illinois villages in the years after 1779 were sinking fast into anarchy. The inhabitants soon recovered sufficiently from their first enthusiasm for liberty to discover that the Virginia paper currency proffered them for supplies was sadly depreciated. Drafts drawn by Clark on Oliver Pollock at New Orleans exhausted Pollock's private fortune long before his patriotism. The French villagers in the Illinois were not so primitive as not to have a somewhat sophisticated view of credit and commercial transactions; they began to withhold supplies. Withholding supplies from Clark's Kentucky backwoodsmen was an ill task, however, and in various ways they supplied themselves. The French were soon at odds with their deliverers.

John Todd and his elected county courts made some attempt to intervene in behalf of the inhabitants. But in November, 1779, Todd left the Illinois forever, designating Richard Winston as his deputy. Of the courts he had established, the Cahokia court preserved its authority and maintained its regular elections until the establishment of county government under the Northwest Ordinance in 1790. The Vincennes court held office until 1787, the justices successfully staving off elections to fill their places. The Kaskaskia court had the most troublous experiences of any, falling victim finally to the opposition of the American settlers.

The year 1779 is important in the history of Illinois as the year of the coming of the first Americans to make their permanent homes in the Illinois. The first settlement in the Kaskaskia district at Bellefontaine dates from this year. In the course of the next year or two appear such names, familiar in later Illinois history, as Moore, Oglesby, and Shadrach Bond. In the Cahokia district the first American settlement was at the Grand Ruisseau. Differing from the French in manners, language, religion, and custom, satisfied of their own superiority, and defiant of law and government not of their own choice, the Americans added to the difficulty of maintaining orderly authority, some of them soon becoming the tools of the tyranny of John Dodge.

John Dodge, coming to the Illinois as Indian agent, in 1780 engaged with Thomas Bentley in buying up claims on Virginia at a heavy discount. In 1781 they went east to collect, but that same year Dodge reappeared. He charged Richard Winston, deputy county lieutenant, with treason and for a time had him imprisoned. The Kaskaskia court did not show what Winston thought sufficient energy in assisting him, and he abolished the court in November, 1782. Next year he returned to Virginia, leaving the Sieur Timothe de Monbreun as his successor, a man whose connection with the founding of Nashville reminds us that a trade on the Mississippi, Tennessee, and Cumberland had already developed. De Monbreun failed to restrain Dodge, who fortified the old fort above Kaskaskia and, with a few American adventurers, ruled with a heavy and corrupt hand over the luckless French inhabitants.

For almost five years a second migration of French across the river to Spanish rule had been taking place. Gibault had gone in 1778, Cerré in 1779. The French who could not transfer their possessions across the river were reduced to petitioning the far-away Congress of the Confederation for relief. On January 5, 1782, the legal existence of the Virginian county of Illinois came to an end with the act creating it. Until the question was settled as to whether the government of the West should be vested in the states or in the nation, the unhappy habitants might look in vain for legal government. In June, 1786, the Kaskaskians petitioned Congress against Dodge, alleging he was the tool of British traders; and Congress took the petition under advisement. In 1787 the Kaskaskians elected a new court; but the political address of the Americans at Bellefontaine secured the choice of Americans for half the places in it. The impossibility of conducting a court so split between races and languages led to its division. General Harmar, the commander of the American troops in the West, visited the Illinois in 1787; but he felt the blandishments and hospitality of Dodge and fell in with his insinuations that the French were unfit for self-government.

The news of the passage of the Ordinance of 1787 threw the Kaskaskia district in deeper anarchy, were it possible. The legal authority of its court could thenceforth be defied as nonexistent. John Dodge in his hilltop citadel with his band of supporters was the very image of the tyrant of a Greek city-state of twenty-three centuries before. The Spanish commandant encouraged Indian raids on the Illinois to attract settlers to the comparative order of the Spanish side, and the Indians robbed and murdered. White men were equally lawless; neither property nor female virtue was safe.

At Cahokia things went better. Despite the theory of French

incapacity for self-government, the court there maintained its authority. When the Americans at Grand Ruisseau sought to set up an independent court, the French court repressed the scheme and put the malcontents in irons. Eventually, however, the Americans of Grand Ruisseau and Bellefontaine were allowed to unite in a court of their own. Even so, disorder was rife. John Edgar, a man of property, one of the later American settlers, in 1789 promised that he could hold out until March, 1790. If stable government did not come by then, he must abandon the Illinois for good. But on March 5, 1790, Governor Arthur St. Clair arrived at Kaskaskia, and the course of the Illinois country as a part of the Northwest Territory began.

We must now turn back to trace the course of events by which the United States secured the Northwest and made the first steps toward providing for its government. The acquisition of the territory was the result of an intricate tangle of diplomacy, internal and external. Since 1778 France had been the ally of the United States and at war with Great Britain. Since 1779 Spain had been involved in the war as the ally of France. Much has been written as to the attitude of those powers toward the young nation. The view that France had dreams of recovering the Northwest and perhaps Canada had the support of Frederick Jackson Turner, who saw in La Balme's expedition a corroboration; but the present balance of authority is the other way. France entered the war with a view to reviving her lost prestige in European politics by the defeat of her old rival, England. She was probably at all times disposed to fulfil the specific terms of her bargain with the United States; but she had also to satisfy her ally, Spain; and to do both was a difficult matter.

Spain had entered the war under the influence of the imperialist revival she experienced in the second half of the eighteenth century. In those years she was extending her possessions in California; she hoped in the war to recover the Floridas, lost to

England in 1763, and the fortress of Gibraltar, lost sixty years before. But her colonial empire was to be one of absolute rulers and docile subjects; and the example of rebellious colonists and lawless frontiersmen was one which she wished to keep far from her borders. She wished to see the American republic remain a little group of distracted states, impoverished in finance, limited in territory, a perpetual object-lesson to subjects against the mirage called "liberty." Any really generous treatment of the United States in the treaty of peace she opposed; and France, striving to satisfy her in this respect, had continually to urge on the Congress extreme moderation in its territorial demands.

Spain found certain of the state delegations to the Congress ready to co-operate. The division of the states into landed and landless is significant. On the one hand, such states as New Jersey, Delaware, and Maryland had boundaries long since fixed at limits rendering them diminutive beside the great belts of territory claimed by Massachusetts, Connecticut, and North Carolina under seventeenth-century "sea-to-sea" charters. Even greater were the claims of New York to the lands over which her vassals, the Iroquois, claimed sway to the West. Greediest and most pertinacious in her claims, however, was Virginia, insisting that the extension of her boundaries west and northwest, as her old charter bade, would throw the greatest part of the old Northwest and all Kentucky into her hands. What equality, argued the small states, could there be in a union of which some members were so vast and others so small? Should the blood and treasure of Maryland and Delaware be poured out in the battles of the Revolution to win fortunes for Virginia speculators? Maryland refused to ratify the Articles of Confederation until New York's cession to Congress of her claims had insured that all the western claims would be pooled for the benefit of the United States as a whole. Virginia finally ceded her claims north of the Ohio in 1784, specifying that the claims of her enemies, the land companies, should forever be barred and that her expenses for Clark's conquest be reimbursed her.

Meanwhile various interests clustered around Maryland. The land companies, such as the Illinois and the Wabash and the Vandalia, who foresaw the ruin of their claims should Virginia make good her hold, and the French agents, anxious that the United States should not insist on too large a territory in the treaty—all looked to Maryland as their advocate. In 1780–81 it was a question whether, losing state after state to the British in the South, the confederacy would not, as Spain suggested, negotiate on the ground of present possession.

The victory at Yorktown changed the military situation in the East, and the fall of Lord North's ministry in England insured the colonies liberal terms; for the Earl of Shelburne, prime minister at the critical time of the negotiations, resolved to secure to Great Britain the future friendship of America and at all costs to detach her from dependency on France and Spain. Possibly the American diplomatists might have gained Canada by more astute play of their hands; but the acquisition of all the Northwest to the channel of navigation through Lakes Ontario, Erie, Huron, and Superior was a triumph great and unforeseen by France.

The solution of two problems regarding the Northwest and the Illinois was reached in the years 1780–84: title was to rest in the United States and its settlement was to take place under the auspices of the United States and for the benefit of the United States as a whole. Whether the new nation would have the strength to hold the West when England under ministers less liberal than Shelburne should repent of her generosity in 1782 and whether the United States could muster the political wisdom necessary to solve the problem of government and empire where both France and England had failed were still open questions.

The first question was to be answered only in the next generation, but the United States' demonstration of her capacity to meet the second comes within the space of ten years. The very fact that the Congress of the United States had a West to develop and needed efficient powers to do so was a contributing factor in the framing of the Constitution of the United States in 1787; the need of an organization under which free government might develop in the West bore fruit in the famous ordinance for the government of the territory northwest of the river Ohio. Congressional action on the problem of western organization really begins with Jefferson's draft of the Ordinance of 1784. In the western country there were already settlements in the present states of Michigan, Indiana, Wisconsin, Illinois, Tennessee, and Kentucky. Jefferson's proposal was to block off the whole acquisition of 1783 into embryo states, ten of them in the Northwest and Kentucky, with extent determined in part at least by physical configuration. Within each of these states the inhabitants might form an almost autonomous government that on reaching a certain population might be admitted to the original sisterhood of states. Slavery, Jefferson proposed to prohibit in the West, North and South alike, after 1800. His proposal was amended and recommitted, and for three years Congress brooded over the ordinance. In 1785 Monroe brought back word that the prairies were a hopeless desert sure never to be densely populated; and Congress decided that the country north of the Ohio should be the basis of three or at most of five states. Congress was again debating a draft ordinance not far removed in form from that finally adopted when a new factor gave an impetus to their work.

Since the close of the Revolution a group of revolutionary soldiers, mainly New Englanders, had been considering the possibility of a settlement founded in the wilderness, where in the economic race they might regain the ground their patriotism had lost them at home. Washington had indorsed their plan, but Congress did nothing; and for a time they thought of settling in the future state of Maine. However, General Rufus Putnam, who had been surveying lands in Maine after visiting the Ohio country, reported the latter incomparably better, and new interest was aroused. An Ohio Company was formed in New England among old soldiers who agreed to contribute Continental scrip and bounty-land warrants to the purchase of a large tract on the Muskingum River. To negotiate the purchase, they sent several agents to Congress, notably the Reverend Manasseh Cutler, Congregational divine, chaplain in the Revolution, botanist, physician, financial negotiator, politician, and future congressman.

On arriving at New York, where the Congress was sitting, Manasseh Cutler was not long in perceiving the strong points in his position. The men of his company, conservative, many of them supposedly favorers of monarchical government in the United States, were the sort of men the growing conservative spirit wished settled in the West to curb its lawlessness. The news of the purchase and prospective settlements by such men would draw additional purchasers. Wealthy New York speculators planned to launch a land company of their own in connection and assisted the Ohio Company in getting what it wanted.

With those influences working for him, Cutler made the best possible bargain. Primarily interested in the financial terms of the transaction, he was concerned incidentally in getting the Northwest Ordinance made a fit thing for New England men to live under. As it finally passed, the local autonomy in Jefferson's draft was modified. In the first stage of territorial government, authority was to be exercised by a governor, secretary, and judges appointed by Congress, selecting laws from the codes of the original thirteen states. With a population of five thousand the territory might pass to the second stage in which the lower house of the legislature was elected by the people, the governor chosen by Congress, and the council elected by co-optation of the Congress and the territorial lower house. With a population of sixty thousand within the bounds designated for a state, the state was to be admitted to the Union on an equality with the older commonwealths. By the famous Sixth Article of Compact, slavery was never to be introduced.

The ordinance, as has been said, represents a reaction from the extreme autonomy of Jefferson's draft of 1784. Yet wisdom there undoubtedly was in dispensing with representative institutions in a frontier settlement that was almost a military outpost; here liberty enough would exist in any case, and stronger government than the community could impose on itself was necessary. The two successive degrees of enlargement, to the second territorial stage and to statehood, were a pledge that the older states would never try to reduce the West to a permanent colonial dependency. Citizens of the old states might go into the new country secure that the political privileges they had enjoyed at home would follow them as fast as they were able to make use of them. So far as a paper plan could settle it, the problem of imperial organization in the West had been solved. Whether the United States was strong enough to hold the territory and put the plan in operation or whether her teeming western population might not develop in allegiance to some other government only time would tell.

CHAPTER IV

The Struggle for the Northwest, 1783–1816

BY THE treaty of 1783 the United States had acquired a title to the Northwest but little more. The Illinois villages, torn by anarchy, would look to her for orderly government; from her borders the headstrong frontier element would pour across the Ohio against the Indians, but that was all the "thirteen fires"—as the Indians named the new republic—could reckon on in 1783. For thirteen years Great Britain retained the posts south of the treaty line that controlled the Great Lakes and the northern part of the Northwest Territory; for twenty years more her citizens controlled the region commercially and encouraged the Indian to make head against the American. Not until 1815 did the British abandon the hope of obtaining a buffer Indian state in the Northwest; not until 1816 did the United States enter on full possession of her mighty empire.

To grasp the difficulties of the years 1783–1816, one must understand a theory and a policy which ran through the writings of Canadian governors and commandants of that generation with respect to American control of the Northwest. The theory is that the negotiators of 1782, from ignorance or folly, had committed a terrible mistake. Running the international boundary through the channel of navigation of the Great Lakes and the Grand Portage from Lake Superior to the Lake of the Woods and the Far West, they had shared with the Americans the control of the lakes and of the routes on which must pass the fur trade of those regions. At every portage on the route the Americans might establish themselves.

49

To Montreal merchants interested in retaining a monopoly of the fur trade this was disaster enough; but the military officers reasoned a step further. Whoever controlled the Indian trade of the Northwest controlled the Indians. Hopelessly fallen away from the independence of his fathers, the Indian must look to his master for blankets, kettles, gunpowder, and rifles. In time of peace the white man's hunter, in time of war his mercenary soldier, employment with one side or the other he must seek. If he were to be employed by the American in time of war—and the British officer judged the American's willingness to employ the Indian by his own—the long unstable line of defense in Canada, stretching from the Straits of Detroit to Quebec, might be pierced by attack from the Chaudière or Lake Champlain, the right flank cut off by an advance at the outlet of Lake Ontario and turned by the attack of an army of western Indians at Niagara and Detroit. One campaign with Indian assistance should bring the Americans to the gates of Quebec. On the other hand, if the Indians of the Northwest were on the side of the British, the right flank at least was safe. At all costs, therefore, the Indians must be held in attachment to the British.

The policy by which this was to be accomplished must necessarily be a delicate one that sometimes trod close to the margin of international comity. So long as Great Britain could avoid surrendering the western posts she held south of the international boundary, she could retain fur trade and Indians alike. But in the long run she must attempt to maintain an Indian buffer state that might stand permanently between the American settlements on the Ohio and the British fur trade on the lakes. Not until 1815 did British officials finally abandon the project and admit that by policy, commerce, and the sword the United States had won undisputed control of the Northwest.

Of course this policy varied from time to time. Until 1790 the British counted on assistance from American sources: the disaffection to the United States in Kentucky and Vermont, then outlying frontiers of the Union but loosely connected with it by law or sentiment, and the supposed friendliness of the Ohio Company settlers to monarchical institutions. When the Nootka Sound controversy was on foot with Spain in 1790, and it seemed that Great Britain would make war for control of the northern Pacific Coast, the British realized that the Americans in the West, if not the United States, might be a useful auxiliary. Toward the end of the century they counted on it also, in the days when it seemed that Spanish Louisiana would pass from the feeble hands of Spain to the vigorous ones of France and that French influence would dominate the tribes of the Northwest and control the Mississippi River route to the sea. For a decade after 1796 the policy of hostility to American interests in the West in view of more immediate danger remained veiled, but then disputes over the rights of neutral trade once more revealed its presence.

The United States in 1783 had plunged boldly into the solution of her difficult problem. She demanded, even if in vain, the cession of the western posts—Mackinac, Detroit, Niagara, and the rest. She gathered the chiefs of the Iroquois or Six Nations and the Indian Nations of the Ohio and Indiana and in a series of treaties, culminating with the Treaty of Fort Harmar of 1789, secured paper cessions of all but the northern part of Ohio. But the treaties and the encroachments of the white settlers goaded the Indians to war, and in 1789 massacre broke out along the Ohio.

The Americans launched punitive expeditions against the country where the Indian villages lay thickest—the interlocking headwaters of the Wabash, the Great Miami, and the Maumee, what is now northwestern Ohio and eastern Indiana; General Harmar's expedition in 1790 ended in something very like a defeat. A year later General Arthur St. Clair, governor of the Northwest Territory, a feeble old man, led a still larger one; it was ill-equipped, ill-supplied, ill-disciplined, and started too late in the year. On November 4, 1791, St. Clair's campaign came to an end when his camp on the upper waters of the Wabash was stormed by the tribesmen in a massacre proverbial to the day when Custer's Last Stand replaced it. The Indians seemed on the point of making good their demand that the Americans give up the claim to the Northwest acquired by the Treaty of 1783 and retire behind the Ohio. The United States, while raising a new army, opened negotiations for peace.

It is hard to state precisely the policy of the British from 1791 to 1795. The home government and the Canadian officials alike had welcomed the pretexts offered by the American failure to live up to the provisions of the Treaty of 1783 that no legal barrier should be opposed to the payment of debts owed to British merchants, in order to retain the western posts and the western fur trade. The local British Indian agents and the British fur traders who wandered unchecked through the territory undoubtedly encouraged the Indian resistance. The higher British officials in Canada were at least complacent about it. They were convinced, or affected to be convinced, that the expeditions of Harmar and St. Clair had for their goal the seizure of Detroit and with it control of the upper lakes and the lion's share of their fur trade. Yet, while they wished Indian resistance to American aggression, they disapproved strongly its reaching the point of war. War injured the fur trade and threatened ultimately to involve Great Britain herself. John Jay was in England endeavoring by a general treaty to settle the various issues, including those of the Indians and the western posts which in 1793 had seemed to be hurrying the two nations into a general war for which neither one was anxious. Therefore when Lord Dorchester, governor of Canada, early in 1794 told the Indians that he would not be surprised at war with the United States, and reminded them that a new boundary must then be drawn by the warriors, he much exceeded the policy of the English ministry. Once the American campaign of 1794 against the Indians began,

Canadian officials had the hard task of retaining the confidence of the Indians without assisting them by any overt act. That they failed is not surprising.

After St. Clair's defeat the British game became indeed a difficult one. Elaborate American preparations against the Indians equally threatened Detroit; and as an outpost to defend it in 1794 the British founded a new fort on American soil at the rapids of the Maumee. They took under their fostering care the negotiations of the United States with the Indians, permitting American commissioners in 1793 to deal with the Indians through British intermediaries. The English officials hoped that the Indians would grant a boundary that the United States could accept and thus assure permanently their desired neutral ground in the Old Northwest. They enlisted the influence of the Six Nations to this end. The Six Nations and the Lake Indians would have offered the United States the Muskingum; but the remainder insisted on the Ohio and the old line of the Treaty of Fort Stanwix of 1768. They refused in the negotiation of 1793 to admit the American commissioners to council until they yielded the Ohio boundary; and the negotiations broke off, as the British believed the Americans intended they should.

While the Indian negotiations of 1793 were in progress, Major General Anthony Wayne had been patiently disciplining a new army and drilling it in open-order formations. In the spring of 1794, Wayne, far different from the daredevil hero of such enterprises as the storming of Stony Point, where the last order was to knock out the musket flints and carry the works by the bayonet alone, had begun his campaign. This Wayne was wise, wily, and cunning, for slowly he crept forward into the Indian country, fortifying a post at each step. Indian chiefs, who knew what good exterior guard was, tried in vain to penetrate his outposts and announced that the Americans had now a new war chief who never slept. On August 13, 1794, he issued a manifesto to the tribesmen bidding them take the choice of peace or war and, receiving no satisfactory answer, passed down the Maumee Valley, devastating their villages and cornfields. On the twentieth of August, advancing in open formation through a windrow of the forest, he came on the Indians prepared for battle. His infantry, trained as Colonel Bouquet had trained them forty years before, fired and advanced in open order at the charge; the cavalry turned the Indian flank, and all was over.

As a military engagement the Battle of the Fallen Timbers was a small affair; the British insisted and probably with truth that but a fraction of the Indian strength was engaged in it; but Wayne, aided by fortune, exploited its full psychological effect on the mercurial Indian temperament. It took place but a little above the new British fort at the Rapids, and the beaten Indians, fleeing to the fort of their British father for shelter, found the gates closed against them by a commandant who feared to give Wayne a pretext to begin hostilities. Wayne put to the torch the Indian villages and the houses of the British traders around the fort, reconnoitering insolently under its very guns. The Indians knew nothing of the diplomatic limitations on the commandant and, disillusioned and discouraged, saw themselves deserted by their British father in the hour of need, and his strength flouted by the common enemy. The news of Jay's Treaty, with its promised surrender of the western posts to the Americans, only deepened their sense of abandonment by the British. Through that winter of 1795 the prestige of the British decayed as that of Wayne, the American war chief who for good or evil had kept his word with them, increased. And when Wayne summoned the tribes to meet him in council at Greenville in July, 1795, the chiefs and the warriors flocked in. This would be no treaty conducted with a handful in a corner. Its results would be definitive and permanent.

As delegation after delegation trooped into the post at Greenville, they were greeted by Wayne with the assumption of superiority and acquiesced in it. When the moment for actual negotiation came, he demanded of them the surrender of everything southeast of a line across northwestern Ohio that stands as the basis of all future negotiations and Indian cessions. Further, he exacted the cession of small tracts at every important post and portage in the West, the importance of which in control of the trade the Indians themselves well understood. Among these was the future site of Fort Dearborn at Chicago and tracts at Peoria and the mouth of the Illinois River. The tribes protested, but protested as individuals and were easily overawed and silenced; and when Wayne at the final session called on each tribe individually to say if it acquiesced, none dared lift a voice against the treaty.

The Treaty of Greenville and the surrender by Great Britain in 1796 of the western posts of which Detroit and Mackinac were the most important end the first chapter of the struggle of the United States for the Northwest. It had acquired an undisputed foothold for settlement and military control of the whole area. It had yet to learn, however, that trade did not follow the flag; and for twenty years more it seemed to hold only the outward symbols of power in a region where influence with the Indians and profitable trade remained with the British.

For Jay's Treaty, in spite of the surrender of the posts, had been a hard bargain. It had reaffirmed the right of British subjects to navigate the Mississippi freely even though it had been ascertained since the Treaty of 1783 that the river nowhere touched British soil. Still worse, it accorded to British traders the right to trade freely in American territory, and the reciprocal provision for the benefit of Americans—the territory of the Hudson's Bay Company being excepted from it—was only a hollow mockery. These objections Madison had urged to Jay's Treaty as sufficient ground for its rejection; but Congress had decided to shoulder the burden.

At this point it is necessary to consider in detail the causes of the British monopoly of the Northwest fur trade. Since the year

1769 the trade formerly enjoyed by the French south of the Hudson Bay trading region had passed into the hands of Scotch traders and firms at Montreal. On the one hand, they established connections with great London firms who supplied the goods for the trade and marketed the furs; on the other, they associated with themselves "wintering partners" in the *pays d'en haut* who supervised the buying of furs from the Indians in their winter hunts. Wintering partners, Montreal merchants, and sometimes London merchants were continually forming loose organizations or pools. Again and again these pools broke down; and resulting trade wars were waged in the West almost to the mouth of the cannon. A pool of this kind existed in 1780, four years before the formation of the famous Northwest Company. From that company or pool there were secessions in 1795, 1798, and 1800, the last year seeing the organization of a new Northwest Company, to reunite with the old after a short commercial war. A Michillimackinac Company, trading almost exclusively in the territory of the United States and comprising some of the firms already engaged in the Northwest Company, appears in the first years of the nineteenth century.

The most natural routes for the trade skirted the international boundary of 1783; its most convenient bases lay in American territory. The easiest route to the Greater Canadian Northwest ran along the channel of the Great Lakes through the Sault Ste Marie to the Grand Portage on the north shore of Lake Superior. The alternative route, through British territory by the Ottawa River from Montreal to Lake Huron, was more expensive; even if one used it, he had to pass American territory at the Sault. From Grand Portage the continent spread out before the trader to the shores of the Arctic and the Pacific; until 1796 it was the main depot of the trade to the farther Northwest. After that year the Northwest Company removed farther north on the lake shore to the Kaministique route and founded Fort William on British territory as a new base. Mackinac Island in American territory remained the best point for reprovisioning the canoes en route to the farther Northwest.

Mackinac was equally important to the Montreal groups that traded in the United States. In 1799 this trade was estimated at $100,000 a year, perhaps the major part of the whole trade. A small part of it on the shore of Lake Superior was engrossed by the Northwest Company, but most of it fell to the Mackinac groups. Until the beginning of the nineteenth century this trade was still in the hands of independent traders who in 1793 went as far down the Mississippi as the mouth of the Illinois. Even Nashville brought its supplies by way of the Cumberland from Mackinac. Prairie du Chien was an important subsidiary to Mackinac, where by 1812 as many as six thousand Indians gathered.

Mackinac Island at the opening of the nineteenth century was almost the trading center of the continent. In the spring of the year from out the rivers of the nearer Northwest came the fur-trading brigades, picking up the members left the preceding fall with their winter's take of furs. Gaining in numbers with every halt, they finally pulled their heavy Mackinac boats or canoes to the island. Here they were met by the Montreal merchants bringing out the Indian goods to be used for the next year's trade; here the picturesque boatmen and traders spent a year's pay in a few weeks' jollity; here the affairs of the pools were arranged and profits divided. From the island in the fall the merchants set out for Montreal with the previous year's haul of furs; and the fur-trading brigades loaded with Indian goods headed out in every direction, dropping individual traders with goods at likely places en route to trade and hibernate until picked up in the spring. Before 1796 it was said that the trade at Mackinac called in eight hundred persons. Sir George Prevost wrote in 1814 to Lord Bathurst:

Its Geographical position [Mackinac] is admirable, its influence extends, and is felt amongst the Indian Tribes at New Orleans and the Pacific Ocean, vast Tracts of Country look to it for protection and supplies; and it gives security to the great Trading Establishments of the North West and Hudsons Bay Companies; by supporting the Indians on the Mississippi; the only barrier which interposes between them and the Enemy, and which if once forced (an event that lately appeared probable) their progress into the heart of these companies Settlements by the Red River is practicable, & would enable them to execute their long formed project of monopolizing the whole Fur Trade into their own hands—from these observations Your Lordship will be enabled to judge how necessary the possession of this valuable post, situated on the outskirts of these extensive Provinces is daily becoming to their future security and protection.[1]

The fur trade of the Continent had long since become in men's imaginations a world trade. Soon after the Revolution the Massachusetts sea captains, debarred from their old trade with the British West Indies, had found their way around the Horn and carried furs from the Pacific Coast to China to be traded for silks, porcelain, and teas for the consumption of the settlements on the Atlantic seaboard. One of the pioneers, Captain Robert Gray, in 1792 had discovered the river he named for his ship, "Columbia," giving the United States prior title to its valley. George Mackenzie of the Northwest Company, exploring to the Arctic in 1789 and to the Pacific overland in 1793, was moved by the desire of forestalling the Americans on the Pacific Coast. In 1802 he projected a trading organization that should span the continent from Atlantic to Pacific and wrest the China trade in furs from the Americans. But the East India Company monopoly barred the way to a British subject, and his scheme was taken up by an American.

American statesmen recognized only too well the fact that the little garrison at Mackinac upheld the American flag over a post at which British capital monopolized a great American trade. To remedy it by force was impossible, and they sought to alleviate it by economic counterorganization or diplomatic finesse. In 1796 they had begun a system of government houses

1. *Michigan Pioneer and Historical Collections*, XXV, 585.

for the Indian trade; and early in the nineteenth century they began to establish these in the Northwest: at Detroit and Fort Wayne before 1803, at the mouth of the Missouri and at Fort Dearborn on the present site of Chicago in 1805, at Sandusky in 1806, at Mackinac and at Fort Madison on the Mississippi in 1808.

The fur-trading houses were latterly run at a loss, and they served to degrade the United States in the minds of the Indians to the position of a trader; they therefore gave no return in counteracting the influence over the Indians of British agents.

Diplomatic finesse and annoyances put in the way of the British trader proved more efficacious. In 1798 British goods were still being brought into the United States for Indian trade without paying customs duties. But in 1802 the new Northwest Company feared that United States customs officials had seized at the Sault Indian goods that had not been entered at Mackinac. In 1808 goods of the Michillimackinac Company had been seized while passing Niagara on the pretext that the embargo forbade all imports to the United States. And even if eventually the United States was compelled by diplomatic means to recede from a seizure of this sort, the Indians had been left without goods and a full year's trade had been lost. Thus the seizure of 1808 had resulted in the dissolution of the Michillimackinac Company in 1810. When the United States acquired Louisiana, on the pretext that it was territory not covered by the Treaty of Paris and Jay's Treaty, all British traders were excluded from a region where formerly the Spaniards had allowed them to roam at will. By economic artifice and diplomatic chicane, American diplomats worked unceasingly to sap the British monopoly.

The British merchants themselves bore testimony to the efficiency of the American policy. In 1808 they assured their government:

That the Indian trade within the American Limits must speedily be abandoned by British subjects, if not protected against interruptions of free navigation of the Lakes, fiscal extortions and various other vexations: that if once abandoned, it can never be regained and with its abandonment, will finish British influence with the Indian Nations residing within [without?] the limits of Canada: that British Traders have materially aided in preserving that influence hitherto, the conviction of which is the strong motive with the American Government for wishing, by every means they can devise, to exclude such traders.

If therefore, the minds of His Majesty's Ministers shall be made up to the loss of that portion of Indian Trade carried on within the American territory (which indeed is nearly the whole, except the North West) and to the extinction of influence amongst the Indian Tribes . . . [2]

the American government might be allowed to pursue its policy unchecked.

In the repeated negotiations of 1805–12 these points came up again and again. In 1809 British merchants urged on their government the creation of a neutral zone in the West in which no duties would be levied by either side. The boundary they suggested was the Missouri River west of the Mississippi and the Illinois River and Lake Michigan east of it. The United States must on no account be allowed a foothold on the Columbia River and the Pacific. On the other hand, American secretaries of state were instructing negotiators never to surrender the right to British traders to enter the Louisiana Purchase.

At last American capital was working into the interior fur trade on a sufficient scale to rival the British. In 1807 Manuel Lisa of St. Louis in association with Pierre Menard and William Morrison of the Illinois country dispatched an expedition up the Missouri to trade. The next year saw the incorporation by the three men of the Missouri St. Louis Fur Company. It saw also the incorporation of John Jacob Astor's American Fur Company. For ten years he had been known to the British. "A German person Jacob Oster," the Canadian government had been informed in a letter from New York of 1797, "who frequently

2. Memorial of October 20, 1808 (*ibid.*, p. 256).

visits Canada, who deals largely in Furs, and is at present ('tis said) in that country, has imported in the last ship from London 6,000 stand of arms and 100 casks of gunpowder (the latter he has advertised for sale)."[3] Astor was not merely importing arms which the Canadian government suspected were to be used in a French uprising. By buying furs in Montreal for export, he learned the fur trade. His American Fur Company was established in 1808 in partnership with Canadian traders and planned on a magnificent scale. His bases for trade were to be Mackinac and Astoria on the Columbia; the two were to be connected by an overland route, and both with New York, by canoe through the Great Lakes, and by ship through the two oceans.

While all these forces were at work sapping the British control of the trade, the United States was engaged in an Indian policy designed to get rid as fast as possible of the tribes of the Northwest. President Jefferson planned to reduce their possessions and by teaching them the arts of agriculture to change them from hunters to farmers; at the same time he and his governor of Indiana Territory, William Henry Harrison, sought cession after cession. As the Indian tribes, corroded like metal on the touch of the acid of the white man's fire water, lost numbers, self-reliance and force, treaties were extracted from the wrecks of the tribes. By 1809 Harrison had obtained treaties surrendering practically all Ohio, eastern Michigan, southern Indiana, and most of western and southern Illinois.

In protest against this policy there rose perhaps the ablest of all the Indian statesmen warriors who have sought to withstand the march of the white man—Tecumseh. Working with the spiritual influence of his brother, the Shawnee Prophet, he drew the Indians away from their tribal chiefs and villages into communities from which the white man, his goods, and fire water were barred. As the Northwest belonged to the Indians in common—so he taught his converts—there must be no more sales or

3. *Canadian Archives*, 1891, p. 155.

cessions save by common consent. Tecumseh, at first so weak that a tomahawk blow inspired by a rival chieftain might have ended him and his movement together, by 1811 had become a menace to American authority; while he was absent from his villages in the Upper Wabash country engaged in cementing a still wider league against the Americans, there came Harrison's expedition against him of November, 1811, and the barren victory of Tippecanoe, which hardly scotched the influence of Tecumseh and the Prophet.

In 1811 the diplomacy of Madison appeared to have reached an impasse; and the belief that British aid to the Indians had rendered the Tippecanoe campaign a necessity swept the West with the war fever. Since 1807 the diplomatic difficulties of Great Britain and the United States over neutral trade had grown more and more acute; and the British government, again compelled to face the possibility of war on the Canadian frontier, had newly enlarged its Indian department. The frontiersmen believed British agents were supplying Tecumseh and urging him on. It was the hope of the conquest of Canada in a single campaign and the ending of the British control for all time that made such typical westerners as Henry Clay of Kentucky demand war. British officials on their side hoped to extort from the United States a treaty by which the Indians "should retain possession of the lands they now occupy and thereby form as long as we remain in friendship with them a formidable barrier to any future attempts of America against His Majesty's possessions in that neighborhood."[4] Both sides looked with confidence to the War of 1812 to settle in their favor the control of the Northwest.

In calculating the advantages of the American position on the Great Lakes, the Canadian military authorities had not reckoned with the imbecility of their first military opponents. The blame

4. Prevost to Bathurst, October 5, 1812 (*Michigan Pioneer and Historical Collections*, XXV, 358–59).

for the disgraces of the War of 1812 has usually been fastened on the militia and volunteer system, but as one studies the army of the United States under the regime of General James Wilkinson from 1796 to 1812, inefficiently managed, honeycombed with intrigue and corruption, one wonders if a part of the blame should not be allotted to it and if a volunteer militia is not as good or as bad as the regular army set to discipline it.

The first campaign in the Northwest beyond all expectations gave the British control of the upper lakes. Madison had not reinforced Mackinac before navigation closed; immediately on the outbreak of war it was attacked by a force of British and Indians from St. Joseph and the commander induced to surrender to avoid an Indian massacre. With Mackinac all the Indians of the Northwest fell under British control; and again at Detroit, August 16, General Hull was induced to surrender by the representations of British officers that they could not hold their Indian allies from massacre in case of victory. The day before, the American garrison of Fort Dearborn at Chicago, retreating from the fort, were massacred two miles away from it.

The British control of the West depended on the naval control of Lakes Erie and Ontario. It was almost impossible for them to transport supplies overland to their western garrisons; and the women and children as well as the warriors of their savage allies must be fed, clothed, and supplied with presents. As the Indian knew no mean between gorging and starvation, his appetite played havoc with ration tables. The necessity of keeping open communications on Lake Erie in 1813 compelled Barclay, the British naval commander, to offer battle to Perry's fleet; and Perry's victory, brilliant and far-reaching in results, compelled the British to abandon Detroit and enabled General Harrison to pursue their army into Canada and defeat it at the Thames.

Had the Americans used their advantage with the proper efficiency, they should have gained permanent control of the upper lakes; but in 1814 the garrison at Mackinac beat off an

American attack and later actually succeeded in capturing on Lake Huron the schooners it was made in. In June, 1813, General William Clark had occupied Prairie du Chien; and a force mainly of Canadians was sent to recapture and hold it under an able young officer, Lieutenant Bulger. They not only kept the Indians of the region attached to the British cause but defeated two American expeditions sent up to retake the post, the second under Major Zachary Taylor. When the operations of 1814 closed, both sides were making great efforts to secure the naval control of the lower lakes for the next year. The territory of Illinois, which then included Wisconsin, was an important field of military operations; within the present state little occurred. Governor Ninian Edwards of Illinois Territory waged a petty war of frontier forts and of raids on Indian towns within his territory. In 1813 Illinois and Missouri were placed under command of General Benjamin Howard of Missouri, much to Edwards' disgust, who aspired to rival as a soldier his neighbor, Governor Harrison of Indiana. Under Howard's orders ranger companies were raised on the frontier and Fort Clark was established at Peoria.

In the Treaty of Ghent, American diplomacy accomplished what American arms had been unable to effect. The British matched second-rate diplomats against the ablest that America could produce; as a result they were defeated on their claim for a buffer Indian state in the Northwest, and the treaty did not repeat the clause of Jay's Treaty giving British subjects freedom of trade. It provided simply for the surrender of all conquests on both sides.

At surrendering Mackinac with its control of the trade to the Americans, Lieutenant Colonel McDonell, the British commandant at the post, and the fur-trading companies alike protested bitterly. They enlarged on its importance to the trade, on the necessity of keeping it at all costs, or at least keeping the Americans out of it; but all to no purpose. Secretary of State

James Monroe knew its value as well as anyone and demanded its immediate return, and Mackinac was surrendered to the Americans on July 18, 1815.

There followed one of those brief periods when the American government seems to act with superhuman intelligence and energy to repair long years of shortcoming. The Americans in the West played with rare skill upon the fact that the Indians of the West felt themselves once more abandoned by the British. They took advantage of the British preoccupation with the Waterloo campaign of 1815. Acting swiftly in the years 1815 and 1816, they prepared for the restoration of the old posts at Fort Dearborn and the occupation of Prairie du Chien and Green Bay to cut off all possible routes of approach to Canada from the Indians west of Lake Michigan. British officials protested that the building of new posts in the Indian country was a violation of the treaty, but to no purpose. In the course of 1816 there were posts at Chicago, Prairie du Chien, Green Bay, Warsaw on the Mississippi River, Rock Island, and Peoria. In 1816 an act of Congress barred all aliens from the trade who did not obtain permits from American Indian agents. The British trader was finally excluded from the region. Astor's American Fur Company took over the remaining posts of the Northwest Company. The future of the trade was in American hands.

For the third time since 1782 the Indian had a right to feel himself abandoned by his British allies, and the Americans acquired an ascendancy they never again lost. New cession treaties were extorted from the Sauk and Foxes, one confirming the St. Louis cession of 1804. With hard words to the Indians the American officers boasted that they had "thrown their British father on his back" and that his Indian children were left at the mercy of his enemies.

Complained an Indian chief at Mackinac to the British:

My Father, I shall in the first place tell you how the Chiefs I sent to St. Louis were treated by the Big Knifes Chief [Governor Clarke] on their arrival there being three Chiefs and several soldiers, they were seated in the circle with the other Indians, the American Chief in going around to shake hands, said that the men I had sent were unfit to talk with him, and that he must absolutely *see me* or my *Head War Chief The Black Hawk*, he added to my Brother, you must immediately send off messengers to tell Lemoite and the Black Hawk to repair to this place in the course of thirty days; *If they do not*, I will ascend the Mississippi *and find them;* those your nation who remain here will be guarded by soldiers, til your Head Chiefs obey my summons. If they are not here in thirty days their Blood will be spilt for their disobedience.

Then addressing the Kickapoos, You have a choice, say you wish for war and we are ready, say you wish for Peace, and it shall be so.—Ye Sauks, Kickapoos, Renards, Poutawatamies you see what you must do, you must never expect to see your English Father again, you have rendered yourselves miserable by following his advice by going to war with us. He did not this year ask you to embark in his Boats, to traverse the Lakes.—We are going to build Forts on the Mississippi, we have driven your English Father from thence and from Michilimackinac, you are miserable, you will not have an English Trader amongst you; *how can they come?*

All this time and while the council lasted guns were pointed at my chiefs [continued Le Moite] and as often as the American chief the Red Head [meaning Governor Clarke] spoke harsh to them, several other tribes who were present would yell with joy, which makes me much ashamed as they were principally our Enemies from the Misouri. . . .[5]

In his dispatches of 1815 and 1816 Lieutenant Colonel McDonell interpreted the American policy. He believed that the Americans were trying to provoke the Indians to hostilities that would put them outside the treaty, for, unsupplied with powder, they were at the mercy of their enemies:

I have taken every precaution to make known the news of Peace, & to put a stop to that predatory mode of warfare, which they are continually waging against the Americans. To effect this *entirely* among so many tribes, having such cause to hate that people, need not be expected. The Govt of the United States therefore, will

5. *Ibid.*, XVI, 194–95.

soon have a fair pretext to glut their vengeance against them & gradually to root them out. They will probably stop all Powder from going to the Mississippi (when they get this place) without which, these nations must perish in the winter; the slow but sure poison of their whisky stills, will effect the rest, and in fifty years time, there perhaps will not be an Indian left between this and the Rocky Mountains, to plague either party.[6]

In these words Lieutenant Colonel McDonell wrote the epitaph of the Indians of the Northwest. The British still tried to hold out a hand to their old allies; General Lewis Cass had to order tribesmen in Michigan to pull down British flags from their lodges; Black Hawk and his band continued to make pilgrimages to Malden for British presents and advice until their overthrow in 1832; but these things could not even retard the displacement of the Indian by the white. The possession of the Northwest Territory and with it of the Illinois had passed to the hands that had held the title; its exploitation was destined to be under American institutions.

6. McDonell to Foster, May 15, 1815 (*ibid.*, p. 104).

CHAPTER V

The Day of Small Things

FROM the passage of the Ordinance of 1787 Illinois had a definite political relation to the United States in theory, and, with the arrival of Governor St. Clair of the Northwest Territory at Kaskaskia on March 5, 1790, the theory became translated into fact; but for many years to come the Illinois country was on the edge of the government thus created. Until 1800 it was a part of the Northwest Territory; from 1800 to 1809 it was a part of Indiana Territory; and only with the creation of Illinois Territory in 1809 and with subsequent statehood in 1818 did it recover a measurable control of its destinies. Its politics throughout the period seem petty factional and personal quarrels, and the only distinguishable motif that runs throughout is the slavery issue.

Slavery gives point to most of the politics of the territory and state from 1787 to 1824. After 1787 the French inhabitants, alarmed by the reports that the Ordinance had abolished slavery, were moving with their slaves across the river to Spanish territory, until they were reassured by St. Clair's decision that the antislavery clause of the Ordinance did not apply to slaves already held in the territory. It was the desire to overturn the Ordinance and introduce new slaves that led in 1809 to the division of Indiana Territory and the setting-off of Illinois. The first constitution of Illinois, protecting the holding of indentured servants, marks a compromise, a breathing space in the struggle between slavery and freedom. Not until 1824 did the six years of contest out of which had emerged the statehood of Illinois and the Missouri Compromise bring forth the definitive decision that thenceforth Illinois was to be free.

What little we know of Illinois from 1789 to 1800 is recorded in the history of government of the Northwest Territory. On April 27, 1790, St. Clair set off the county of St. Clair with boundaries including all Illinois south of the Illinois River and west of a line drawn from the mouth of Mackinaw River to Fort Massac on the Ohio. Official records tell us that one of the judges of the Northwest Territory, George Turner, took part in the old controversy between Kaskaskia and Cahokia, ordering the records of the local court to be kept at Kaskaskia; to settle the difficulty, in 1795 the county of Randolph was created with Kaskaskia for its county seat. Until 1798 the governor and the three federal judges legislated for the Northwest Territory, supposedly selecting laws from the codes of the older states. When the territory passed to the second state of territorial government and had a legislature with an elected lower house, St. Clair County sent the senior Shadrach Bond and Randolph County John Edgar to sit among the twenty-three representatives. The laws passed by this legislature in 1799–1800 reenacted by territorial and state legislatures in Indiana and Illinois formed the basis of the Illinois code for thirty years to come; but one wonders how far some of them were ever enforced. Laws for the settlement of the poor which prohibited their free movement, laws that unmarried insolvent debtors must work out their debts in seven years' servitude for their creditors, match strangely with a frontier community on the edge of the wilderness.

It must not however be forgotten that the government over the Illinois in this period was more aristocratic than it ever has been since. The officials sent out by Congress to govern successively the Northwest, Indiana, and Illinois territories were accorded the position and consideration of gentlemen. The men who led the opposition to them claimed likewise to be gentle-men. And the rank and file of the population of the territory willingly conceded gentlemen the right of political leadership. Under the Northwest Ordinance the suffrage was restricted to the small group of freeholders. While it was subsequently ex-tended, not until the Jacksonian revolution in Illinois was the control of the aristocrats of the territorial period finally dis-carded.

Of the actual life of the Illinois country when it was a part of the Northwest Territory we know little or nothing. The hand-ful of French inhabitants was being supplemented by a handful of American frontiersmen. They lived a rude life in stockaded "stations"; some of them forgot all religious training, while others welcomed the first volunteer Methodist and Baptist preachers who came in. As early as 1787 the Baptist James Smith preached in the Illinois. The first Baptist church was founded at New Design in 1796. The first Methodist preacher, Reverend Joseph Lillard, appeared in 1793. In 1803 Benjamin Young was assigned to ride the circuit in the Illinois. Roman Catholic priests only occasionally visited the land that had witnessed the labors of Marquette, Allouez, and Meurin. By 1800 there were per-haps 2,500 souls, almost evenly divided between French and Americans within the present state. In 1806 there were 4,300 in Illinois and the present Wisconsin. In 1812 there were 12,282.

Increase was doubtless retarded by the slow evolution of the government's machinery for disposing of the public lands. The Act of 1796, providing for sales at two dollars an acre on a year's credit in tracts not less than a section or 640 acres, placed the land beyond the reach of the average frontier farmer. In 1800 William Henry Harrison, as delegate to Congress from the Northwest Territory, had secured a more liberal measure which permitted sales in 320-acre tracts with a credit extending over four years. In 1804 lands in Indiana Territory, of which Illinois was a part, were sold in 160-acre tracts.

This legislation in practice did not help the dwellers in the future state of Illinois because, before the federal government could begin surveys and sales of public land, it had to determine what claims to land under ancient French grants and under its own promises of donations were actually binding on it. In 1788 Congress had granted 400 acres to each French head of a family resident in 1783; in 1791 it had extended the grant to all heads of families resident in 1783 and added a grant of 100 acres to each militiaman not benefited by other grants; further, it had confirmed all holdings, no matter how shaky in title, if they had been improved in good faith. In confirming titles by grants and donation rights, Governor St. Clair had been lavish and careless; Governor Harrison of Indiana Territory for a time was as bad. The greater part of the French inhabitants had long since despaired of realizing on congressional promises and had sold their rights for a song to aggressive American speculators like John Edgar and the Morrisons. Many claims put forward by those and other men seemed to require examination.

The investigation of a commission into the mass of titles, confirmed and unconfirmed, produced startling results. Not only had the speculators bought up numerous French claims good, bad, and indifferent; they had actually manufactured false headright and improvement claims, basing them on affidavits sworn to wholesale by bibulous Frenchmen under the influence of brandy and had transferred the claims to themselves by fraudulent conveyances. So complicated was the problem and so bitter the opposition to investigation that it was not until 1809 that the commission reported and not until 1810 that the acceptance of the report by Congress cleared the way for the survey of townships and the sale of quarter-sections at the land offices of Shawneetown and Kaskaskia.

The investigations into land frauds probably had their influence on the development of political parties in the territory. The period, whether blessed or not, in which Illinois had no history, had passed. Barely had William Henry Harrison, now governor of Indiana Territory, arrived at Vincennes on January 10, 1801, than the contest between Harrison and anti-Harrison parties opened. In the Illinois country, Edgar and the Morrisons, the speculating interests, ranged themselves against the governor. Among the governor's friends were the Shadrach Bonds, uncle and nephew, Dr. George Fisher, and Pierre Menard, an able and benevolent Frenchman born in Canada who had come to the territory in 1790. Both factions in the beginning were proslavery as was Harrison himself. They were reduced to differing as to the method of overruling the prohibition in the Northwest Ordinance and introducing slaves. Harrison's following sponsored petitions to Congress for the relaxation of the Ordinance; in 1796 and 1800 the Illinois country had so petitioned without effect. In 1802 Harrison summoned a convention of the territory which drew up a memorial to Congress asking among other things admission of slaves for ten years. A committee of Congress finally reported favorably on it, but nothing was done. Meanwhile, in 1803, Harrison and the territorial judges had adopted an indenture law allowing Negroes to be indentured and brought into the territory to serve long terms of years.

The anti-Harrison element at first advocated proceeding to the second stage of territorial government as a means of getting a delegate in Congress to voice the plea for slavery. In 1804 Harrison swung around to support the proposal; and his opponents, placing party before consistency, changed their positions and opposed the measure they had before advocated. Harrison's proposal carried in a popular vote, and a pro-Harrison lower house of the legislature was elected with George Fisher, William Biggs, and Shadrach Bond as members from the two Illinois counties. In 1805 and in 1807 this body passed indenture laws under which whole families of Negroes down to the babe at the breast were indentured to long terms of servitude. The same years saw repeated a series of petitions from the legislature and the inhabitants of the Illinois for a modification of the Ordinance to permit slavery. Congressional committees reported them favorably but did no more. The story has been set forth that these petitions were blocked by Jefferson, who twenty years before had dispatched James Lemen to the Illinois country, making a secret compact with him that they would work together to keep slavery out of the Northwest. There is no proof that the alleged documents upon which this claim is based are more than clumsy forgeries.

In 1807 the question approached the crisis. The elevation of Bond and Fisher to the territorial council had left their seats in the lower house to be filled. The new members were John Rice Jones and John Messinger, both of the anti-Harrison faction. Indiana proper was no longer agreed on the subject of slavery; men with anti-slavery sentiments had begun to settle in Dearborn County; in 1805 they had petitioned Congress to be annexed to the free state of Ohio. They hoped that, if the pro-slavery bloc of the Illinois country was detached from the territory, they might be able to turn the balance in favor of freedom. The Edgar-Morrison group had for some time been working for separation from Indiana; in 1803 they sought to have the Illinois villages annexed to the newly purchased Louisiana Territory across the Mississippi; in 1805, 1806, and 1808 they had petitioned for the erection of a separate territory in Illinois, the last of the three petitions being opposed in a counterpetition of the Harrison group.

The session of 1808 saw a political bargain for the election of Jesse B. Thomas, the Dearborn County member as territorial delegate to Congress, under pledge to work for the division of the territory. As Thomas was a slippery politician, the Illinois members took his bond for specific performance of the bargain. All worked out as expected. On February 9, 1809, Congress set off Illinois Territory, including the present state of Wisconsin. As a fitting commentary on the factional strife that led up to the division, Rice Jones, the younger, was assassinated on the streets of Kaskaskia, and the anti-Harrison speculating group tried to fix complicity in the murder on their enemy, Michael Jones, the land commissioner.

Fortunately, the organization of the new Illinois Territory was with one exception intrusted to new men. Jesse B. Thomas came back as territorial judge, but his colleagues, Alexander Stuart and Obediah Jones, soon replaced by Stanley Griswold, were strangers. So was the secretary, Nathaniel Pope, and his relative the new governor, Ninian Edwards of Kentucky. Edwards adroitly refused to take sides with either faction and based his appointments to office so far as he could on popular referenda. In 1812 the territory voted almost unanimously to proceed to the second grade of territorial government; and Congress in 1812 extended the suffrage to all adult males resident a year and paying taxes, for the older freehold requirement would have barred the majority of the population. In October, 1812, the junior Shadrach Bond was elected delegate to Congress, and a territorial legislature was chosen.

The only measure at issue in the local politics of Illinois Territory concerned the legislature's attempt to regulate the terms of court held by the federal judges; ultimately it gave up the struggle and created courts independent of those provided by the federal government. But the history of Indiana Territory repeated itself in the formation of political factions for and against the governor. Some men such as Pierre Menard and the Bonds were neutral. Young men like Elias Kent Kane and John McLean, who came to the territory to seek their fortunes, joined the opposition; others like Pope's relative, Daniel Pope Cook, gathered round Edwards.

The close of the War of 1812 saw a rapid development in Illinois. Harbingers of civilized community life such as newspapers appeared. In 1814 the *Illinois Herald* was founded at Kaskaskia, continuing under several changes of name. In 1818 at Shawneetown, now the natural gateway to Illinois from the East, Peter Kimmel founded the *Illinois Emigrant*. Population flooded into the territory. By 1818 it seemed quite possible that statehood was attainable. Daniel Pope Cook in 1817 began a campaign for it in the *Western Intelligencer*, as the *Illinois Herald* was then called. Opinion seemed to favor the measure, and in Congress Nathaniel Pope as territorial delegate introduced a bill for an enabling act.

The result is a high tribute to Pope's political skill. He managed to maneuver the bill through both houses; the best testimony to his address is the fact that a similar bill concerning Missouri was introduced too late and failed of passage. The terms obtained for Illinois were most liberal: of the proceeds of government sales of land within her borders, Illinois was to have 3 per cent for education and 2 per cent was to be expended by Congress for roads leading to the state. In addition, she received Section 16 in each township for schools, a whole township for a seminary of learning, and all salt licks. Her northern boundary instead of being the east-and-west line through the foot of Lake Michigan, as the Northwest Ordinance prescribed, was set as it now stands, some sixty miles farther north. Pope, in advocating the change in the terms of the Ordinance, emphasized the importance of giving the new state a footing on the Great Lakes and territorial propinquity to both North and South. At present the importance of the change secured by Pope is best measured by the fact that 60 per cent of the population of Illinois lies in the territory he secured. In the days of the slavery struggle the voters of the section turned the tide for the election of Lincoln.[1]

The enabling act once passed, a constitutional convention was speedily elected. It began its labors on August 3 and concluded them twenty-three days after. With but little difficulty it framed a very rudimentary government in which practically all

1. Lincoln carried the state in 1860 by 12,000 votes plurality. His plurality in the district must have been over 25,000.

of the legislative and most of the appointive power was placed in the General Assembly. Territorial experience with governors and judiciaries united with current political theory to leave the judiciary subject to the regulation of the legislature and to intrust to the governor and judges sitting as a Council of Revision only a veto power that could be and usually was overriden by a majority of members elected to the legislature.

Again the slavery question was the burning one. Slavery and antislavery had been the issue in the elections to the convention; both sides had filled the newspapers with their articles. The antislavery party lost the elections, but prudence lest Congress refuse to accept the constitution made its provisions on slavery nondescript. It confirmed the territorial indentures but prohibited the further introduction of slavery. Without submission to a popular vote the constitution came before Congress. There, with the Missouri struggle impending, northern men challenged the Illinois constitution as a violation of the Ordinance; but on December 3, 1818, Illinois was formally admitted to the Union.

For six years more slavery remained the great political issue in the state. The Missouri struggle that began in the very session in which the Illinois representatives first took their seats riveted men's attention to the course of their representatives on the question. John McLean, the state's first congressman, was defeated for re-election by Cook on the issue of McLean's vote for the admission of Missouri as a slave state. Ninian Edwards and Jesse B. Thomas were the state's senators, and both were on the side of slavery. To Thomas was intrusted the introduction in the Senate of the famous amendment embodying the Missouri Compromise providing for the admission of Missouri as a slave state on condition that slavery be barred from the rest of the Louisiana Territory north of thirty-six degrees and thirty minutes. A strong opposition to both men developed because of their proslavery attitude.

The victory of the slavery forces on the Missouri question apparently encouraged the advocates of slavery in Illinois. Repeatedly it had been said in debate that the Northwest Ordinance prohibition of slavery could not bind a sovereign state after its admission to the Union. A slave state across the river from Illinois, already dominating Illinois trade from its metropolis of St. Louis, would attract away the well-to-do southern emigrants so long as Illinois remained free. Young men of means in a frontier community resented the fact that their wives for want of domestic help had to toil at household tasks and hoped for a state of things in which housemaids would be a purchasable commodity. Missourians, indignant that antislavery sentiment in Illinois had meddled with their domestic concern of slavery, planned to retaliate. The Shawneetown saline required labor to build fires and carry water; and Adolphus F. Hubbard reminded the Illinois legislature that these were duties for which divine Providence had pointed out the Negro. A campaign for the amendment of the Illinois constitution to admit slavery was soon under way.

Much turned on the election for governor in 1822. Four candidates were in the field. Of them, Judge Joseph Phillips was proslavery, James B. Moore perhaps was antislavery, Thomas C. Browne nondescript, and Edward Coles, a stiff Virginian of the Jeffersonian school, lately come to Illinois, avowedly antislavery. By a narrow margin Coles was elected.

A resolution submitting to the people the calling of a convention to amend the constitution came up in the General Assembly of 1822–23. In the senate the proslavery forces had the necessary two-thirds majority. In the house at first they lacked it by one vote. There was, however, a contested election in Pike County between John Shaw and Nicholas Hansen; the technical merits of the contest are in doubt. But Hansen was seated early in the session, apparently to get a vote against Ninian Edwards for United States senator. When Hansen voted against the convention resolution, the house by a majority vote reopened the question of his election, reversed its former decision, seated John Shaw in his stead, and, with Shaw's vote, passed the resolution. A two years' campaign before the people began at once. Coles, by his position the leader of the anticonvention forces, drew to his aid Morris Birkbeck, the English radical, who had sought in Illinois a refuge from the aristocratic control of English politics and had been one of the founders of the English settlement in Edwards County. Other antislavery men rallied to them. The *Edwardsville Spectator*, although its editor, Hooper Warren, was personally hostile to Coles, became the antislavery organ; soon the antislavery men gained control of the *Illinois Intelligencer*. Eastern Quakers contributed antislavery pamphlets for distribution. In newspapers and public meetings two years' incessant argument ran on. The Jonathan Freeman letters of Birkbeck are the ablest contribution to the controversy; they were intended to drive home to the small farmer the fact that the presence of slaves in the community would be a degradation of the dignity of labor and of the man who worked with his hands. On religious, on economic, and on moral grounds the argument was waged; in the election of 1824 the people registered their verdict against the calling of a convention by a vote of 6,640 to 4,972.

With 1824 the slavery issue disappeared from Illinois politics so completely that the advocates of a convention like Kane, Kinney, and McLean later fared far better in politics than the men like Coles and Birkbeck who opposed it. The search for a reason for this last fact brings us to the exigencies of factional politics in the state. The Edwards and anti-Edwards factions as such had not taken sides in the convention struggle; and factional alliances were in the twenties the most potent factors in making or marring men's political fortunes.

For about ten years after the admission of Illinois to the Union the Edwards and anti-Edwards factions had contested the control of the state. In 1818 they seem to have reached a tacit

SHADRACH BOND (1773–1832)
Courtesy of Illinois State Historical Library. Original portrait owned by Chicago Historical Society.

ACHSAH (MRS. SHADRACH) BOND
Courtesy of Illinois State Historical Library

agreement on a division of the offices. Bond and Menard, at that time allied with neither group, became governor and lieutenant-governor, respectively; indeed, with such a disposal of offices in view, the constitutional convention had for Menard's special benefit modified the citizenship qualification for the lieutenant-governorship. Of the anti-Edwards faction, Kane became secretary of state and Thomas senator; of the Edwards group, Edwards was elected senator and Pope was appointed federal judge. In the only contest of anti-Edwards and Edwards men, McLean beat Cook for Congress.

The party contests between the factions do not seem usually to have been carried into elections for the state legislature; there the personal popularity of the candidates, save when the slavery issue was introduced, determined the result. The main contests between the factions before the people came in the successive elections for Congress in which year by year Cook defeated one after another the strongest candidates of the anti-Edwards group: McLean in 1820, Kane in 1822, Bond in 1824.

Meanwhile in the Senate, Edwards, now Cook's father-in-law, was engaged in a bitter quarrel with Jesse B. Thomas, partly at least over patronage. The presidential question also entered in. Ever since 1817 the candidates had been groomed for the succession to Monroe in 1824. Henry Clay of Kentucky, William H. Crawford of Georgia, John Quincy Adams of Massachusetts, John C. Calhoun of South Carolina, De Witt Clinton of New York, and Andrew Jackson of Tennessee stood out as candidates, dividing the Illinois state factions into partisan groups. Of the two senators, Thomas was for Crawford and Edwards for Calhoun. Edwards, throwing himself too hotly into the war on Crawford, was caught contributing to a Washington paper anonymous articles signed "A. B.," attacking Crawford's relations as secretary of the treasury with western banks; he resigned from the Senate in 1824 under a cloud.

The presidential election of 1824 was hotly contested in Illinois. That of 1820, the first in which the state had taken part, had been a foregone conclusion for Monroe and had excited no interest save among candidates for elector to vote for Monroe. Now, Jackson, Clay, Adams, and Crawford all had their candidates for elector in the field in the three electoral districts into which the state was then divided. The result was close and marked by sharp jockeying on all sides. Jackson electors were chosen in two districts, an Adams elector in the third. Cook, however, believed he had received a mandate for no candidate, and, when as sole congressman for Illinois he had to cast her vote in the House of Representatives voting by states, he cast it for John Quincy Adams—an act that was to plague him thereafter.

In 1826 Ninian Edwards determined to seek rehabilitation for his part in the "A. B." scandal by seeking election as governor. At the same time his son-in-law, Cook, was running for a fourth successive term in Congress, under the supposed handicap of having disregarded the expressed will of his constituents in casting the vote of Illinois for Adams rather than for Jackson. But heavier than this weighed upon both father-in-law and son-in-law their relationship and the fact that they avowedly stood forth as leaders and candidates of a faction. They were opposed by two young men latecomers to the state and not in the popular mind connected with either faction, though both doubtless had the full support of the anti-Edwards group. In the election Edwards beat Thomas Sloo, Jr., by but a few hundred votes, and Cook was defeated by Joseph Duncan, a young Kentucky veteran of the War of 1812. Cook did not survive his defeat a year.

With this election the first era of Illinois politics comes to an end. The slavery question for over a generation had been the one real issue; for almost a generation men had acquiesced in seeing the spoils of office contended for by political factions aristocratic in their leadership based frankly on family alliances and personal likes and dislikes. In one form or another these factions had influenced Illinois elections for the first eight years of statehood, and at length people were weary of them. In the defeat of Cook and the unexpectedly close election of Edwards they showed their disgust.

A new system of politics was slowly emerging, a system in which national issues and national parties would divide the voters and make the Illinois Whig nearer akin to the New England one than to the Illinois Democrat. The period of close party organization and of loyalty to national parties was at hand. In these years the conviction was developing that it was for the people to decide on political questions, to elect their party leaders, and to control their party machinery. All this was the antithesis of the system of aristocratic political factions represented by Edwards and Cook. In 1826 the voters of the state registered their disapproval, but eight years were to elapse before the old factions had completely disintegrated and the new Democratic and Whig parties had come in their stead.

CHAPTER VI

The Frontier

BETWEEN the establishment of the first English trading posts to the west of the Alleghenies about the year 1740 and the formal announcement of the United States Census Bureau in 1890 that the frontier had disappeared we count a century and a half. During that period a mighty flood of population from the older America and from most of Europe had spread over an area of three million square miles of swamp, prairie, oak barren, forest, mountain, desert, and plain, had laid hold of whatever land was immediately fitted for the use of man, and had established upon it thirty-one commonwealths, fused into one great nation. Such an achievement the world has not before recorded. Part and parcel of it, representing a certain stage of progress in it, in some details resembling the rest of the movement, in others unique, is the founding and development of Illinois.

In the first half of the eighteenth century the interior valleys of the Alleghenies were a seething trough in which was forming a mixture of Anglo-Saxons, Scotchmen for a few generations resident in Ireland but not of it, and Germans driven from their homes by the wars and persecutions of the eighteenth century. From New York and Pennsylvania and the colonies farther south the human elements poured in, tending ever westward and southward. The chance of travel might separate members of the same family by a thousand miles until, of the stock that entered the valley at the north in 1740, a half-century later traces might be found all the way to Georgia. By 1740 the flood was already surging up the western barrier of the Alleghenies. The Seven

Years' War—the French and Indian War as America named it—for a time restrained it, and the Proclamation of 1763 and the British ministerial prohibition restrained it a little longer; but by 1774 the trickles of population running out into Kentucky were becoming torrents. By the time of the adoption of the federal Constitution fifteen years later Kentucky was already a populous state. Tennessee was ready for admission to the Union in 1796. Six years later Ohio was admitted. The western tide flowed on, more slowly until after the War of 1812, then with a rush which within five years of the Treaty of Ghent brought five new western states into the Union: Indiana, Mississippi, Alabama, Missouri, and Illinois. It is at this stage and for the succeeding generation that the human torrent engages our especial interest. It defies description. Eddying in it were specimens of distinct social strata, distinct modes of life, thought, and opinions; from year to year, from district to district, its outward appearance varied. But some generalization about it and the economic, social, and political organizations it developed in Illinois must be attempted.

Long before 1818 new settlers were converging on Illinois from different directions. They came from North Carolina, Tennessee, Virginia, Kentucky, Maryland, Pennsylvania, New York, even from New England. At this period, however, the Ohio was the main highway to the state and Shawneetown its gateway. Drifting down the Ohio on flatboats large enough to house a settler's horses and cattle, before 1796 equipped with log breastworks against the lurking Indians, steered down in later years in keelboat or steamboat, the emigrants came. A few of them found their way across the Wabash from Indiana, a few came by the roads or rivers of western Kentucky converging on the Ohio and merely crossed it to reach the state; but the main travel in the early years was by the Ohio. Later, the rivers were supplemented by the Cumberland Road, the great national highway from Wheeling on the Ohio across the states of Ohio and

Indiana, and by other land routes. Along them passed the emigrant wagons loaded with the "plunder" of the newcomers, their horses and their cattle.

The classes that traveled the routes to the West were diverse as might be. The firstcomer was the typical outlier of civilization, imbued with the love for the wilderness, a lone wolf, often scarcely more than a savage, with a savage's cruelty, ignorance, and superstition. Men of this type flitted before the advancing tide of settlement. After them came the squatter, stopping a year or five years in a place to build a cabin and clear a few acres of corn for his family to supplement the spoils of his rifle, until he sold his improvements to a more permanent settler and moved on. Sometimes he was shiftless and indolent, sometimes he was merely cursed with a poverty that would not permit him to buy land of his own. A fortunate sale of his improvements, a year or two of lucrative wages paid him by a wealthier settler, and he might succeed in entering a tract of land and become a solid member of the community.

After the squatter came the farmer, the man with stock or capital who did not settle on any land save what he owned or expected to be able to buy. Primitive in his first living arrangements on the frontier, he kept in his mind the ideal of approximating as soon as possible the comforts of his old home back East. Like the squatter, his household arrangements in the West might begin with a half-faced camp of logs rolled up to afford shelter on three sides, with an open fire on the fourth to which the sleeping family stretched its feet for warmth; but this was speedily to be succeeded with the farmer by the single or double log cabin, with puncheoned floors, chinked walls, and, finally, efficient doors and windows. The small-caliber rifle, the spinning wheel, wool cards, and heavy plow were the essential possessions. A few bits of finer portable furniture might recall the comforts of the old home. The clock was a sufficiently important adjunct to erect clock-peddling into a separate calling, recognized by Illinois law. The farmer of the type outlined was the backbone of the new community.

Rising above him in gentility of birth and breeding, in good social position, and in education were the young men who came to the frontier to seek a fortune. Notable examples were Ninian Edwards, who abandoned a Kentucky judgeship in 1809 to take the governorship of Illinois Territory and make a fortune in land and trade, and Elias Kent Kane, of a good New York family, a Yale graduate, who came on a similar errand and at length became the Jacksonian leader in the state.

Wherever a fall of water existed or could be artificially induced there was a potential mill site to be eagerly contended for by speculators. On it millwrights, skilled in constructing out of a dozen kinds of wood, each with its own especial virtue and purpose in the mill wheel and the mill machinery, labored to set up a gristmill and sawmill. Patronized by the local farmers, it often became the nucleus of a trading hamlet.

In the little frontier towns high and low rubbed elbows. Such places as Shawneetown, Kaskaskia, and Edwardsville were little communities with a few brick and many more log buildings, set in streets of bottomless mud where lawless backwoodsmen and keelboatmen turned Sunday into a day of revelry. Yet in their streets the fine lady might encounter the squatter's wife; the lone wolf trapper, the young college graduate alert for a land speculation.

The stores of these villages advertised not only the hardware, rifles, powder, blankets, rough stuffs, and calicoes demanded by the frontiersman and the squatter and his wife, but the fine wines, brandies, cigars, lemons, spices, boxed sweetmeats, the silver tea services and jewelry, the broadcloths, linens, silks, and laces to which the more aristocratic classes were accustomed. The advertisements of the stores are an index to the diverse standards of life of the frontier community.

The towns such as these were the centers of the little commercial life of the early twenties. Their stores sold wholesale to storekeepers in the little outlying hamlets, Golconda, Carmi, Vienna. Of local customers they took produce in exchange for goods—furs, skins, honey, corn, whiskey, venison hams, barreled beef and pork—and shipped it to New Orleans by flatboat, keelboat, or steamboat on their own account. Often farmers would consign produce to them on commission. Sometimes a farmer would build a flatboat, freight it with his produce, and, with a neighbor's boy or two to man it, float down the Wabash or Illinois to the market at New Orleans. The merchant's notions of merchandising were not modern. Apparently a man pricing goods was expected to buy. The glass of whiskey sealed every trade even to the smallest, and a dramshop was called a grocery. In the Lincoln-Douglas debates Lincoln thought it necessary to deny Douglas' description of him as a prominent grocery-keeper of the earlier day. Sales were on long credits, and newspapers were filled with advertisements calling on delinquent debtors to settle at once. The storekeeper in turn bought on long credit in Baltimore, Norfolk, or Philadelphia; in the thirties New York merchants sent out traveling salesmen to the West; occasionally merchants in places convenient to Lake Michigan made the trip to New York to select their stocks and gathered tales to relate at home of the theaters, the beauties, the dandies, and the fast trotting horses of Broadway.

This trade, meager as it was, was carried on in spite of a circulating medium rather than with it. The 1820's were cursed with a financial problem that was never solved partly because it was never understood. Illinois in the days of early statehood suffered like every other young community for lack of capital. Money was needed to buy from the East the hardware and the other goods necessary to establish civilization in the West. What good money there was drained speedily out of the country to pay debts owed to the East or by way of the government land offices to the eastern branches of the Bank of the United States.

Against its additional debts to the East incurred for goods brought at ruinous transportation charges across the mountains and down the Ohio, it could set only the credits due it for produce shipped to New Orleans. But the produce that the West poured down the Mississippi was more than New Orleans could use or export: surplus foodstuffs piled up on its wharves; beef and pork salted with the cheap western salt instead of the fine imported article spoiled in the sun. Above all, the exchange mechanism furnished the country by the Second Bank of the United States and its branches did not enable the credits accumulated by the West at New Orleans to be set off against the debts it owed to the East. Financial ruin stared the West in the face.

It is difficult by mere description to make clear how bad was the currency situation in the West. There banks had sprung up, good, bad, and indifferent, in response to the crying need of the country for capital, misunderstood as a need for more money. Money these banks provided in the form of bank notes and credits; the former mingled with the flood of notes from eastern banks of all the reverse degrees of excellence and in circulating deceived the ignorant at twenty different discounts. In those days counterfeiting was merely an offense against state law. There was no federal secret service to track down counterfeiters; and counterfeit notes of genuine banks, notes of imaginary banks, and genuine notes of failed banks all added to the confusion. Many of the state banks established in the Northwest states were badly managed; sometimes the banks persuaded farmers and merchants to take loans they never could hope to repay in order to take possession of their lands and business by foreclosure. The Second Bank of the United States and its branches were in this respect as great offenders as any. They sought first to harass the state banks by presenting their notes for specie redemption; after June, 1818, the Bank of the United States refused to accept the notes of western banks deposited with it by government land-office receivers except for collection.

Secretary of the Treasury Crawford had labored at the problem with a patience and wisdom for which he has not been given due credit. Confronted by the refusal of the United States Bank to function as fiscal agent in the West, Crawford sought to keep the machinery of finance running by selecting western banks of fair repute as government depositories, requiring them to transmit at par to the East the notes of such western banks as they should notify the land officers they would accept. Crawford was accused by his foes, perhaps with truth, of granting favors in this way to his political allies. He was accused also of having lost some money in government deposits in failed banks; but it is a question whether he did not save in this way government funds not otherwise recoverable and give some alleviation to the hardships of the West.

Unfortunately by 1822 the whole scheme was dropped. Meanwhile Illinois had sought relief for the inability of her citizens to get advances to repay their loans and for the general shortage of money by the creation of a state bank. The legislature in 1819 authorized one which was never established. In 1821 it created another with branches, ostensibly to loan money to citizens who needed it! The unconstitutionality of the bank under the clause of the federal Constitution forbidding a state to issue bills of credit was so patent that the bank dared not sue to collect from its debtors. Its notes depreciated, and when the legislature tried to maintain them by making them receivable for taxes, the state suffered heavy financial loss before it finally got rid of them. Of the earlier state-chartered banks, the bank at Edwardsville had failed and the Bank of Illinois at Shawneetown had suspended business. The whole experience of the twenties left a latent distrust of paper money and a latent impression that banks were leeches to suck the blood of the farmer. In local trade barter replaced the use of money of any kind. All these things were to play their part in the support accorded Jackson in his war on the United States Bank and in the movement of the forties against banks and "bank rags" in general.

The commerce, trade, and finance of the new state were, however, slight things beside the exploitation of its land and the making of farms and homes upon it. To understand this, a brief consideration of the federal land laws is necessary. Since 1812 lands had been purchased at government land offices in Illinois, first at Shawneetown and Kaskaskia, later at Edwardsville also, in tracts of 160 acres at a minimum rate of two dollars an acre, of which amount one-fourth was payable down and the rest in payments extending over four years. The theory on which this policy had been adopted in a series of federal acts beginning with 1800 was that the farmer could thus pay for his land out of the first four crops. Actually such a thing was almost impossible. Farmers had taken advantage of the act to get farms; but speculators also had used it to acquire options on choice tracts at fifty cents an acre on the chance of selling at a profit before further payments were due. Disappointed hopes filled the West with debtors to the government who could not and would not pay and who were too numerous to be dispossessed. In 1820 Congress, in spite of the protests of speculators, abolished the whole credit system and provided for cash sales at one dollar and a quarter an acre, after each tract had been put up at auction. Very little land was bought in Illinois for ten years thereafter. Meanwhile the government in a series of relief acts offered to the delinquent purchasers full title to an amount of land equivalent to the sums they had actually paid in.

The land speculator was at work in Illinois from the beginning. Young men came to seek their fortunes in the territory, with money to invest by entering fertile tracts, mill seats, or possible town sites. Town sites especially offered on every side; advertisements in every newspaper detailed the advantages of these future emporiums of trade. The competition between town-site speculators when the convention of 1818 was in session in Illinois led the convention to locate the state's second capital at Vandalia in the wilderness where the state might reap the profit from the sale of town lots. Eastern speculators worked through western agents or bought up claims of veterans of the War of 1812 to tracts of 160 acres in what is known as the Military Tract—the section between the Illinois and Mississippi rivers.

Speculation in agricultural land of course was determined by the lands considered most desirable; and here the choice was a strange one. Eschewing the broad prairies except for grazing, men chose uplands heavily timbered with hard wood. This has been ascribed to the following syllogism: if land that will support the heavy growth of hardwood timber is better than scrub oak barren, scrub oak barren in turn must be better than land that grows no trees at all. The more likely reason is, paradoxical as it may seem, that a man by ax, by fire, and by neighborly assistance in a logrolling, by girdling trees and planting corn among the decaying stumps, could accomplish more than he could on prairie land without a team of heavy oxen to turn the first tough sod. From 1818 Morris Birkbeck, the founder of the English settlement in Edwards County, Edward Coles, and others labored to teach their fellow-citizens ways of dealing with the problem of the prairies.

Even in the thirties, however, when population was sweeping over the prairies of northwestern Illinois, there was still a problem. Breaking prairie cost several dollars an acre, splitting rails and putting up rail fences cost several dollars additional, and more still if the necessary timber was not close at hand. Even then, when men were locating farms on the prairie, they took care to build their homes on elevated ground near good water and to take a part of the farm in timber. A man who located his entire farm on the prairie had to steal his timber for building and fencing from government land or the land of a nonresident. Speculators were able to keep control of great tracts by locating the fractional sections that covered timbered land along the water courses.

The attitude of men toward the land system varied from decade to decade. For ten years after 1820 little land was entered in

EDWARD COLES (1786–1868)
Courtesy of Illinois State Historical Library

NINIAN EDWARDS (1775–1833)
Courtesy of Illinois State Historical Library

southern Illinois. What few sales were made were in the central part of the state. Men either acquired title from speculators or squatted on unsold government lands. In 1828 William Lee D. Ewing, the receiver of the Vandalia Land District, reported 1,100 legal electors in the district and total sales since the beginning of 17,586 acres of land. Ewing wrote:

> The citizens of this country are all aware of the discussions that have been had in Congress on the subject of the reduction of the price of those lands. They believe (which is very natural for them to do) that the price should be reduced; and finding, too, that they are supported in this opinion by many of our most enlightened legislators, and believing that efforts will again and again be made until the object be either effected or totally defeated, they will not enter their lands, except in particular instances where places are found to possess some peculiar advantages; but will continue (as they have long done) to cultivate a still stronger faith in an understanding among themselves not to enter each other's improvements, nor to let any one else do it, until government affords them some relief in the shape of the reduction of the price of its lands.
> This position may be more satisfactorily illustrated by the following facts:
> In the county of Clay there are about one hundred voting inhabitants, of whom there are not more than twenty freeholders.[1]

The land policy appealing to western men as the ideal one was the policy advocated by Senator Thomas Hart Benton of Missouri known as "graduation"—the reduction year by year of the price of lands remaining unsold until finally, having reached a price of twenty-five cents an acre, they should be donated to the states. Joined with this was the right of actual settlers to preemption—the right to buy the lands on which they had settled at the minimum price. Of such a policy there was no chance so long as the East had the majority in Congress. It was twenty years before the federal government permanently recognized the principle of pre-emption, ten more before it applied that of

1. *American State Papers, Public Lands,* V, 556.

graduation on unsold lands, and ten more before it adopted the homestead principle.

In Congress the West had to wage a long battle against New England and other sections that opposed western settlement, lest their population be drawn off, their lands depreciate in value, and their manufacturers lack cheap labor. Western representatives, therefore, had to bargain for support where they could find it. For southern support of a reasonably liberal land and Indian policy they had to sacrifice other things. The building of roads and canals and the improvement of rivers at government expense appealed to the westerners, who desired better routes to carry their produce to market; similarly, they desired a protective tariff to foster the household industries of nailmaking and weaving. Both these things could have been had by alliance with New England and the Northeast; both had to be sacrificed to conciliate the South.

In studying the intellectual and moral forces that played upon pioneer Illinois, the striking thing is that the Illinoisan developed and improved for himself on his former habits. In the back country religion and religious organization, education and schools, politics and strong government, did not follow close on the pioneer; he had to learn the need of them and to evolve them out of his past experience with a little assistance from organizations back East. Of such organizations he was essentially suspicious and borrowed as few as possible of their ideas.

As to religion, the first westward push outran it. Away from ministers and services, men forgot church and Sunday observance. The deism of the eighteenth century, denying the supernatural and indeed all save the moral teachings of Christianity, had shot through American life and thought. In the West it often took the form of a sort of diabolism that rejected and opposed all organized religion as hypocritical and superstitious. Against it the churches had to contend for very life.

The Baptists were the first in the field. The Baptist church order, essentially congregational, made the organization of churches an easy affair. Every zealous lay preacher, no matter how ignorant, who migrated to the West was the possible seed of a little Baptist church. The first in Illinois, at New Design, dates from 1796. Similar churches sprang up everywhere with little denominational connection, individually marked by strange and unorthodox beliefs—such a one as that of the anti-Mission Baptists who held attempts to convert men a rebellion against divine predestination that had decreed from the beginning the lost and the saved. The elements of order, coherence, and unity were first brought among the scattered Baptist churches by such missionaries as John Mason Peck of Connecticut, founder of churches, Sunday schools, temperance societies, newspapers, of Shurtleff College at Alton, who labored some forty years, slowly overcoming narrowness and distrust in the order.

Of the Protestant denominations, the Methodists were next on the ground about the year 1801, but Methodism implied organization. Organized into circuits, the Methodist church was an aristocracy of service presided over by bishops, ruled by the circuit-riders, who retained their voice in affairs so long as their devotion and their bodily strength enabled them to ride the bottomless roads, swim the rivers, and preach with all the power of a rough oratory and a deep-seated conviction to the vast camp-meeting audiences that gathered from near and far. Great natural orators like James Axley and Peter Cartwright, when God's gifts were strong in them, could sway multitudes like fields of grain in the wind, until sinners by hundreds, with shouts and cries, were torn by spiritual agony to find at length spiritual peace.

Ranking below the circuit-riders were the settled, or superannuated, ministers and class leaders, without voice in the government of the church but continually teaching and fortifying the converts and the faithful generally. Methodism in its earlier years preached simplicity in apparel and life, the abandonment of dancing, card-playing, and other frivolous amusements; its preachers withstood to the face the vice of drinking and the sin of slaveholding. In later years, as Methodists waxed in wealth, pioneers like Cartwright bewailed their growing laxity.

Presbyterianism was in Illinois at an early day, but as in the West generally it increased slowly, mainly because of its insistence on an educated ministry to teach the Calvinist theology. By a bargain of 1801 with the Congregationalists, known as the Plan of Union, the Presbyterians refrained from pushing their organization further in New England, and Congregationalists agreed that the two denominations should unite their missionary activities in the West and that Presbyterianism should be the form of organization there. Their set missionary activity aroused western distrust, and their insistence on a learned ministry alarmed the simple Methodist and Baptist preachers; but they pushed on. Determined on having their educated preachers, they dotted the West with their colleges, such as Illinois College, Knox, and Blackburn.

Congregationalism, however, had begun to infiltrate in defiance of the Plan of Union as New England emigrants, accustomed to that form of church government, came in the thirties. The stricter Presbyterians believed that the great Congregational elements already absorbed by the Plan of Union did not take the Presbyterian discipline with due seriousness. Yale theology came to be in bad repute; finally, in 1837, the conservative Princeton theologians, attracting the South to their support, drove the lax Presbyterians of the West out of the church. In Illinois and elsewhere the church divided into old school and new school, the New England and other theologically liberal elements either falling into the new-school Presbyterian organization or becoming Congregationalist. The Plan of Union, so far as it hindered the establishment of Congregational churches, was abandoned; and Presbyterians and Congregationalists quarreled over colleges like Knox which they had formerly combined to establish.

Other denominations were active: the Disciples or Christians, made up of offshoots from the Presbyterian, Methodist, and Baptist orders, taking the Bible as their sole guide; the Cumberland Presbyterians, an offset from Presbyterianism in the great revivals at the beginning of the nineteenth century; and various others.

Roman Catholicism slowly made its way again into the land consecrated by the devotion of Marquette. In the year 1809 the Trappist Fathers established themselves on the great mound of Cahokia.[2] With the founding in 1808 of the diocese of Bardstown, Kentucky, priests again began their labors. Illinois was a part of Bardstown and of dioceses successively set off from it, Vincennes, St. Louis, and Chicago, founded in 1844. The bishops struggled with the problem of finding competent priests to take charge of the scattered but growing flocks. The Irish who came to Illinois to labor on the works of internal improvement increased the number of the church; but its real development necessarily came with the great European migration after 1870.

As an intellectual force, organized religion was relatively more important in the pioneer community than in the later day. The sermon, save for the political speech, was for the great mass of the population the only intellectual and emotional stimulus, the only example of creative art. Western Christianity developed certain characteristics all its own. Thrown into a wilderness, compelled to do battle with openly hostile deism and unbelief, it became strenuous, vigorous, even violent. No Methodist circuit-rider could hold a camp meeting unless by force of address he could cow the bullies who sought to break it up. Mocking a preacher on the road was good sport for ungodly young people. Theological belief and religious convictions had to be

2. This fact gives rise to the name of Monks' Mound by which it is sometimes known.

backed by one's fists on occasion. The church had none of the protection afforded it by the conventions of polite society. Compelled to fight for life, it battled to destroy its adversary. Intolerance was the fruit of the contest between religion and irreligion where the stakes were life and death.

The pioneer outran education also in his movement to the West, but this was not a serious matter. The English organization of society had long taken it for granted that the church was the means of education for the masses. In the southern states, from which the mass of Illinois' earlier population was drawn, there were no public school systems, and a large proportion of emigrants to the state were illiterate. The western states, however, were accorded one section in each township in their bounds for local schools; and, in addition, Illinois had a percentage from government land sales and a township of land for a seminary. Her pioneers came with divers opinions on the subject of the employment of this endowment. Some believed the lands should be sold at once so that the present generation might be educated. Others thought that they should be held as a great fund for the future. Southerners were averse to taxing rich men to educate poor men's sons, and only gradually, as the northern elements came in, was school taxation established. A law of 1825 allowing localities to lay school taxes was repealed, and another was not passed until 1845. The state appropriated the 3 per cent fund for other uses, paying interest on it to the schools; local land grants were rented and the rents used for local schools.

The earliest schools were most casual affairs. They were kept by drunkards, by men with the barest smattering of knowledge, unfitted for other purposes by physical or moral defects. Pupils studied whatever textbooks their families possessed and were taught out of them by primitive and brutal methods in which flogging played an important part. Schoolmasters ruled only by superior force. The barring-out was a favorite custom, the pupils some day attempting to keep the master out until he capitulated and provided a treat in which whiskey played an important part. In the late thirties, however, teachers began to be paid from local and state funds according to the number of their pupils and the number of days they attended school. The grade of teachers improved; young men on their way through college to a career in law or politics would teach school to get a start. By the forties thinking men were thoroughly imbued with the necessity of an organized and standardized system, and around the new office of Superintendent of Public Instruction one began to be evolved. The newspapers began to discuss educational systems—the Prussian, the New England.

Higher education from the earliest years of statehood had been available for those able to pay for it. Peck's Rock Spring Seminary was soon duplicated by many another high school teaching more or less successfully Latin and other academic subjects. Select girls' schools began to develop both in Illinois and across the river in Missouri. Above all rose the college.

College education came primarily from the churches' realization of the need of college-trained ministers. Colleges were at first definitely denominational; the Illinois legislature, suspicious of religious connection with politics, refused for a time to incorporate theological institutions to grant degrees. In the thirties Shurtleff for the Baptists, the outgrowth of Peck's seminary, McKendree for the Methodists, and Knox and Blackburn for the Presbyterians all developed. Before any of these came Illinois College, the fruit of the ambition of a group of Yale men—Theron Baldwin, Edward Beecher, Julian M. Sturtevant, Jonathan B. Turner—to build a greater Yale on the Illinois prairies. Their college they had designed as the center of a great educational system; as such their dream was never realized.

Newspapers one naturally includes among intellectual forces; but the newspapers of the twenties were comparatively slight and unimportant. By the end of the decade they hardly exceeded a dozen in number, each with but a few hundreds of circulation.

They were small weekly sheets of four pages mostly filled with advertisements and official publications, laws, etc. Their remaining space was taken up with news anecdotes and scientific scraps clipped from eastern papers, with occasional "communications" by local talent, literary, political, satirical, in prose and verse of no very high order. So far as the editors had any policy, it was dictated by the factional leaders whose henchmen they were, and revealed itself in feeble attacks on chiefs of the rival factions. Save for James Hall, at one time editor of the *Illinois Gazette*, none of the pioneer editors showed even mediocre literary ability. The influence of their papers was correspondingly slight. The awakened democracy of the thirties and forties gave life to the newspapers. Enlarged in size, with editors, if not able at least vigorous, contending with one another on measures of state and questions of principle, they reflect the life and thought of their time as the artificial little papers of the decade of 1820 do not.

Government in the primitive commonwealth was a simple affair. The state government was no more than a legislature meeting biennially, three or four administrative officials doing their work at first almost without clerks, and a supreme court. Local government was essentially county government—county commissioners' courts to manage local finances, circuit and probate courts and justices of the peace to judge locally, and sheriffs to maintain order. Roads in theory were created by action of the General Assembly or of the county commissioners and maintained by a labor tax; in practice they were usually bottomless seas of mud until the twentieth century. Town governments for many years after 1818 were rudimentary. Police forces were nonexistent. The only laws that could be enforced were ones the local community would enforce itself. When public opinion was slack, bands of robbers on rivers or prairie robbed and terrorized at will until the community was roused to the point of suppressing them by main force.

The social life of the frontier can be described more voluminously than accurately. Recollections of such merrymakings as the corn-husking, the logrolling, and the cabin-raising abound, but contemporary descriptions and allusions are infrequent; in the contemporary newspapers they are scarcely mentioned. One wonders whether reminiscence, enforced by the earlier published accounts of frontier life, did not assign them undue importance, or a general one instead of one confined to certain localities and periods of the frontier movement. At all events they are depicted for us as meeting places, evidences of neighborly helpfulness, concluded by jollity, dancing, and whiskey. Wedding celebrations and dances offered additional opportunities for frontier merrymaking. They were marked, one judges, often enough by coarseness, but rarely by anything worse; but the Methodists labored to substitute for them the emotional joys of religion.

Certain other occasions for meeting were afforded by official duties. The periodical meeting of the circuit courts called into the county seats suitors and jurymen who learned the news of the outside world from the judge and lawyers riding the circuit, were regaled with speeches by political aspirants, and sat down to dinner in the local tavern all at the same table. The periodical musters and trainings of the militia offered other opportunities for escaping the loneliness of frontier life; but by the forties the militia had become a mere source of military titles.

The conquest of the frontier and the clearing of the land took their tolls in health and life alike. As forest was cleared away or prairie sod broken, vast masses of decaying vegetable matter were exposed to the sun—underbrush, decaying logs, the debris of centuries—from these and from the stagnant pools and swamps came wasting diseases. Intermittent fever and ague wrecked the health of strong men; and women and children succumbed pitifully to hardships and disease. The generation that began the founding of Illinois was a stalwart one. The men of the second generation were connoisseurs in ill-health and medicines. Calomel and whiskey was the most common dose; but the newspapers were filled with glowing advertisements of elixirs and patent medicines warranted to cure all known ills from tuberculosis to warts. Ill-health in the forties and fifties became fashionable in the United States; the pale and sickly interesting young man and the fragile girl dying of consumption are the romantic figures of the period.

The gloom of sickness and death hung over the lives of the people. They did not know the cheerful, lighthearted merriment of the French peasant. Their wit was keen, their humor boisterous, their laugh a guffaw put on over sickness and gloom. The man typical of the wit of the frontier at times masked with a seemingly inexhaustible fund of droll stories a gloom that made him fear to carry any weapon with which he might attempt his life. A literary master has hit off the spirit of the Illinois of the pioneer period in the phrase "a valley of shadows."

But mingled with the gloom there was a great and inordinate pride. The conquerors of the wilderness were their own men. The same impulse had moved them to the West, that restless spirit of adventure, the search for better things beyond the horizon; but they had obeyed it as individuals. They needed not to bow their heads to any man for meat. So long as the wilderness stretched before them and their hearts were whole to attempt it, they need be no man's servants. They obeyed no laws save those the community public opinion enforced by the threat of lynch law. They cringed to no public official. They were not like the peasantries of Europe, humble in the mighty presence of the land, that great mother that for twenty generations had molded them in her bosom. The wilderness to the American pioneer was no mother but a terrible foe; yet one that, encountered with fire, ax, a brain, and a stout heart, could be transmuted into a little cornfield, a farm and a home. Man knew that if he would, he might be greater than his environment and remake it to his use; and the thought ennobled him.

The pride of the frontier becomes most visible when it takes the form of patriotism. Even the most ignorant rejoiced in the heritage of freedom given him in trust for the world's benefit and looked down with contempt on the slaves of despotic government in Europe. He was firmly convinced that his military powers as a freeman could bid defiance to the world. Angered at the thought of the galling defeats of the War of 1812 that seemed to contradict his heroism, he was prone to ascribe them not to his undisciplined lawlessness in the day of battle but to his feeble and intriguing leaders at Washington. His eye turned more and more to the figure of one man: a backwoodsman, violent, irascible, chivalrous to women beyond the chivalry of romance, true to a friend, stern to a mortal foe—a man who accomplished what he set out to accomplish whether it was bringing a mutinous army to subjection by sheer will-power, crushing hostile Indian nations, saving the outlet of the Great Valley from the invader, or teaching a foreign power it could not afford immunity to the violators of American soil. Winged by the news of the great victory at New Orleans, there drifted over the whole West the report of a character inaccurate in details but true in essentials, the very incarnation of the frontier—Andrew Jackson.

CHAPTER VII

Jacksonian Democracy

THE first quarter-century after the admission of Illinois to the Union saw a revolution in the nation's political life. The people of the United States as a political entity came into being and consciousness. Tired of having their President selected for them by conclaves of congressmen in caucus at Washington, they democratized party machinery to nominate and elect him themselves; they devised the democratic organization of nationally organized political parties to support him in carrying out the will of the people in office. In the political history of that quarter-century the outstanding figure is the man who instinctively grasped the direction in which the spirit of the times was turning and who as President made himself the incarnation of the people's will—Andrew Jackson. No Illinois citizen was so vital an element in the Illinois of his day as he.

When first a candidate for President in 1824, Jackson was fifty-seven; at the time he retired from office he was sixty-nine. As a mere boy the savagery of the revolution in the Carolina upcountry in which he had taken an active part and had lost by untimely death his whole family made him a good hater; twenty-five years in Nashville on the frontier of Tennessee had made him more western than the West itself, the truest of friends, the fiercest of foes, duelist, horse-racer, cockfighter, Indian hater, hero of hairbreadth escapes that related in sober truth sound like the episodes of a dime novel. Nature had created him a leader among leaders, who in the War of 1812 led armies of lawless frontiersmen trained to obey only such orders as they liked,

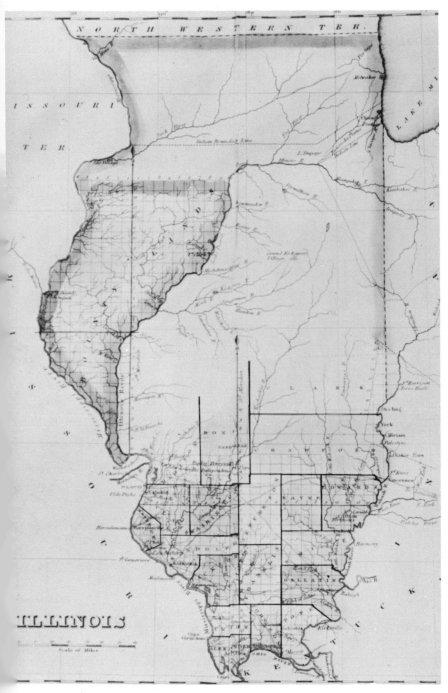

ILLINOIS—1819: NINETEEN COUNTIES

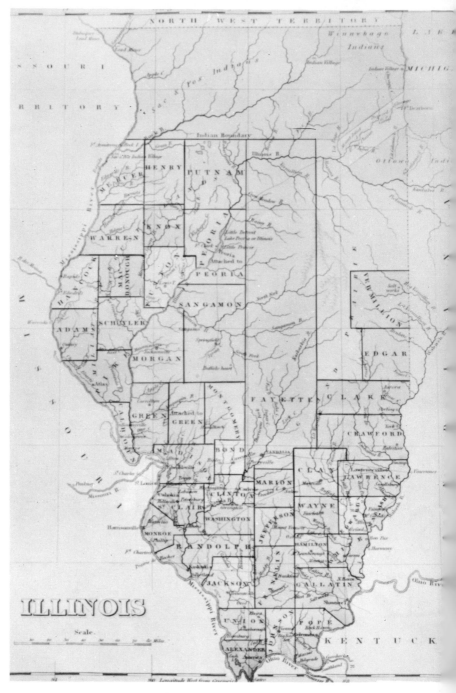

ILLINOIS—1826: FORTY-FIVE COUNTIES

ILLINOIS—1833: SIXTY COUNTIES

This map was published in 1836, and the state had grown too fast for the cartographers to
▪ up with it.

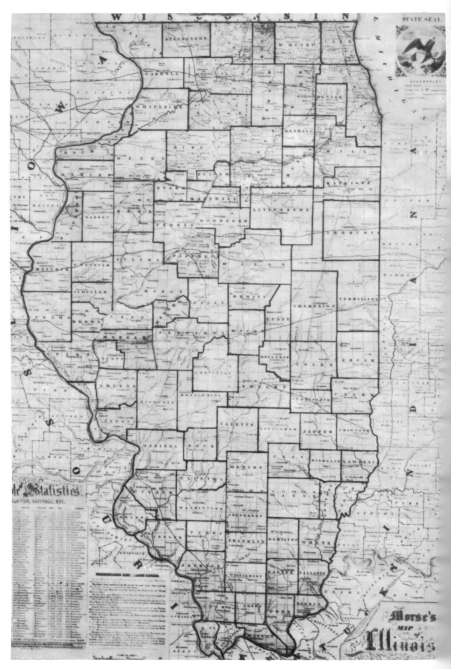

ILLINOIS—1854: ONE HUNDRED COUNTIES
Two more were created to make the present number

ruling them by sheer force of will, a general who won such victories as that of New Orleans by the light of natural military genius, a man whose spirit burned like fire and was not consumed. That figure would have been a significant one whereever placed in the world's history; in the America of 1815 it was the apotheosis of the frontier.

The politics of the United States of the early nineteenth century were not organized to promote the elevation of such a figure to the presidency. It was traditional that the nomination of presidential candidates lay with the leaders of the parties. Since 1796 the candidate of the Republican party for the presidency had been designated by the Republican members of Congress meeting in caucus at Washington. From 1800 to 1824 the nomination of the Republican caucus had been equivalent to election. Men justified the system by saying that only so could the party be united on a candidate; that otherwise candidates would spring up in the various states and sections of the nation; that no man could have a majority of the electoral votes; and that the House of Representatives, voting by states, would have to choose among the highest. In caucus or in the House, Congress must choose the President; and its choice fell naturally on the political leaders it knew, men from their youth up expert in politics and statecraft.

For twenty years the United States had acquiesced in this arrangement. But transportation was improving; men were traveling from state to state more than formerly; the age of national conventions was on the horizon. The western states were entering the Union with constitutional provision for manhood suffrage. The older states were casting aside the property qualifications for the ballot that had survived the Revolution. In state after state the system of choosing presidential electors by the state legislature was being abandoned and their choice by popular vote substituted. The nation, retrieved to a new life by the favorable termination of the War of 1812, felt itself conscious of a fresh unity and a new strength, of liberation from the chariot wheels of European politics, of freedom on the broad continent that stretched to the west to work out its own destiny. The people reached out for the tools of democracy and began to prove them.

The presidential election of 1824 was the first opportunity for their national use. When Monroe had been elected President in 1816, everyone had taken his re-election in 1820 as an accomplished fact; and, almost disregarding the aged President, half-a-dozen younger men of ambition stretched out their hands toward the prize of 1824. There were John Quincy Adams of Massachusetts, secretary of state, a liberal and a forward-looking man; Secretary of War John C. Calhoun of South Carolina, still a nationalist; William H. Crawford of Georgia, secretary of the treasury, representative of the old strict-constructionist Republicans. These men had their eye on the honor and were on the ground at Washington to pursue it; and they disregarded such competitors from the outside as De Witt Clinton, maker of New York's Erie Canal but not on good terms with Martin Van Buren and the state machine, or General Andrew Jackson. The popular appeal of Jackson all of them at first disregarded. But the attempt in Congress and the cabinet to censure him because, sent to stop the raids of the Seminoles on the United States from Spanish Florida, he had done it in his own way without regard to the letter of his orders, the immunity of British subjects, or the *amour propre* of Spanish officials had disclosed the fact that very many of his fellow-countrymen admired him intensely for these very headstrong acts. He stood forth, after his vindication by Congress, as a national candidate for the presidency.

Edward Patchett of Pittsburgh wrote to his friend James Hall in Illinois in 1823:

And for our next President, General And$^{w.}$ Jackson has the full & free voice of the Citizens of Pennsylvania. We sometime since had a meeting in the Courthouse where about 800 of the citizens were present; the names of the several candidates were placed on the nomination list. Calhoun was first balloted for, & had four or five votes; Clay next had five, Adams six; Crawford one; Clinton twelve, or upwards; Jackson was finally brought forth, and in a voice of thunder the Courthouse rung, for the Hero of New Orleans. Jimmy my son, you have been an officer in the last war, your sword was then drawn in defence of your Country—and now let you your pen in time's of peace be wielded in vindicating the just claims of your old General, as old *Hickory* is the best hoop for national Safety.

But still I am well aware—there will be many objections set up against General Jackson, both by the Governmental Editors, and the office holders; 1ˢᵗ because he hath not been schooled, educated and brought up at the feet of Gamaliel, in the Presidential Academy in the City of Washington; 2ᵈ Because he hath never drank deep that fountain of Political intrigue & corruption, and were he elected President might take away the Loaves and the fishes from Bladensburgh cowards, and feed the poor starving officers & soldiers who fough[t] our battles during the last war at New Orleans 3ᵈ Because he is a man of prompt, energetic mind and would as soon put a rascal to death as he would an Indian or an Ambrister, 4ᵗʰ objection, altho' he has made the best General in the known world, yet we are afraid to trust him for our President, yet the people may answer—Washington was the greatest General in the world, and made the best President; never the less we can gull the ignorant, and palm a coward on them, for what right have the swinish multitude to interfere in making a President. It shall be done by Legislative Caucus, according to law, 5ᵗʰ & last great objection He might do us a great deal of injury as he is so fond of fighting, who knows but what he might declare war against the world and bring down the vengeance of the allied Sovereigns on our heads; and to a moral certainty he would disperse our political nest at Washington City, break up our Presidential Academy, where the great Crawford, Clay, Calhoun & Adams have received that omnipotent nostrum, of political slang. Thus Jimmy my son, you must be prepared to ward off the blows, for all these obstructions and a great many more will be cast in the way of the worthy Chieftain to the Presidential chair; but let us go to work like true Pioneers and clear off the rubbish—we will have a host on our side, we will have all the true Soldiers and all who are true and faithful freemen to rally round the standard of Jackson and Liberty, as none but trembling cowards—office holders and office hunters will vote against him. . . . But where Jackson was, let a grateful nation answer by their votes at our next Presidential Election, for he hath earned them at the mouth of a British Cannon.[1]

The nomination of Crawford by the congressional caucus was a foregone conclusion. The friends of the other candidates at once began an outcry against caucus nominations that found a popular response. In one way or another the candidates were got before the people, and a real campaign was on. Illinois had cast in 1820 but 1,443 votes for her electors to go through the empty form of voting for Monroe; now she could choose between three or four candidates. After hot contests in her districts, she chose two Jackson electors and one Adams elector. The result in the nation was to give no candidate a majority and to send Jackson with 99 votes, Adams with 84 votes, and Crawford with 41 votes to be voted on by the House of Representatives voting by states.

There Illinois was destined to play a part all out of proportion to her weight in the Union. In the House the sole representative of Illinois, Daniel Pope Cook, could cast a vote as potent as that of the whole delegations of New York, Pennsylvania, or Virginia. The local factions in Illinois politics had not divided on the presidency. Cook was left to estimate from the vote for the electors throughout the state which candidate had the plurality in the state's choice. If one elector run under the "Jackson or Clay" label was counted for Jackson, Jackson would have the plurality. Were he counted for Crawford, the probable source of his vote, Adams would have it. Cook was persuaded by his own partiality to Adams to decide in his favor and cast the vote of Illinois to elect him.

The charge, probably false, broke forth throughout Illinois and the nation as well that Adams was elected by a corrupt bargain in which Clay, bribed by the office of the secretary of state, had swung his strength to elect Adams. It stirred up a deep feeling of moral indignation that the old soldier, the hero of New Orleans, the first choice of the people for the presidency, was

1. Eddy Manuscripts, Illinois Historical Survey, University of Illinois.

pushed aside for a politician and closet statesman. That indignation did not die away but grew deeper and deeper during Adams' ill-starred term. It was fanned by politicians, especially those of the Crawford following who in Illinois and elsewhere, when their chief withdrew from politics, went over to Jackson. It was given validity by the fact that the alliance of West and South on the basis of free trade, no internal improvements, a liberal public land policy, and a white man's Indian policy naturally cemented itself around a man like Jackson, both western and southern. But, when all is said, it was deep anger that the people's will had been disregarded by the people's servants that gave Jackson the vote of Illinois in 1828 two to one and swept the old hero into the presidential chair on the first of American landslides. The elder statesmen might well shake their heads and repeat the axiom that a President chosen by a great popular majority would be a dangerous one. Such a one had been called by the people, and he knew his call.

The Jackson enthusiasm in Illinois was destined to destroy the older factional politics. Probably it was discontent with his factional affiliations rather than with Cook's vote for Adams that caused his defeat for Congress in 1826; but three years later politicians, looking back in the light of Jackson's meteoric course in Illinois, naturally ascribed it to Cook's defiance of the people's will. Sensing the fact that the day of factional politics was past, the Crawford element in the anti-Edwards following became Jacksonian, and more exuberantly Jacksonian than the Jacksonians of 1824. After 1828 no man might be elected to an office by the general vote of Illinois unless he professed himself a supporter of Jackson. Ninian Edwards hesitated between Jackson and the Adams-Clay group, clinging to both. He sought the support of Adams men to stay up his disintegrating personal faction, and on that account he was condemned by Jackson and his supporters, whose ear at Washington former Crawford men like Kane and Kinney had obtained. True, John Reynolds, professing to be a good Jackson man and at the same time quietly bargaining for Adams votes that could be delivered unobtrusively, with Edwards' support slipped into the governorship in 1830, defeating the "whole-hog" Jackson candidate, William Kinney. Again in 1834 Reynolds was elected to Congress by Adams votes. But this time he promptly repudiated his Adams following as soon as elected and thenceforth marched under the Jackson banner only.

The rise to prominence of men like Kinney and Reynolds is in itself an indication of the democratic revolution in politics. Both had arisen from the ranks of Illinois frontiersmen. William Kinney was a storekeeper, a Baptist preacher by avocation, so far illiterate that it is almost impossible to disentangle the sense of his letters from the handwriting, spelling, and grammar in which they are couched. He was nevertheless an outspoken man of keen mother-wit, always expressing itself in homely epigrams. John Reynolds, in later years the historian of pioneer Illinois in volumes that are literary curiosities, had a smattering of education which he strove to stretch to the appearance of erudition. Always an office-seeker, always searching for the popular side of every issue, fawning on his friends when he needed them and discarding them when they could no longer serve him, he shuffled his way through Illinois politics from 1818 to the days of the Civil War. That such a man could become governor and congressman is proof that the day of aristocratic dignity in Illinois politics had passed.

The years from 1828 until 1834 when the Democratic and Whig parties fully separate out of the amorphous political mass are years of confusion. To begin with, the Jackson movement of 1828 had been one mainly of sentiment and personal attraction. But Jackson's political ideas developed fast after his election. They developed on such questions as internal improvements and tariff in the direction of the limited construction of the powers of the federal government that had characterized the Republicans of 1798 and the former Crawford men. When in 1832 the issue of the recharter of the Bank of the United States was forced on Jackson by the Clay-Adams group, he seized on it to rally his western and southern constituencies where hatred of banks and above all of the Bank was rife. He vetoed the renewal of the Bank's charter and, succeeding in the presidential election of 1832, withdrew the government's funds from the "monster" and put them in the hands of the state banks. Moreover, his removals from office hardly coincided with his nonpartisan and reform attitude of 1817 and 1823. In all these directions his policy alienated in Illinois and elsewhere many men who had been his ardent followers in 1824 and 1828.

As a result there was from 1830 to 1834 a steady secession of Jackson men to the ranks of the Clay-Adams opposition; and many men who continued to call themselves Jackson men and to run for office as Jackson men opposed again and again the Jackson measures in Congress. For instance, Joseph Duncan, sole congressman from Illinois from 1826 to 1833, did this until 1834. Then he ran for governor of the state against a field of William Kinney and Robert K. McLaughlin, out-and-out Jackson men, and James Adams, Whig. Duncan did not repudiate the Jackson name until after the canvass and was easily elected. In that same year six candidates opposed one another in the three congressional districts of the state, all six declaring themselves Jackson men, but some of them indorsing a United States Bank.

In order to strip malcontent Jacksonians of the party name and force them to support the measures of the party or to leave it, the Democratic party was formed in Illinois between 1834 and 1836, its party chiefs evolving the ideas of party regularity and the convention system. Briefly stated, these are that no man may run for office as a Jacksonian or a Democrat—a term one may at length use—unless he supports the measures of Jackson as set forth in party platforms. In order to secure the election of loyal Democrats, all Democrats must give up the former right of appearing as candidates for office whenever they wish; they must submit their claims to conventions held in the district in which they are to run and must agree to support loyally the candidate chosen by the convention as the party standard-bearer. Otherwise the party vote may be divided, and the opposition triumph.

Over the party machinery thus devised a fierce controversy waged within and without the party. Resolutions denouncing the convention system were introduced in the Illinois legislature in 1835 and bitterly contested. On one side it was alleged that the convention system was democratic—that it enabled the poor but upright young man of ability to run for office with united party support and deprived the man of prestige, wealth, and social position of the advantage those gifts would give him in the race were he free to enter whenever he saw fit. This undoubtedly was one reason why men of this latter sort gravitated to the Whig party. On the other hand, conventions were denounced as subject to fraud and manipulation, dens in which wily politicians could defeat the will of the voters; and no doubt too often was this the case.

The convention system, however, adopted in Illinois some years after the Jackson party in both Ohio and Indiana had adopted it, was to have a rare record of efficiency in the state. In 1838 and 1842 it enabled the Democrats to substitute one candidate for another in the midst of the race for the governorship. In 1838 their first choice, James W. Stephenson, was proved a defaulter; Thomas Carlin was substituted for him and elected over Cyrus Edwards, the Whig candidate, brother of Ninian Edwards. In 1842 Adam W. Snyder died during the canvass, and Thomas Ford was put in his place and beat handily Governor Duncan.

The system had its real test in the Democratic party in the troublous years 1837–42. Those years began with the great Panic of 1837 caused by inflation of credit through the lavish issue of bank notes and deposits by state banks enjoying government deposits. To repair the evil, Van Buren, now President of the United States, proposed the subtreasury system: the divorce of the government from all dealings with banks, the collection of government dues in specie, their deposit in strongrooms or subtreasuries under care of government officials, and the making of all disbursements in specie likewise.

It was only after a desperate struggle that the Democratic party in Illinois was brought in line with this policy. The senators, R. M. Young and John M. Robinson, both comparatively obscure men, were in favor of it. All three congressmen, Zadoc Casey from the southeast, Adam W. Snyder from the southwest, and William L. May from the north, were elected as Democrats; all three opposed the subtreasury. The Democratic papers of the state, generally in favor of the measure, declared war on the congressmen. Zadoc Casey was in a district where the Democrats were not yet in favor of conventions; his personal popularity secured his re-election in 1838 and 1841. Then in 1843 in a redistricted constituency he was badly beaten. But Adam W. Snyder was compelled to decline a re-election; and in the northern district in 1838 Stephen A. Douglas was substituted for May as the Democratic candidate by a convention and was beaten only by a hair's breadth by John T. Stuart, Whig. Douglas especially prided himself on his share in introducing the convention in Illinois politics; by 1843 it was in full use by the Democrats throughout the state in both state and local elections.

Douglas' rise in Illinois politics had been sensational. Born in Vermont in 1813, he had come to Illinois penniless at the age of twenty and had settled in Jacksonville. He attached himself to the Democratic party and rose from office to office—public prosecutor in 1835, state representative in 1836, register of the United States Land Office at Springfield in 1837, secretary of state in 1840, judge of the state supreme court in the same year, congressman in 1843, United States senator from 1847 to his death in 1861. A man of ready wit and tongue, a personality who charmed men and women alike, it was his fierce willingness for political battle at any time and at any odds, his strong partisan spirit and his deep patriotism, that made the physically diminutive "Little Giant" the idol of millions of his countrymen.

The Whigs were slower in adopting close organization. This was inevitable, as at first they were in considerable degree but a congeries of elements thrown off from the original Jacksonian group as the Democratic party was crystallizing out of it. A personal grudge, dislike of Jackson's Bank policy, of his removals from office, of his opposition to the tariff or internal improvements—any one or all of these might have determined the secession of a man or a group from the Jackson party. In 1832 a certain group had tried to run electors for Jackson and R. M. Johnson instead of Jackson and Van Buren. Some of the group ended as undoubted Democrats, some as Whigs; and besides there were, of course, the Anti-Masonic and Clay tickets supported by open opponents of Jackson. In 1836 also the Whig policy was "divide and conquer." In Illinois an electoral ticket was run pledged to vote for either the liberal William Henry Harrison or the conservative Hugh White for President, whichever had the better chance; and apparently the elements supporting the two candidates were not in perfect harmony.

The campaign of 1840 is illustrative of the same tendency. The Whigs nationally nominated the liberal William Henry Harrison for President and an extreme state-rights man, John Tyler, for Vice-President, without a platform. By the use of frontier symbols and appeals to mob psychology, they sought to reawaken for their candidate the genuine enthusiasm for the Jackson of 1828. So monster mass meetings were held, attended by thousands of people marching by delegations from all parts of the state to Springfield, bringing floats of log cabins with coonskins nailed to the door, latchstrings out, and barrels of hard cider at hand, all to prove that Harrison was a man of the frontier, simple, hospitable, a brave general, charitable to old soldiers. A sort of feast of tabernacles, it was commemorative of the hardships of the pioneer days already passing away; and when in the midst of cities of the East, bankers, merchants, and mechanics met around log cabins to pledge one another in tin mugs of hard cider, they sought to impress on men that the golden days of the past with their imagined simplicity and democracy would return with the election of Harrison.

Harrison swept the nation. He lost Illinois because the Democratic organization was too strong; also because the Whigs had been placed in the position of seeming to deny to unnaturalized aliens the right to vote in state elections. Moreover, in supporting a Whig, Alexander P. Field, in his attempt to hold the office of secretary of state against Governor Carlin's attempt to remove him, they seemed to advocate the undemocratic position of unlimited tenure of office. The rest of the nation, for all the fruits of their victory the Whigs were destined to reap, might as well have followed the example of Illinois. Harrison died a month after his inauguration, and John Tyler, bound by no platform, vetoed the Bank bills and other Whig measures. Full of wrath, the Whigs deserted Tyler, save a few like Daniel Webster, who served him two years more as secretary of state. In Illinois as elsewhere Tyler's strength was but a "corporal's guard" recruited from both Whigs and Democrats, plus those men willing for the sake of office to be all things to all men.

Naturally the Whigs did not repeat their mistake. In 1844 they ran undoubted Whig candidates for President and Vice-President on a party platform. But many of the Illinois Whigs still shrank from adopting in state politics the Democratic system of party organization. In 1842 no convention to nominate a Whig candidate for governor was held; the party newspapers persuaded all the Whigs who put themselves forward, except Joseph Duncan, to withdraw. In 1846 it was seriously proposed that the central committee nominate the candidates for state offices, as in effect had been done in 1838; and the convention of 1846 was hardly more than one in name. In a famous manifesto published in 1843 Lincoln, with two other Whigs, laid to the lack of conventions the defeat of the party in the elections of 1842; in answer, Governor Duncan preached the older Whig doctrine of the iniquity of conventions.

The control of the Democratic party in the state after 1843 seemed to rest in the six Democratic congressmen elected in that year. As a result of the redistricting of 1843 the Whigs could count on but one seat in Congress, that in the Seventh, or central, District contended for by John J. Hardin, E. D. Baker, and Abraham Lincoln, among the most prominent of the younger Whigs of the state. The six Democratic congressmen, led by John Wentworth of the Chicago District, Stephen A. Douglas, and John A. McClernand, controlled the federal patronage, governed the party in the state, elected Douglas senator, and silenced the *Illinois State Register* at Springfield, the state Democratic organ, when it dared raise its voice in protest.

The opinions and characteristics of the two parties deserve a word in closing. The Whigs in national politics were supporters of the Bank of the United States and after 1837 opposers of the subtreasury; they were favorers of protective tariff and internal improvements at national expense. Their public land policy was Clay's distribution bill, and they had to prove as best they might that the doles of money Illinois would receive under it would counterbalance the indefinite continuance of the price of one dollar and twenty-five cents per acre. More generally they were a party of the middle classes, sentimental, reading sentimental papers, appealing to sentiment in elections as in 1840. Their party name of Whig recalled the days of the English revolution of the seventeenth and eighteenth centuries and indicated their stand for the independence of the legislative as against the executive.

The Whig politician of Illinois typical of the party was Orville H. Browning. He had come to Quincy in 1831, a young lawyer educated at Augusta College, Kentucky. He became equally famous in the tax-title litigation so important in the Military Tract and in defenses of criminals that moved jury and audience to tears. As a politician he was a skilled debater, a suave and florid orator, but a man with a personal fastidiousness, elegance, and self-conceit that contrasted with the democratic exterior affected by his rivals, Douglas and Richardson. In his later years he was to be a senator and secretary of the interior in Johnson's cabinet; now he doubtless considered himself in ability and in grace the superior of his Whig associates, Hardin, Baker, and Lincoln.

The principles of the Democratic party began with the motto which Blair set at the head of the party organ, the *Washington Globe:* "The world is too much governed." Their policy was strict construction of the Constitution with respect to internal improvements and the chartering of corporations like the United States Bank. At the same time the Illinois that had applauded Jackson's vigorous onset on nullification by South Carolina saw nothing in strict construction incongruous with the most outspoken nationalism. That the government of the United States was a government of limited powers did not mean that the United States was not a nation. The western Democrats sought to enforce on their party a public land policy that would give the actual settler his choice of a farm at a nominal charge or none at all. Some of them had a hankering after national internal improvements in spite of the declared party policy on it. The more radical group in the Democratic party, the so-called "Locofoco" element in New York City and the great masses of the party in Illinois represented by John Wentworth's *Chicago Democrat* and the *Illinois State Register*, were in favor of human rights as against property rights. In East and West, as time went on, an element increasingly apparent opposed all banks, state or federal, and preached an agrarian democracy.

In the Democratic party thus developed in the Illinois of the middle forties the democratic elements of the frontier had found full expression. The one ominous thing was the unnatural alliance in the same party of the western farmer, believing in the dignity of labor and the rights of man, with the great mass of southern slaveholders. From the middle forties the democracy of northern Illinois increasingly chafed against the predominance of the slavery element in the councils of the party. The wave of frontier enthusiasm for Andrew Jackson had developed into a party democratic in name and in some of its ideals; but, as the increasing importance of slavery in the Lower South divided that section's interests from those of the Northwest, a fissure on the surface of the party became more and more apparent.

CHAPTER VIII

The Expansion of the Frontier Commonwealth
1830–46

THE 1820's had seen the population of Illinois overleap the inferior lands between the Wabash and the Mississippi in the southern part of the state and attain the rich Sangamon River country. It had crossed the Illinois River into the present counties of Calhoun and Pike and began to press northward in the Military Tract. In the thirties new tides of population pouring in from the South or by way of Chicago, the Great Lakes, and the Erie Canal from New York and New England were to flood over into all the country north and west of the Illinois and Kankakee rivers. By individual settlers, by colonies, the flood seeped in. Farms and towns developed overnight. Speculation in real estate ran riot, and men began to dream of great transportation systems to create a vast economic empire in the valley; their dreams for the moment were unattainable, but they only faintly foreshadowed the development a half-century was to make in northern and northwestern Illinois.

The early thirties saw the disappearance of the Indians from the prairies. The relics of the Illinois, the Kickapoo, and the Shawnee had all been removed by treaty beyond the Mississippi. The Winnebago of northern Illinois and southern Wisconsin, responsible for the little flurry of 1827 characterized in Illinois history as the Winnebago War, followed in 1832, after the Black Hawk War. The Potawatomi of Lake Michigan made their last cession in the state at Chicago in 1833. Two years later they came for the final payments on this country under the treaty; as they held their last dance on their old assembly ground at the Chicago River, they were in the midst of the streets of the new village of Chicago. Fort Dearborn, garrisoned two years longer, was swallowed up by 1858 in a bustling city. Within a young man's memory the modern metropolis had replaced the frontier trading post.

The Sauk and Foxes, who still dwelt to the east of the Mississippi, were not easily got rid of. In 1804 they had made their first cession, good or bad, at St. Louis; the Treaty of 1816 after the British desertion of the Indians had compelled them to ratify the earlier treaty. A group from the two tribes under the malcontent war chief, Black Hawk, adhered still to the British, made pilgrimages year by year to Malden for the presents and advice of their British father, and clung to their cornfields and the graves of their ancestors at Rock Island, which by treaty they were privileged to occupy until it should be sold by the United States. The frontiersmen could not wait in deference to Indian sentiment. They began to occupy and improve the site of Black Hawk's village. The Indians resented it, and, forced across the Mississippi, Black Hawk began a last, pitifully hopeless war against the white men.

For a time in 1832 northwestern Illinois was kept in terror by Indian raids and murders; the incidents of frontier Kentucky— the gathering of settlers in blockhouses, attacks on small parties of militia—were repeated from time to time. Black Hawk was soon chased into the unknown wilderness of southern Wisconsin. The regular infantry of the United States Army was at a disadvantage in a war with mobile mounted savages, and the mounted militia and volunteers mustered from Illinois and from Wisconsin Territory were a better reliance. One volunteer soldier of skill Illinois produced, General James D. Henry. A blacksmith by calling, Henry delighted in the reading of military books. Nature had given him the ability to lead undisciplined

VANDALIA STATE HOUSE

Erected in 1837, this was the third building used as the seat of government in Vandalia, state capital from 1819 to 1839

Courtesy of Illinois Department of Conservation

BLACK HAWK (1767–1838)
From an old portrait

men and an instinct for tactics and strategy that led him right where men with better systematic training went wrong. His claims to the honors of the Black Hawk War were disputed by the Dodges of Wisconsin and by regular officers, but any careful student must concede to Henry much of the credit for the battles of the Wisconsin and the Bad Axe, which reduced Black Hawk and his band to abject submission. Black Hawk was held a prisoner, and his Indians removed across the Mississippi. A century and a half after Marquette had first met the Indian in the Illinois country the white man had finally expelled him from it.

The Black Hawk War has an especial interest to Illinois history for the reason that many a promising young politician with a career before him answered the call of duty and marched with the militia to put down Black Hawk. Most of the Illinois statesmen of later days who were in the state at the time entered in their records the campaign of 1832. Abraham Lincoln served as a captain of militia in it and accepted a land bounty for his service, which he later immortalized in a richly humorous comparison of its bloodlessness with the military record of General Lewis Cass.

With the passing of the Indian there was nothing to impede the advance of the white man. Everywhere farms were carved out of the wilderness before the government had opened it for sale. As tract after tract was put up for sale in the new land offices opened at Galena, Chicago, Quincy, and Danville, settlers who already had fenced and broken tracts of land and put up cabins or had bought the improvements of earlier squatters thronged to the sales to buy the tracts on which they had already established their homes. At times in the thirties temporary pre-emption acts protected them. When they did not, the settlers protected themselves. In land districts before lands were put on sale the settlers formed settlers' committees which first adjusted disputes between actual settlers as to overlapping claims and then attended sales in force to overawe any speculator who dared to bid on a settler's improvement.

The methods of the war with the soil were changing. Men had conquered their dread of the prairies; but they took care usually to enter sections that included a bit of woodland for cabin, fence rails, and firewood. If they did not, they had to borrow those necessary articles from the lands of nonresidents or, if the settler had a New England conscience, from the land still belonging to the United States. Good springs and healthful home sites were other things to look for. The men who came to this district in the thirties had money to spend; and definite rates for service established themselves: two dollars and fifty cents an acre for breaking prairie, two dollars a hundred for cutting rails, hauling them, and building a rail fence. Often the claim and improvements of a squatter who lacked his one dollar and twenty-five cents per acre to pay in at the land office were for sale and made that much easier the establishment of a new home. Squatters and day laborers could and did by industry earn the money to enter quarter-sections of their own. The day of promise seemed fully dawned for every man able and willing to work.

Everywhere through the district was to be found the track of the speculator. For years eastern speculators had been buying up choice tracts in the so-called Military Tract west of the Illinois River, and many a veteran of the War of 1812 parted with his bounty land in Illinois for a song. Now speculators were busy in the new reaches opened up for sale in northwestern Illinois. A favorite trick was to buy up the quarter-sections of woodland along the rivers and resell at a handsome profit to the heedless man who located his tract entirely on the adjoining prairies. But the town sites offered even better picking. To serve as county seats in the new counties springing up and as commercial centers, old forts, trading posts, and fords were developing into towns—Warsaw, Oquawka, Savanna, and Rock

Island on the Mississippi, Peoria and Rockford in the interior, and, above all, Chicago.

The following advertisement may serve as a specimen of the speculative towns of the day:

PUBLIC SALE OF LOTS IN THE TOWN OF HURON

On Monday 21st of August next, will be sold on the premises to the highest bidder, 100 Town Lots in Gay's addition to the town of Huron, Sangamon county, Illinois. Huron is situated on the south bank of Sangamon River, at the point before known as Miller's Ferry, about 30 miles from Beardstown, 30 miles from Jacksonville, 30 miles from Freemont and Pekin, 30 miles from Springfield, the seat of government of the State—also at a point where the canal from Beardstown must intersect the Sangamon River, (by an act of the Legislature) which has already been surveyed. It is likewise about the geographical center of that part of the Territory of Sangamon county, which by general consent, it is conceded, must in a short time become a new county—is surrounded by fertile and healthy country, now containing a large and industrious population, and which is constantly and rapidly increasing. It must command a large portion of the trade of Pecan bottom, a tract unrivaled in fertility and beauty by any in the State, as well as a large extent of rich and fertile country adjacent. And in the event of the construction of the canal (which from the nature of the river, precluding almost the possibility of its ever becoming navigable) which the interests of the country and of the stockholders require, Huron will possess the advantages of an immense water power, that cannot fail to build it up at once into a flourishing and populous town. There is one saw and grist mill now in operation about 4 miles from Huron, and two more building within six miles. The water is of the first quality. There are two state roads running through Huron at right angles, and the principal part of the travel to the upper part of the Military Tract is thro this place. The town lies on the second table, and principally about 30 feet above high water mark. Should the State take a fancy to make the Sangamon River navigable, (which might be done by digging a channel 150 or 200 miles) then Huron possesses the advantage of being one of the most prominent points of the river.

We say that Huron possessing all these advantages must become an important place, and is worthy the attention of persons who wish to make good investments, or who seek favorable locations for business.

Terms—Six and twelve months credit.

G. W. GAY, *Agent*

297 ts.

Huron, July 7, 1837
Sangamo Journal, Aug. 5, 1837

Chicago in the middle thirties was the happy hunting ground of the speculator. Into the Chicago River crowded schooners and steamers expeditiously bringing emigrants and their household goods, merchants and their stores from the head of Lake Erie, where De Witt Clinton's Erie Canal opened up the way from New York and New England. Some of the newcomers swarmed out into the rich lands of northern Illinois; but many stayed in Chicago. The city grew rapidly year by year in population. In March, 1837, it was incorporated. Town lots sold for one hundred dollars a front foot; speculators made fortunes in the city's real estate.

Speculation was not merely local to Illinois. In those years it ran throughout the Union and throughout the West in particular. The deposit of federal funds in state banks had given the banks great assets on which they were eager to reap profits. They would readily lend to the speculator the precious bank notes that would buy at the land office the sections and quarter-sections of rich western land. The attention of the speculators fluctuated from state to state; Indiana this year, Mississippi that, Illinois another, led the sales of lands in terms of millions of acres where a decade before barely hundreds of thousands were sold. Until Jackson checked the mania by prescribing that only gold and silver be received for public lands, speculating was easy and sure wealth.

Throughout the states of the Northwest men's imaginations ran riot. They were fired by the matchless beauty of the untouched prairies with their lavish succession of flowers from the spring violet and grass flower, the pink, the crimson phlox, the physostegia, the purple liatris, to the blue and gold of the fall aster and the goldenrod. Their cupidity was quickened by the promise of the rich farms that lay beneath, by brisk and thriving villages grown overnight, by commercial metropolises whose buildings in sober reality grew as through a mirage. The promise of wealth nature stretched out to them on every side with lavish hands. Only adequate means of transportation and capital seemed needed to enjoy it at the fullest; and, with optimism run wild, men in the middle 1830's set about securing both these things.

The General Assembly caught the contagion and once more began to think in terms of millions. It had, about 1830, painfully wound up the affairs of the State Bank of Illinois; it had seen the Bank of Edwardsville fail and the Bank of Illinois at Shawneetown, while solvent, suspend business. It had despised not the day of small things and had debated with praiseworthy economy of the people's money appropriations of hundreds or thousands of dollars, and with Republican virtue had looked closely to its own small per diem. But the boom times of the thirties awoke it anew. It began once more the chartering of banks. The Bank of Illinois in 1835 was rechartered for a capital of a million. The new State Bank of Illinois was created in the same year to have branches and a capital of $1,500,000.

These friendly institutions would doubtless supply to a growing and progressive country the money it needed, but how was the state to obtain the transportation required to pour into the world's markets the produce of the Illinois prairies? True, there was the grant of federal land obtained for the Illinois and Michigan Canal in 1827 by Daniel Pope Cook—his last service to the state. Alternate tracts to a depth of five sections along the route were a valuable nest egg. Illinois had discussed various projects, had debated the advisability of canal or railroad, and finally, in spite of engineering difficulties, had decided on a canal. In 1836 the state at last decided to undertake the work on funds raised on credit, trusting to the sale of canal lands and the tolls of the canal to pay the debt. That same session of the legislature saw the passage of a flood of bills for private corporations to construct railroads, canals, turnpike roads, with powers stated in all degrees of looseness. In view of Marshall's decision in the Dartmouth College case that a state may not change corporate powers it has granted, one shudders at the thought of what an ungovernable transportation system Illinois would have endured had these bills been anything but a pleasant mirage.

The excitement was satirized most ably by William Kinney, in a speech that may serve as a specimen of his style:

MR. CHEERMAN—The gentleman *what* has just taken his seat says, he is decidedly in favor of railroads, and that upon the joint stock principle, the state subscribing one third and individuals the residue; a railroad should be constructed from the city of New Jerusalem, about to be built on the Rocky Mountains, through Peoria to the City of New York—For he says, there are actually people now residing at Peoria! And report says there are even some (*besides Indians*) beyond there.—He knows every inch of ground in the whole state of Illinois—and has surveyed the same from the center to the circumference—and Peoria is exactly three miles, twenty three chains, eleven and eleven sixteenths links from the geographical center; and in all respects the most suitable and practicable location for a seat of government in the universe; and is in fact the only place under the sun where all the turnpikes, railroads, highways, canals and water courses, both natural and artificial, must eventually terminate.

The gentleman in flights of fancy has disdained to confine himself to this little dirty planet, earth—in his vast and fertile imagination he has constructed a double track railroad to the moon, and traveled thither on a locomotive at the rate of 75,000 miles per hour—thence he has thrown a summerset and landed straddle of the north pole—then vaulted into the regions of eternal space, and there with a dead rest and unerring aim, has shot at eternity.

Some men are born *poets*, and all women are born *singers*, but as to *that air critter* what has just taken his seat, any body can see Natur has made him an Orator![1]

1. *Belleville Advocate*, December 9, 1841.

But southern Illinois had at length caught the internal improvement fever. The oldest settled part of the state, she had seen the rich lands to the north fill up while her own counties remained unpeopled. A great transportation system might redress the balance. Accordingly in the session of 1836–37 the legislature set enthusiastically to work out a vast system of internal improvements to be constructed on the credit of the state. The Wabash, Illinois, Kaskaskia, and Rock rivers were to be improved. There was to be an Illinois Central Railroad from the terminus of the Illinois and Michigan Canal to the mouth of the Ohio River at Cairo, two east-and-west lines, the Southern Cross and the Northern Cross railroads, the former from Alton to Mount Carmel, the latter via Quincy and Springfield to the Indiana state line; and divers other enterprises. All this was supported on the most enthusiastic calculations of profits from the work and the distribution to the states of the surplus federal revenue. The Council of Revision, consisting of Governor Duncan and the justices of the supreme court, vetoed the bill, but it passed over the veto.

The internal improvement system had been adopted because at the same session the question had come up of a relocation of the state capital. The capital had been located for twenty years at Vandalia merely as a speculation in town lots by the state. Now, as the twenty years neared its end, Alton, Jacksonville, Peoria, and Springfield were all aspiring to the dignity. The Springfield delegation in the legislative session of 1837, the famous "Long Nine"—headed by Abraham Lincoln—traded their votes on the internal improvement system for the location of the capital at Springfield.

As Abraham Lincoln was one of the leaders in the internal improvement movement and in his earlier life typified the ambition for material progress that characterized it, it is fitting here to recall to the reader the main facts of his earlier career. He was born in central Kentucky in 1809. His father was of the pioneer type and drifted with the advancing frontier, from farm to farm in Kentucky, to southern Indiana, and then, in 1830, to eastern Illinois, to Decatur, and to Coles County. Abraham Lincoln, now of age, struck out for himself, settling at New Salem, then included in Sangamon County. His physical strength and his wit made him a leader, and he went into politics, running a close race for the General Assembly in 1832 and being elected in 1834, 1836, 1838, and 1840. He soon was counted among the younger leaders of the Whig party in the state. First an unsuccessful storekeeper in New Salem, he took up the study of law by himself and in 1836 was admitted to the bar. He removed to Springfield in 1837, marrying Mary Todd, daughter of an aristocratic Kentucky family, five years later. With the exception of a term in Congress (1847–49), he devoted himself to the practice of law at Springfield and on the eastern Illinois circuit until the repeal of the Missouri Compromise in 1854. To his contemporaries he as yet seemed little more than a good jury lawyer who sought the law of his cases by intuition rather than study, a clever and honest politician, and a companion whose wit made him the life of his company.

When the internal improvement system went into effect, in accordance with the law, construction was begun simultaneously at many different points. The Panic of 1837 cut off the bonus of federal money. The State Bank, to which the state had subscribed paper capital, expecting to receive huge specie profits, was deep in difficulties. The legislature of 1839 at the behest of southern Illinois laid a heavy tax compared to what the state had hitherto known; twenty cents on the one hundred dollars was an argument to use in approaching English bankers for a loan. Opposition to the system had already been gathering, and this tax turned the scale. Demands for a classification or a repeal of the system began to spread.

Meanwhile the fund commissioners of the state floated what bonds they could in New York and then turned to the firm of

John Wright in London. Commissioners for the canal bonds and the internal improvement bonds were soon competing in the market. Blocks of bonds from the hands of bankrupts began to come in the market and depress it. Governor Carlin considered for a time the contract with Wright illegal, held it up long enough to cause the failure of Wright's house, and then ratified it. Work on the system stopped in 1840. By 1841 the state could no longer pay the interest on its bonds; its work stopped, and the whole system came crashing down. The banks had suspended specie payments; the State Bank had speculated wildly, its notes circulating at an increasing discount, and ruin was everywhere. A member of the General Assembly stated that in his district constables and magistrates were the only businessmen.

The roseate hues of speculation and optimism no longer colored life. Northern Illinois, distrustful of the imperial destiny of the state, began to look longingly toward debt-free Wisconsin Territory, and many men proposed that the Northwest Ordinance be obeyed and the northern boundary of the state be the line through the foot of Lake Michigan. Trade had degenerated into barter. It is of these days that old residents of Chicago used to delight in telling how they had refused an offer of the future site of Marshall Field and Company for an old set of harness. Certainly one-hundred-dollar-a-foot values were no longer in evidence.

The solution of the state's difficulty was achieved in 1842 in the election of Governor Thomas Ford. His opponent in the election, former Governor Joseph Duncan, had rather looked to the tariff of a Whig national administration in 1845 and money doles to the state from the federal government to extricate it. Ford's scheme compelled the state to rely on itself. The winding-up of the State Bank, and an agreement by which the state's creditors should advance funds for the completion of the canal on a pledge of its lands and tolls, was the solution finally adopted and adhered to by both sides. Population and business now flowed to Illinois, and the debt of fifteen millions no longer seemed a serious matter. Illinois had extricated herself by her own efforts from the effects of her folly. She had been too optimistic of the future in 1837, but her destiny was unfolding rapidly. The railroads came fifteen years later than she looked for them; but the material progress they brought outran the wildest dreams of 1837.

The state, however, owed her immediate rescue to a man of the age that was passing. Poverty had beset Thomas Ford throughout his life. It had condemned him as a young man to a role in politics below his abilities and in his middle years to the meager pay of a circuit judge. In the vain hope it might be a legacy for his children, he left at his death a "History of Illinois" that is a remarkable work. Approaching the period of the state's history through which he had lived as an example of the futility of American politics, he dissected with a merciless scalpel both politicians and political methods. John Reynolds in particular writhed in agony at the acid recounting of stories revealing his littleness at which the bar at its circuit dinners had doubtless roared many a time. The future careers of Douglas, Trumbull, and Lincoln were, of course, beyond Ford's knowledge; and he drew all his characters on the same scale. To him the period was one of little measures and little men. The pessimism with which one of the keenest commentators on American political life regarded it is more in the fashion of the present age than of his own.

In the face of the great change that was to come over Illinois in the decade of the fifties, we may consider two incidents typical of the frontier period of the state on the eve of its passing. Only in the frontier stage of development could the dual tragedy of the Mormon settlement and the Mormon war have been staged. Mormonism, according to the Mormons, began in 1827, when the Angel of the Lord surrendered to Joseph Smith mi-

THOMAS FORD (1800–1850)

MORMON "PROPHET" JOSEPH SMITH WITH
NAUVOO TEMPLE IN BACKGROUND
From 1847 etching, courtesy of Illinois State Historical Library

raculous golden plates that had been buried for some fifteen centuries on the hill at Palmyra, New York; marvelous plates that told long histories of emigrations to America in days before Christ and in the early Christian Era, of the preaching of the gospel and the founding of churches here, of wars and the wiping-out by barbarians of all trace of the divine message. These plates, translated by Smith through miraculous interposition into the Book of Mormon, laid the foundation of the Latter-Day Saints, a religious group molded into a community economically and politically subservient to Joseph Smith and his family and a few other leaders.

The Latter-Day Saints moved from place to place, and always persecution followed, once in Ohio, twice in Missouri. The second persecution by the Gentiles in Missouri was the bitterest, and about 1840 the Saints sought refuge at Nauvoo in Hancock County on the Mississippi. Here the faithful began to gather together, some converts by Mormon elders in the East, more from England and Europe. A city of perhaps twenty thousand, the largest in the state, grew up in a few years. Mormons scattered into the outlying districts, but even so Nauvoo had hard work in finding enterprises to keep her impecunious thousands in food.

From the beginning Smith had sought to trade off the thousands of votes he controlled for political privileges. He obtained a charter for Nauvoo that gave it an independent militia organization and local legislative power concurrent with that of the General Assembly. In 1840 his followers voted for Harrison, in 1842 for Ford and the Democrats; but in 1844 Smith aspired himself to be a presidential candidate.

Meanwhile ugly rumors about Nauvoo and the Mormons began to circulate. Scabrous recruits to the colony like John C. Bennett, when expelled from it, began to tell stories of debauchery and plural marriage that went on in it. Reports that it was a refuge of horse thieves antagonized the local farmers. In 1844 the city government under the Smiths forcibly suppressed the *Nauvoo Expositor*, a newspaper that began to attack their management and morality. A few weeks later the Smiths, surrendering to arrest at Carthage, the county seat, on the charge of rioting, were committed to the jail where they were set upon by a mob and murdered.

Thereafter the Gentiles of the surrounding country took up arms again and again to force the withdrawal of the Mormons from the state. Nauvoo was twice attacked by military forces from surrounding counties; once the governor mustered the power of the state to protect it. But Brigham Young, stronger and abler than ever the Smiths were, had seized control of Mormondom, expelled all hostile elements, and prepared to lead the colony to the Far West, where his power would be absolute. In 1846 all but a remnant of the Mormons had left the state on their way to Salt Lake.

Today a little village of a few hundreds nestles in the heart of what was once a great religious metropolis. Taught by French pioneers, the people of Nauvoo manufacture a blue cheese and in an annual festival celebrate the wedding of wine and cheese. A few brick houses survive out of the homes that once sheltered tens of thousands. The great temple, completed before the Mormons left, said in its day to be the most imposing building beyond the mountains, can be traced only by its foundations.

Much may justly be said in condemnation of the violence that drove the Mormons out of the state at the point of the rifle; much more of the murder of the Smiths. But it must not be forgotten that the Mormon community was growing with frightening rapidity and that it had fastened itself in a body politic so rudimentary that it could not itself expel the intruder. Smith had striven to set his community outside the law of the state; by political bargaining, he had nearly accomplished it. The state had no police force adequate to deal with the menace of autocratic government and defiance of law and morals at Nauvoo.

The frontiersmen took the law in their own hands when the simple government they had erected in the state for their simple needs proved inadequate. In the frontier stage that was passing in the forties action was taken that in the more advanced state of a decade later would not have been condoned.

CHAPTER IX

The Coming of the Railroads

THE years in which Illinois was called to the foremost place in the nation's councils in deciding the great questions of slavery expansion, war, and reconstruction were also years in which she was in the throes of a mighty rebirth. Between 1850 and 1870 she was transformed from a simple frontier rural community to an industrial state, with large cities growing into mighty ones as cities had never grown before in the world's history. Suddenly she was compelled to meet the problems of a social, economic, and political life made many times more complex. Innumerable factors worked in the accomplishment of the change, but the greatest of them was the railroads.

The railroad era represents one of a series of mighty strides forward that the modern world was taking. In the sixteenth and seventeenth centuries if a savant had been asked what the civilized world in material achievement had added to the heritage of Greece and Rome, he could have mentioned only the mariner's compass, the application of gunpowder to war, and the contribution of the printing press to the rapid spread of the written word among men. By the end of the eighteenth century he would have had to add that the application of steam to manufacturing had made possible the increased machine production of the industrial age. After 1830 he would have seen the remaking of the farm and the multiplication of the crop that could be reaped by a single man with the harvester and other agricultural machinery; he would have witnessed the revolutionizing of transportation, the binding of city to city, state to state, nation to nation, by the ocean steamship, the telegraph, and the railroad in a degree that transcended the imagination of the most gifted taletellers of the past.

The railroads of the thirties had failed because the state had embarked on an overambitious scheme dictated by political alliances and roseate hopes rather than by sound economic considerations, and for the funds to attempt its construction had pledged her credit to credulous financiers ignorant of local conditions. How capital had accumulated in the eastern United States and how, why, and in what combinations it began to look to Illinois railroads for investments are questions that cannot be answered until the economic history of the United States is adequately written. But by the late forties capitalists were beginning to bid for charters that would carry railroads across the state to St. Louis or at least to Chicago at the terminus of the Illinois and Michigan Canal. That canal, opened in 1848, was already carrying away the grain and other products of the Illinois River country from St. Louis to Chicago, en route for eastern ports by the Great Lakes. The old cry of federal aid for internal improvements re-echoed; and, though such things had no part in the program of the Democratic party, western-minded Democrats like Douglas and Wentworth set about to get them. Douglas believed that funds to make navigable the rivers of the state could be obtained by the imposition of state tonnage duties. For the construction of a railroad in the state to link Lake Michigan and the Ohio in 1850 he secured a federal land grant.

Years before this, Senator Sidney Breese had been working for federal aid to the Illinois Central Railroad projected in 1836–37; Douglas took up the scheme, satisfied state-rights Democrats by making it a donation to the state for the construction of the road and bore back in triumph a federal land grant along the lines of the projected road—a Y connecting Galena and Chicago with Cairo—that was to net the Illinois Central Railroad Company two million, five hundred thousand acres. A group of eastern capitalists promptly undertook the work; and eastern Illinois, then almost a desert, blossomed as the rose with towns and farms. Meanwhile the state legislature was besieged with requests for charters for lines to cross the state and connect the Mississippi with eastern trunk lines. Here local interests contended obscurely with one another. Each locality, of course, opposed the railroad schemes designed to help its rivals; but Alton especially in the name of "state policy" sought to prevent its rival, St. Louis, from being the terminus of any line crossing the state. In spite of the fact that Governor French and some of the most prominent Democratic politicians were in favor of a St. Louis terminus, the advocates of "state policy," in a called session of 1849, passed a general railroad law with a provision that the General Assembly must approve routes and termini. In 1851 the Assembly approved the routing of the Ohio and Mississippi Railroad from Vincennes to Illinoistown opposite St. Louis. The Terre Haute and Alton project, however, aided by the Ohio and Mississippi Road, until 1854 blocked the chartering of the Atlantic and Mississippi— a connection between Terre Haute and Illinoistown. Bribery of the legislature was freely charged on both sides. The Atlantic and Mississippi was not undertaken until 1865; but Lieutenant-Governor Koerner, by inserting a joker in a local railroad bill, secured a connection between Alton and Illinoistown that made Alton only a way station on a route from Terre Haute to St. Louis.

Meanwhile other roads had appeared with magical speed. The Galena and Chicago Union, later part of the North Western system, incorporated in 1847, had fourteen miles in operation in 1849 and reached Freeport in 1853. It soon added an air line west from Chicago to Fulton. In the same years a network of roads in northern Illinois and southern Wisconsin developed, ultimately to be combined in the North Western system. Between 1851 and 1854 the Chicago and Rock Island was constructed; and by 1854 the Chicago and Alton. Within a year or two separate roads from Quincy to Galesburg, from Galesburg to Mendota, from Galesburg to Burlington, and from Aurora to Chicago were united into the nucleus of the Chicago, Burlington, and Quincy. Connections with the East had already developed. In 1850 the Michigan Southern and the Michigan Central, built by rival capitalist groups, were seeking to block each other out of Indiana and Illinois. Ultimately they entered the state over spurs, built under state charters for the Michigan Central by the Illinois Central and for the Michigan Southern by the Rock Island. Chicago interests feared a junction outside Chicago from Joliet to La Porte and felt that a union of eastern and western lines even five miles out of the city would ruin its prosperity.

This was of course but the outline of the Illinois railroad net of the present. Year by year new roads and connections developed, a dozen projects dying ingloriously for every one that came to fruition. More than one relic of the mania of 1837 was galvanized into a hectic life.

"I was creditably informed," wrote J. C. Allen to Governor French on December 9, 1851, "a few days since, that General Pickering, the indefatigable proprietor of the Mt. Carmel and Alton Rail Road, in his zeal for the completion of his favorite work, has actually hired an Irishman and set him to work on it, he (the Genl) acting as Superintendent."[1]

Men learned to use the railroads as soon as they came. By 1853 the *State Register* noted the discontinuance of the last of the lines of stages for which Springfield had been noted. The bar, riding the circuits through the state, speedily learned to abandon the buggy, the wagon, or the stage and to pick its way even by roundabout routes from one railroad line to the next. Complaints of crowded cars occur before 1854. The next year the Illinois Central introduced sleeping cars. In 1857 the first through Chicago–St. Louis sleeper was put in operation. The coal-burning locomotive came in to take the place of the engine burning wood.

1. French Manuscripts, Illinois Historical Survey, University of Illinois.

Accidents began to happen. The superintendent of the Chicago and Alton issued an order in 1853 that an hour before evening trains were due section-masters should pass over their sections on handcars to drive all cows off the track. Unfenced rights of way had their dangers, and the companies set to fencing them as speedily as they could.

In the years between 1849 and 1856 the population of the state was changing rapidly. The restless frontier elements of pioneer Illinois were flowing out to the newer West. Migration to California in 1849-50 caught the popular imagination. The *Ottawa Free Trader* of March 23, 1850, wrote:

> Our town has for the past week been every evening so crowded with California teams and emigrants, that the hotels have not been able to accommodate all. We can scarcely look out of the windows but we see California teams, some drawn by oxen, some by horses, some by ponies, some by mules—every species of conveyance seems to have been brought into requisition and every known contrivance to get through. On Fox River we are credibly informed, the migration will average one out of every six able bodied men . . . while in our own County, although not as large as this, the proportion is yet fearfully large. You can scarce pass a wagon, wrote an Illinois emigrant, but 'tis the common inquiry of "Where do you hail from?" the certain response is "from Illinois"; "what county?" and you may have an answer from every county of the state.[2]

Similar banded migration to Kansas and Nebraska from 1853 on, and to Pikes Peak in 1859, attracted attention. The steady drift of the restless to other parts of the newer West, revealed by the census of 1860, passed without comment.

Population poured in far more rapidly than it poured out. Eastern Illinois between 1850 and 1856 settled as if by enchantment. The Illinois Central Railroad held its lands as high as fifteen dollars an acre. Speculators like Governor French hastened to make locations along it in central and southern Illinois on government lands that still sold as low as twelve and one-half cents.

2. *State Register*, May 31, 1849.

Men and even neighborhoods in "Egypt" that had improved farms on government land without troubling to enter it, trusting to the rifle to protect them against intruders, were threatened with loss of their lives' earnings of four or five thousand dollars.[3] In 1849 almost fifteen million government acres, or two-fifths the area of the state, remained unsold. In 1857 there were but 294,149 acres left. In four years the railroad changed Jonesboro from a village of fifty log huts to a town of two thousand population. A man who in traveling over the Illinois Central from Mattoon to Odin in 1857 had only the conductor and brakeman in the car with him, in 1864 passed through thriving villages every six miles where formerly there had been but open prairies or bare station-houses. Between 1850 and 1860 the population of the forty-nine counties through which the Illinois Central ran was said to have increased from 335,598 to 814,891. Similar results appeared in the Military Tract and to a less degree in most other parts of the state.

Southern and eastern Illinois at last were settled. The new population came from New England; it came also from Germany in the shape of political idealists, seeking a land of liberty after the disaster of 1848; it came from other parts of Europe also. There were colonies of Frenchmen as at Nauvoo, of French-Canadians in the Kankakee country, of Swedes at Bishop Hill. Norwegians pressed into the state. The foreign-born population tended toward towns; by 1860 Chicago had more foreign-born than native-born population.

At the coming of the railroads, the McCormick harvester and the many other makes of reaper had already foreshadowed the revolutionizing of Illinois agriculture. In the Civil War young men by hundreds of thousands could leave the farms of Illinois for the battlefield, secure that the reaper could gather crops that would feed the United States and Europe as well. No longer was

3. Both the United States and the Illinois Central granted liberal terms to such squatters.

a man's planting limited by the amount he could reap by the scythe in a harvest season. In the middle fifties, the tedder and the steam plow were taking their place beside the reaper. Skilled farmers who had been in Illinois since it was a state had been eager to teach their fellows all the scientific agriculture known in their day. Now the instruction was enforced at firsthand by the great cattle-feeding ranches, the great farms, the great fruit orchards that stood as incentives to the ambitious pioneer farmer. Agricultural societies and agricultural papers spread the information of how the excellence of these things might be copied. The shiftless farmer and the dilapidated farmhouse were migrating or amending. The Illinois farm, the basis of the state's prosperity, was already being revolutionized before 1848 or 1850. The railroad accentuated the progress.

One of the most striking characteristics of the period was the development of Chicago. By 1859 men mentioned with pride that Cyrus H. McCormick's reaper works gave support to two hundred and fifty families; but manufacturing was the least of the city's achievements. The completion of the Illinois and Michigan Canal had resulted in the shipping by Chicago and the Great Lakes of great amounts of grain that formerly found its way by the Illinois to St. Louis and the East. Holding that her lake route to the East was her greatest commercial asset, Chicago feared lest railroad cut-offs to the East should deflect trade, unconscious of the bounty the railroads were to fling in her lap. Chicago was a better outlet for produce to the Atlantic seaboard than St. Louis through New Orleans. The Alton and the Illinois Central contributed their share to bringing produce into Chicago and distributing merchandise from that point. The roads that in the fifties reached out to the Mississippi and to the Greater Northwest beyond diverted great masses of freight that formerly had followed the Mississippi to St. Louis. For instance, receipts of lead there between 1851 and 1857 declined from 503,751 to 200,402 pigs; and on the ground of obstruction to river traffic St. Louis vainly made war, legal and illegal, against the Rock Island bridge across the Mississippi, the symbol of the ruin of her commercial empire in the north.

Chicago business became hectic as today, as a description of the Chicago grain dealers of 1859 may show:

> They get up at sunrise, bolt their steak and rolls, and rush down town to the "first board," which meets at a well known corner between eight and eleven o'clock. There they buy and sell—till it is time to attend the "second board," at the Board of Trade rooms. There they investigate the bulletin boards, note the receipts and the shipments.—Half-past eleven o'clock comes, and all eyes are turned towards the telegraph office across the way. The New York dispatches are expected; and nothing can be done till they arrive. . . .
>
> The "third board" has met—on the corner before mentioned (some call it Gambler's Corner), and the same operations described on 'Change are repeated—only with more recklessness. . . . And thus it goes till six o'clock. . . .
>
> . . . What! go home at six o'clock, and not return to the city again! The steamer might come in with a decline, and thus thousands of dollars would be lost—or not won—which is all the same. . . . No; they must attend the "fourth board" at the Tremont House—or rather on the sidewalk opposite the Tremont. . . . It meets at 7 o'clock P.M.[4]

Chicago in population increased from 29,963 in 1850 to 80,000 in 1855, 109,000 in 1860, and 298,977 in 1870. The other towns of the state increased also. The little trading centers of the forties numbering two, three, four, or, as at Chicago, eight or ten thousand began to grow in earnest. In 1850 Springfield, Alton, Peoria, Cairo, Quincy, Belleville, Beardstown, and Ottawa were all thriving towns. By 1860 the largest of them, Peoria and Quincy, exceeded twenty thousand.

Naturally such municipalities had their problems. Before 1850 the Illinois municipal law, applicable to little towns of a few hundreds, was highly rudimentary. Now with a greater concentration of population regulation became essential. Boards

4. *Chicago Press and Tribune*, July 4, 1859.

sinking in abysses of mud could not take the place of sidewalks. Hogs wallowing in muddy streets and cows chewing their cuds in repose across footways sorted ill with the ambitions of young metropolises; and one after another in the fifties the Illinois cities from Chicago down wrestled with the problem as to whether hogs and cows should be barred from the public streets. Once that was done, there arose the problem of the garbage formerly piled high in the gutters for hogs to remove, of drains in the open street, of polluted water supplies; and, while the towns toiled over their ABC's of sanitation, epidemics of cholera swept over them in 1848, 1850, and again in 1851.

On such matters no city could be the first to cast a stone at a rival. Said the *Illinois Journal* (Springfield) of September 7, 1853:

Our city Hogs are a very industrious and refined race as evidenced by their labors and amusements. They are now in the enjoyment of the city, find plenty of "grub" every where, and feel no anxiety for the coming morrow.... The peach stones found about the streets and crackled by the swinish herd, are used as a dessert. They amuse themselves by digging holes in the gutters, some of them at the corners of the streets—some several feet deep—the one at the corner near the State House is probably three feet deep—into these they collect all the moisture in the neighborhood and stir up a most beautiful batter. It is about the consistency of cream or perhaps mush. Now, every thing ready, his swineship takes a walk about the city. He notices, especially, all newly painted fences and houses within his reach....

Thirteen years later even a worse story could be told of Chicago.

Men had to learn that living so close together they must do many things jointly that before they had done each for himself. In 1850 Chicago was preparing to instal gas lighting, a sewage system, and a water system. In 1853 Quincy and Peoria put in gas plants; in 1855 Springfield and Quincy had waterworks. The presence of many little children in cities too dense to allow of family cows created the necessity of dairies; and, until men learned to regulate these, the innocents were massacred by milk

STUMP-SPEAKING, PAINTED BY GEORGE CALEB BINGHAM

The original painting is owned by the Boatmen's National Bank of St. Louis

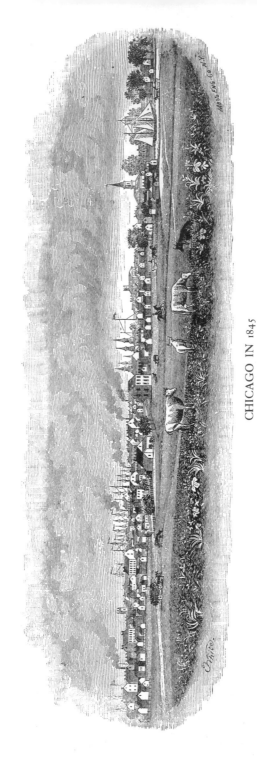

CHICAGO IN 1845

From J. Wellington Norris, *A Business Advertiser and General Directory of the City of Chicago for the Year 1845–46*

from cows fed with distillery mash. Buses appeared in Chicago in 1850, streetcars in 1859; and, until the coming of the automobile set individuals once more at liberty from the mass, men in cities used public utilities and traveled and lived together in ever increasing degree.

Some of the problems of the age were not so easily settled. The descendant of the New England Puritan, the zealous Methodist, had modes of life quite different from those of the German or Irish emigrant and with his greater political experience and skill set about enforcing his own theories of sobriety and decency upon them. No question existed that the doggery, grocery, or saloon, where whiskey was dispensed freely, was a bad thing, at its worst along the line of the canal where a whiskey consisting of a concentrated extract diluted with water was sold the "canal Irish"; and the Puritan set about reforming it altogether. In Chicago the citizens accustomed to the use of beer and wines on the Sabbath succeeded in defeating everything but a high license system; but in one downstate town after another prohibition was tried in the middle fifties and then abandoned. Between 1851 and 1853 a law, practically a dead letter, prescribed that liquors should not be retailed in quantities less than one quart; on its repeal the temperance advocates began to press for a "Maine law" prohibition. However, the slavery question pushed temperance into the background for two generations; and Illinois saloons continued to reflect the lawlessness of pioneer days until the 1920's saw the desperate device of prohibiting the use of alcoholic beverages. The New Englander fought with the German and Irishman over Sunday observance also; but on this question for the time being the Puritan Sabbath came off second best.

Some of the problems lay deeper yet in the future. The very massing of population in the cities was a sign that the day of opportunity for the landless man to become landed was passing. As early as 1852 the grant to the Illinois Central and the seizing on the public lands by speculators had produced an antiland monopoly agitation. In the middle thirties a man of strength, sobriety, and industry in the Northwest could earn in a year or two the one hundred dollars that was the price of a half quarter-section of government land. Now, on wages of seventy-five cents to one dollar a day in cities where rents were high, there was no such chance. Men worked ten- and twelve-hour days and found, when wheat was one dollar and forty cents a bushel, they could not feed or clothe their families; the hard winters of 1854 and 1857 brought suffering. The democracy of Wentworth and Douglas had sought to relieve these men by a homestead act, but that act passed in 1862 was to be the work of the Republicans. Meanwhile, the high prices of the Civil War finally brought trade-unionism to Chicago, with strikes, and the modern phase of the struggle of labor and capital.

Other problems were on their way. The simple rural democracy of the forties had regarded banks as the work of the evil one. Beaten in the election for the constitutional convention of 1847, while they had excluded a banking clause from their constitution, they had admitted a proviso that a system of state banking with notes secured by bonds might be submitted to popular vote. The constant demand of the new industrial order for banking facilities was too strong. Men like George Smith of the Wisconsin Fire and Marine Insurance Company did a prosperous business in note issue at Chicago in defiance of law. In 1851 the state legislature over the governor's veto submitted to the people of the state a banking law allowing institutions to incorporate and to issue notes secured by federal or state bonds. The passage of the measure by a vote of 37,650 to 31,413 was one more sign that the old order was changing.

The system for some years worked with fair success. Some banks fell by the wayside in the panics of 1854 and 1857; but the great majority stood until the secession of the southern states depreciated the value of their bonds. Then bank after bank gave up the struggle. In May, 1861, notes of fifteen banks were depreciated to fifty cents, fifty-three went from sixty to ninety cents on the dollar, and only six remained at par. The issue of the greenbacks and the National Banking Act and its tax on the notes of state banks left the surviving banks to carry on a strict banking business without issue until the system of state-supervised banking was adopted in 1887.

The railroads themselves brought the worst problem of all on the unsuspecting community that welcomed them so innocently. From the beginning the eastern capitalists who in most cases had subscribed the majority of the capital assumed control. The representatives of the minority holdings in Illinois, and of subscriptions by towns and counties, were powerless. Even in the fifties rates were manipulated to favor certain localities. After 1861 the Mississippi competition was shut off by the Civil War, and the railroads proceeded to raise their rates for passengers and freight to unheard-of figures. This, with discrimination in favor of long hauls over short, ownership and monopoly by railroads of grain elevators, added to the difficulty in ways but too familiar. Men proposed additional canals to offer competition—canals from the Illinois to Rock Island, a ship canal along the Illinois and Michigan Canal. Failing these things, they sought to establish competing lines. In 1868 the *Paxton Record* protested that at railroad rates wheat could be teamed to Chicago at a profit. The regulation of the railroad by state or nation was for the future. This was its day of power to be arrogantly used.

The solution of the problems of the fifties was made more difficult by the change that had come over Illinois politics; the day of small things had passed. Eastern capitalists had much to seek at the hands of the state government: the calling of special sessions of the assembly to grant railroad and corporation charters; favors in the funding or acknowledgment of the state's indebtedness. Certain groups were ready to check each other's schemes by means none too scrupulous. Stories of bribery and counterbribery of state executives and state legislatures circulated freely, with how much truth it is impossible to say.

Beyond question, however, a new type of men was coming to the front in politics, men who as financial associates or legal advisers had private relations with interests with which they might have to have public dealings. Governor French (1846–52), though opposed to banks, was an inveterate speculator in lands enhanced in value by railroads and in his official position had to favor by his acts one or the other of rival railroad interests; Governor Bissell had been a railroad attorney and was accused of formerly driving sharp bargains for his clients with the state.

Most significant is the career of Governor Joel A. Matteson, elected in 1852 as a supporter of the banking system. He had made a speculative fortune from small beginnings, was interested financially and as an official in both the Illinois Central and the Alton railroads, and was accused of using money and the influence of those roads and of colonizing voters to aid Douglas in 1858 and 1860. He was caught in 1859 defrauding the state in the refunding of its indebtedness and was compelled ultimately to reimburse the state. Though his case was an extreme one, the taint of corruption hangs on much of the politics of the period. Even where no actual corruption existed, politics and business alike seem often leavened by sharp practice that moved close to fraud and dishonesty. The nature of men was no more debased than formerly, but temptations were greater.

The problems that arose in the era of the railroads had almost swamped the available governmental machinery. At the outset of the period Illinois had adopted the new constitution of 1848. The constitution of 1818 had placed practically all the legislative power, and very much of the appointive power, in the hands of the legislature, had left the supreme judiciary of 1824 practically to hold for life or good behavior, and had assigned to the executive but a shadow of authority.

The constitution of 1848 was the work of an age suspicious

of government. It provided that practically all officials, even supreme court judges, were to be elected by the people. It left the governor a veto that could be overridden by a majority vote, but by a great enumeration of prohibitions it sought to bind the hands of the state legislature. It provided for popular referendum on certain subjects of policy and, by limiting salaries of officials and the pay and length of sessions of the General Assemblies, sought to enforce a Jeffersonian simplicity.

The framers of the constitution had their eyes on the age that was passing and not on that which was arriving. Barely was their work adopted before its defects began to appear. Officials were insufficiently paid; General Assemblies in sessions limited to a few weeks had to deal with floods of private incorporation acts full of jokers and outrageous provisions, passed literally in batches, so that they could be neither checked nor amended.

All through the fifties a new constitution was confidently awaited; when a convention met in 1862, it was unfortunately in the height of the excitement of the Civil War. The convention was overwhelmingly Democratic. The constitution it drew up prohibited private acts of incorporation, provided that all future charters be subject to amendment and repeal, and prohibited new banks and the circulation of bank notes after 1866. In homestead exemption and mechanics' lien clauses it sought to appeal to the poorer classes. Popular excitement was raised against it, because of the partisan character of the provisions for apportionment, and it was rejected by a popular majority of 16,051.

The last years of the old constitution were by far the worst. The legislative session of 1867, marked by an appropriation of three million dollars for a new state capitol, the establishment of a penitentiary in southern Illinois, and the location of the state university at Urbana, was an orgy of logrolling, with charges of corruption freely passed on all sides. The financial interests that could gain or lose in the new Illinois by franchises in the gift of the legislature were too powerful to be bridled.

Private bill legislation swelled the statute-books of the sixties to huge proportions. Corporations of any and every sort could and did buy themselves charters. Governors like Palmer in vain interposed the veto to check the orgy. Threats of railroad regulation became merely a means of blackmail.

Early in the session the old schemers, anxious to replenish a depleted exchequer, introduced in the senate a bill for an act to regulate the passenger and freight tariff on railroads, and today it passed that august body. Contrary to their expectations, the railroads did not imitate Zaccheus and come down, but they could not recede from their position. It is a matter of grave doubt whether the legislature can place restrictions upon those companies already incorporated; in fact, I believe it is generally conceded that the only application the proposed law can have is to the companies hereafter incorporated. To Southern Illinois this is a most unjust and iniquitous measure.[5]

Decorum passed along with decency. The *Aurora Beacon* of March 21, 1867, wrote:

Dignity in our Senate is thrown to the dogs. A spirit of innocent playfulness pervades that institution, that is like Artemus Ward's Kangaroo, "highly amoosin." In the first place the Speaker is a very interesting animal. He handles himself with a great deal of grace and agility. The way he uses the gavel would do credit to a stone cutter; and the way he *don't* preserve order would astonish a country school master. . . . The twenty-five senators are a very nice body of men. They have a free and easy way with them that is decidedly refreshing. In order to dispatch business as rapidly as possible, and save the State expense, they usually omit the useless ceremony of addressing the Speaker, and ordinarily from six to ten of them have the floor, and all speak at once. . . . Those who are not engaged in making speeches, usually employ their massive talents in manufacturing paper balls and throwing them at each other, or in occasionally varying the proceedings by hurling books at the speaker's or some Senator's head. . . .

Under the conditions of the new era the constitution of 1848 had broken down. Once the issues of the Civil War were settled, a new constitution was inevitable.

5. *Cairo Evening Bulletin*, January 16, 1869.

CHAPTER X

The Beginnings of the Slavery Issue
1837–56

SO TERRIBLY was the generation that followed the Civil War impressed by the mighty storm that shook the foundations of the Union that in writing the history of the years before 1860 they made the slavery question a cloud menacing ever since the Compromise of 1820. In doing so, they unwittingly distorted the facts. The slavery question in the thirties was a cloud no larger than a man's hand and went almost unnoticed in the Illinois politics of the period; not until the forties did it become a danger to be reckoned with; not until the repeal of the Missouri Compromise in 1854 had led to a split in the Democratic party and its defeat in the state it had controlled for a quarter of a century did men dream of the terror of the years 1858–65.

The defeat by popular vote in 1824 of the proposal to call a constitutional convention that might introduce slavery into Illinois was followed by years of profound quiet on the slavery issue. Kidnaping of free Negroes resident in the state attracted little attention; the free Negro, most men agreed, created a problem. The supreme court of the state slowly defined the rights or lack of rights of the Negro and the servant indentured under the old territorial laws of 1807 and 1812. The verdict in general was that whatever validity the indenture system had was given it by the constitution of 1818. Time did its work. By the fifties the

last traces of slavery among the French inhabitants and the indentures of the territorial period had disappeared.

The slavery question first excited passing attention with the
rise of Garrisonian abolitionism and the question of excluding
abolition newspapers from the mails and the gagging in Congress of abolition petitions. The Illinois congressmen on these
points were generally orthodox. The state legislature in 1837
delivered itself of its opinion on the subject in forcible terms in
a set of resolutions. Only seven votes were cast against it; two of
the voters, Dan Stone and Abraham Lincoln, spread on the journals of the house a moderate protest. From the beginning Lincoln was a hater of slavery.

Abolitionism, however, had already reached Illinois. Elijah P.
Lovejoy, a young New England Presbyterian minister, in 1833
had begun editing a denominational paper in St. Louis. Driven
to the Illinois side of the river by mob violence, he set up at
Alton the *Alton Observer*, assailing in Miltonic invective with
the biting scorn of the Puritan every vice and sin. Inevitably he
turned to the subject of slavery. In the thirties northern men,
however much they might disapprove it in the abstract, believed
the criticism of the peculiar institution of the South fraught
with danger to the Union and therefore to be discountenanced.
Lovejoy could be discountenanced neither by rebuke nor by
threats of violence. Two of his presses were destroyed by mobs.
The fear of personal violence for him drove his wife to the verge
of insanity. His death, he knew, would leave his family destitute.
Yet driven by a force stronger than himself he went on. He pro-
cured still a third press, and, while defending it against a mob,
he fell on November 7, 1837, rifle in hand.

The news of the tragedy rang through the Union, binding the
name of Lovejoy forever to the name of Alton. New Englanders
believed in later years that the town was accursed for Lovejoy's
blood. In Illinois, however, though men were indignant at the
violence by which Lovejoy had met his end, the vast majority

disapproved of the course that had brought him to it. His slayers went unpunished; the men associated with him in the defense of his press were indicted "for unlawfully defending a certain warehouse." And the Baptist organizer, John Mason Peck, himself a New Englander, who had hated the uncompromising young Presbyterian, believed that by refraining from public denunciation of the murder he had brought about a blessed outpouring of divine spirit in the form of a gracious revival.

The blood of the martyrs is the seed of the church. Lovejoy had taken the new-school side in the Presbyterian schism, from distaste of the proslavery alliance of the old school. The eve of his death had seen at Alton the organization of a state antislavery society. As the standard fell from Lovejoy's hand it was caught up by the old antislavery editor, Benjamin Lundy, who published at Hennepin the *Genius of Universal Emancipation.* Lundy, that he might write as he thought, cultivated a little farm. A wheat harvest in 1839 overtaxed his strength, and a fever silenced his journal forever. But a year later the Lowell *Genius of Liberty* replaced it; within three years, its name changed to the *Western Citizen,* it was removed to Chicago, flinging defiantly to the wind on its headline the haughty challenge by which the Puritan in age after age has made weak things to confound the mighty: "The Supremacy of God and the Equality of Man."

The antislavery movement grew fast in northern Illinois. Antislavery societies spread, Congregational churches wrote the doctrine in their confessions of faith, and the Liberty party was organized in Illinois in 1840. Garrisonian abolition had demanded the centering of attention on the crime of slavery and passive resistance to it; Garrison himself decried all participation in politics. The Liberty group, on the other hand, prepared to fight the evil with the citizen's weapon, the ballot. Many men in the group looked on the contest with slavery as but one phase of a contest for human rights and liberty for all men. Intellectually such men were not far removed from Democrats like John Wentworth, who, interested in human rights as against property rights, believed they could be maintained only by the alliance with the democracy of the South. Meanwhile Wentworth recognized that the ideas of the Liberty party were working through New Englanders both Democrats and Whigs and forebore to antagonize it. By 1846 the Liberty party held the balance of power in thirteen counties of northern Illinois.

The slavery issue entered national politics in the question of territorial expansion. Demagogues like John Reynolds sensed the popular enthusiasm in Illinois at the prospect of expansion and of war with the old enemy. In a speech built around the twin ideas of the annexation of Cuba and war with Great Britain, Reynolds stated:

> Mr. President, as Hannibal swore eternal hostility to the Romans, so I swear eternal hostility to monarchies, especially to them that dont let us alone. I have nothing to say against the English people but to their cursed government I have sworn war. It is generally the case, Mr. President, that when a man is cavorting against another; that the cavorter is wrong and the cavortee is right, but when I am cavorting against the English government I am not cavorting for nothing. I have heard my father tell of their oppression and tyranny. I know of the sufferings of the Irish under their persecution—I have read of their butcheries in China and other parts of Asia. I have read of their paying savages in the revolution for the scalps of our men, women and children. . . .[1]

The Democratic platform of 1844 demanding the reannexation of Texas and the reoccupation of Oregon voiced Illinois sentiment. True, there was a gasp of disappointment traceable in the state newspapers when Polk instead of Van Buren was the Democratic nominee; but they loyally set themselves to elect him. Then came the disappointments in his policy. He vetoed river and harbor improvement bills of vital importance to northern Illinois; he proposed a tax on tea and coffee, the lux-

1. *Illinois State Register*, January 17, 1846.

uries of the white laborer. Worst of all, he compromised with Great Britain for a half of Oregon, while he drew the sword on Mexico in behalf of the extreme boundary claims of Texas. To avoid war with the ancient enemy, he sacrificed territory destined to be the abode of freedom, while he shed American blood to spread more slave plantations over the free soil of Mexico. Northern Democrats like Wentworth believed that southern slavery dictated Polk's foreign policy and reared in the party harness.

In the Mexican War, Illinois had her full share. Of her regiments, the First and Second under Colonels Hardin and Bissell fought at Buena Vista, where Hardin—"our best Whig man," Lincoln called him—fell at the head of his regiment. The Third and Fourth regiments served under Scott, with James Shields as their brigadier at Vera Cruz and Cerro Gordo. Two more regiments served in Texas and on the Santa Fe expedition. Illinois soldiers were magnificently brave and magnificently undisciplined. General Wool said to Hardin, "I will take away your commission, sir."

"By God, you can't do it, sir," replied Hardin.

Popular enthusiasm for the war compelled the Whigs in Illinois to disguise their dislike of the grounds on which it was made. Lincoln had introduced in Congress resolutions expressing a doubt as to whether the first American blood had not been shed on a spot beyond the American border; and the nickname of "Spot" Lincoln was fastened on him by the Democrats to imply that he had refused to vote supplies for the army. Another Illinois Whig, in words later famous, cynically remarked that he had ruined himself politically by opposing the War of 1812 and that thereafter he was for "war, pestilence, and famine."

The immediate answer on the part of the North to Polk's war in Mexico was the Wilmot Proviso—that in any territory acquired from Mexico slavery should be prohibited. Wentworth indorsed it; so did the northern Democrats of Illinois generally.

A river and harbor convention held in Chicago in 1847 in the interests of forcing adequate federal appropriations to river and harbor improvement in the face of opposition from southern democrats marked how close Wentworth was to rebellion against his party. Lincoln was made authority for the statement that the administration had issued orders to defeat him even though a Whig should be elected. Wentworth stopped at the brink of party revolt. He professed to believe that the nomination of Lewis Cass for the presidency, even on a platform without the Proviso or river and harbor improvement, would set all straight. But 1848 was the year of the Free Soil revolt in the Democratic party and of the Free Soil independent candidacy of Martin Van Buren. Cass went down in defeat before General Zachary Taylor, hero of the Mexican War, slaveholder, and Whig nominee for the presidency. Illinois remained Democratic, but the party in the Chicago district especially was splintered by the Free Soil defection.

The presidential election of 1848 settled nothing of the slavery difficulty. The question of the disposition of the spoils of Mexico—whether California should be received in the Union as a free state, whether the territories to be organized in the Southwest should be free or slave—threatened to disrupt the Union. Southerners like Calhoun were calculating the value of the Union to the South, talking secession, and affirming that slavery could constitutionally be excluded from not an inch of the territory of the United States. Northern men were insisting that there be no further compromises with slavery; that the peculiar. institution might be tolerated where it already existed but not elsewhere.

To settle this question, Henry Clay proposed the Compromise of 1850: admission of California as a free state, organization of Utah and New Mexico without mention of slavery, and a fugitive slave law. When the compromise first offered by Clay in the form of a single measure had failed, Stephen A. Douglas succeeded in getting the provisions adopted in the Senate one by one. The Illinois delegation in the House, Richardson and Mc-Clernand in particular, assisted in the passage of the compromise. The Illinois senators, Douglas and Shields, were compelled by instruction of the state legislature to vote for the Wilmot Proviso; Wentworth and E. D. Baker alone of the Illinois delegation did so in the House. The final passage of the Compromise set Illinois forward as the savior of the Union; and Stephen A. Douglas, her brilliant young senior senator, stood forth as the representative of the Union sentiment of the West.

In northern Illinois feeling had been divided between support for the Proviso and sentiment for the Union. The dread of danger to the Union prevailed. Douglas, returning from Washington to Chicago on one of the great triumphs of his career, October 23, won over a hostile meeting to resolutions in support of the Compromise as necessary to the Union. The Free Soil strength passed as suddenly as it arose and the great majority of party men in Illinois accepted the Compromise; but the Democrats found it expedient to nominate for governor in 1852 Joel A. Matteson, a protégé of Wentworth, at this time supposed to be so decidedly antislavery that a radical like Jonathan B. Turner was ready to vote for him.

In 1852 Illinois offered a candidate for the national Democratic nomination in Douglas, the champion of the Union and the savior of the Compromise of 1850. He was a young man's candidate; but the *Democratic Review*, his national organ, was too outspoken against "old-fogyism" in the party, and the "old fogies" had their revenge in the nomination of Franklin Pierce. Pierce easily carried Illinois, but discontent in the northern districts with the proslavery attitude of his party sent to Congress three Whigs pledged to free soil and again elected John Wentworth in the Chicago district in spite of the fact that his opposition to the Democratic platform on the point of slavery was well known. The passage by the General Assembly in 1853, in accord with the state constitution, of an act[2] allowing free blacks who entered the state to be sold into terms of servitude

2. Drawn up by John A. Logan (*Chicago Tribune*, January 16, 1865).

aroused indignation among Democrats and Whigs alike. It was said less than half-a-dozen papers in the state openly approved the law.

With the inauguration of Pierce in 1853, the old issues of politics seemed worn out. Regular Democrats wished to keep away from the issues of the Compromise of 1850. Bank, tariff, and subtreasury seemed dead. Douglas and the western Democrats were pushing a graduation act actually passed in 1854, selling unsold lands for as little as twelve and one-half cents an acre. They were advocates of a homestead measure, but they could hardly commit their party to it. Douglas was endeavoring to get rid of the river and harbor issue that was perplexing the party in Illinois by proposing the levy of tonnage duties for local internal improvements at the place of collection; above all, he was for expansion, for a Pacific railroad for the extension of white settlement to the regions of the Upper Missouri. This led to the Kansas-Nebraska Bill of 1854 and to that fatal repeal of the Missouri Compromise that split his party and the Union.

Douglas' motives have been the subject of historical controversy for three generations. Was the repeal of the Compromise a damnable betrayal of the interests of the free North, opening the Great Plains north of the 1820 line of 36° 30' to slavery and designed to purchase the vote of the slaveholding South for the presidency? Was it a bargain in which the North got the undoubted advantage of the location of a railroad to the Pacific with its terminals in the North in return for the concession to the South of the empty right to carry slaves to a territory where nature had decreed that slavery could not thrive? Was the repeal of the Compromise of 1820 the fruit of factional warfare in Missouri? Did Douglas sacrifice it to open the territories to settlement? Or did Douglas really believe that the doctrine of popular sovereignty—that right of the people of the territory to determine untrammeled by congressional action, past or present, the conditions of their life—was a carrying to new heights of the old frontier democracy of Jackson? Mortal man can only surmise.

At all events late in 1853 Douglas introduced in the Senate his bill for the organization of Kansas and Nebraska territories, with its provision for popular choice in the territory in the territorial stage between freedom and slavery. Later he admitted the amendment, repealing the part of the Missouri Compromise of 1820 that forever prohibited slavery in the Louisiana Purchase above 36° 30'. Despite opposition from northern Whigs and some northern Democrats, he and his chief lieutenant in the House, William A. Richardson, congressman from the Quincy district and chairman of the House Committee on Territories, drove the Kansas-Nebraska Act through. His colleague in the Senate, Shields, supported him; but in the House the four Whig congressmen, with two Democrats, John Wentworth and William H. Bissell, a majority of the delegation opposed it. By the time the measure had finally passed, the Northwest was all in flame.

The Republican party had its beginning in these days in the coalescence of Whigs and antislavery or anti-Nebraska Democrats with more radical antislavery groups into a new party based on opposition to slavery in the territories. In the states surrounding Illinois the reaction was almost instantaneous. In Illinois it took a year or two. The Whigs generally opposed the repeal of the Missouri Compromise from the first, as did the anti-Nebraska Democrats; but both held aloof from the comparatively insignificant Republican party, which was at first made up largely of the more extreme Free Soil or abolitionist elements. In 1856 the extreme abolitionists withdrew; a great part of the anti-Nebraska Democrats entered it, and most of the Whigs, save the group that rallied round the anti-Catholic, anti-foreign element to form the Know-Nothing party and those who sought refuge in the Democratic ranks.

At the beginning the leadership of the Illinois Democratic

party was against Douglas. Even old wheelhorses whose political careers were mainly in the past, like Sidney Breese and John Reynolds, were anti-Nebraska, perhaps because they hoped for a return to power from the overthrow of Douglas. But the ablest men of Douglas' own political generation—John Wentworth, John A. McClernand, William H. Bissell, Lyman Trumbull—and the best of the younger men, such as John M. Palmer, were also in the opposition. On September 1 Douglas tried for hours to defend the bill before a howling Chicago mob, finally shouting, "It is now Sunday morning—I'll go to church, and you may go to Hell!"[3] Newspapers and public meetings, without regard to party, protested. It was small satisfaction under the circumstances that county conventions in central and southern Illinois generally indorsed the Nebraska doctrine.

As early as March 18, 1854, at Rockford a mass meeting resolved that "the free States should now blot out all former political distinctions by uniting themselves into one great Northern Party."[4] The movement was slow in developing. The anti-Nebraska Democrats hoped to control their party on the issue and not divide it. The Whigs tried to maintain their distinct organization on anti-Nebraska lines and capitalize the issue to carry the state they had been seeking in vain for twenty years to win. At Ottawa on August 1 the extreme antislavery elements, in imitation of those in Wisconsin and Michigan, first assumed the name "Republican," but when a Republican convention was held at Springfield on October 4 and 5, it was distinctly of a Free Soil cast. Lincoln, with his eyes on the senatorship at Whig hands, adroitly stayed away and failed to act on a state committee to which the convention appointed him.

With the anti-Nebraska elements holding aloof from each other, the congressional elections of 1854 were a strange affair. In the Chicago district there was a four-cornered race between

3. Arthur C. Cole, *Era of the Civil War*, p. 132.
4. *Rock River Democrat*, March 28, 1854.

an anti-Nebraska Democrat indorsed by Wentworth, a Nebraska Democrat, a Whig, and a Republican, James H. Woodworth, the Republican, winning. Elihu B. Washburne and Jesse O. Norton, anti-Nebraska Whigs, were indorsed by the Republicans and elected in the First and Third districts. In the Alton district Lyman Trumbull, running as an anti-Nebraska Democrat with Whig support, beat Foulke, convention nominee and a Nebraska Democrat. James Knox was re-elected in the Peoria district. But in the Springfield, Quincy, Decatur, and Cairo districts, Douglas or Nebraska Democrats were successful. The General Assembly elected in the fall was anti-Nebraska, and it had to elect a senator. Lincoln nearly succeeded. He had the votes of the members of the Whig antecedents but could not gain the necessary anti-Nebraska Democrats, and finally, rather than see Matteson elected, he threw the Whig strength to the anti-Nebraska Democrat, Lyman Trumbull.

The election of 1854 had made evident a sharp sectional division in the state. The *Chicago Weekly Democrat* of December 2, 1854, wrote:

In the Northern half of Illinois not a Congressman nor member of the Legislature, nor a county officer friendly to the Nebraska bill, or opposed to Harbor and River Improvements, has been elected to any office this year—Whilst in the southern half, all of two-thirds of the men elected are of opposite sentiments!

This is accounted for in the fact that the northern half of Illinois is settled generally by emigrants from the free states, whilst the southern half is settled by those from the slave states.

For a year or two there was political chaos; and it was the opportunity of the native Americans or Know-Nothings. They represented the old anti-foreign and anti-Catholic prejudices of the Whigs and offered a shelter for members of that group hard pressed to decide between the antislavery and Democratic groupings. The existence of this group temporarily helped to check a movement of the antislavery foreign groups such as the

Germans from the Democratic party because it was represented to them that the anti-Nebraska men must be nativists. Further, they distrusted the New England Republicans in northern Illinois as "Maine Law men" or prohibitionists. In the course of 1855 schism developed even in the fraternal ranks of the Know-Nothings, a more liberal group known by the cant term of "Jonathan" being antislavery and merely anti-Catholic as distinguished from "Sam," who was inclined to be Nebraska and anti-foreign generally. Representing a prejudice rather than a principle, there was little stability in the Know-Nothing group.

The approach of the presidential year compelled the anti-Nebraska Democrats to choose finally between their principles and their party. In convention at Decatur the anti-Nebraska editors of the state reached harmony in the winter of 1856. At a convention held at Bloomington on May 29, the Republican party was formed. Whigs like Orville H. Browning imparted a tone of conservatism to its platform. The brains and conscience of the Democratic party—Wentworth, Koerner, Bissell, Trumbull, John M. Palmer—threw in their lot with the new party. Breese, Reynolds, and McClernand fell back into the old line. Save for the American group, the Whigs disappeared. Some of them, such as E. B. Webb, their candidate for governor in 1852, J. W. Singleton, and R. S. Blackwell, joined the Democrats. At last the lines were clearly drawn.

The presidential election of 1856 was hotly fought. Buchanan in Illinois was barely successful over Frémont. But four Republican and four Democratic congressmen were elected, and the state ticket headed by William H. Bissell was victorious over Richardson and the Democrats. For the first time since party lines had been sharply drawn in Illinois, the Democrats had been defeated in a state election. Sectional parties had been formed in the Union and had taken root in the state also. A sharp geographical line divided Republicans and Democrats. It followed the southern boundaries of Henderson, Warren, Knox, Stark,

and Marshall counties and swung to the south to include Mc-
Lean, Logan, Piatt, and Coles. Tazewell, Macon, and Edgar
counties were debatable; Republican outposts in the south lay
in Edwards, Madison, Bond, and St. Clair. The citadels of the
two parties centered, respectively, in a group of northern counties stretching diagonally northeast from Henry to Du Page and
Lake and in the old Democratic bloc between the Mississippi
and the Wabash rivers.

CHAPTER XI

The Climax of the Slavery Struggle
1856–65

OUT of the Kansas-Nebraska Act came the formation of the Republican party; on the heels of the Dred Scott decision and the Lecompton Constitution followed the Civil War. Douglas in the repeal of the Missouri Compromise had let slip the forces of sectional strife, and they had rent in twain his northern democracy. Representatives of the slaveholding South, whether or not they coveted the northern territories, stood on principle for the rights of slaveholders in them. Between southern Democrats and northern Republicans contending for principle, Douglas stood vainly trying to compromise on grounds of expediency to save his party and the Union. He fought his losing battle magnificently and heroically. In the end he saw the prize he had sought so long escape him and fall into the hands of his old opponent, Abraham Lincoln. Then for the last months of his life he upheld the hands of Lincoln, seeking at last to save the Union by force when he could no longer save it by compromise.

Barely had Buchanan been inaugurated in 1857 when the Supreme Court of the United States handed down the medley of divergent opinions known in our history as the Dred Scott decision. Starting with the simple question as to whether a slave carried to a free state and to a territory made free by the Missouri Compromise was thereby enfranchised, Chief Justice Taney—apparently with a majority of the Court behind him—laid down among other dicta the saying that the Missouri Compromise was unlawful and that there was no power in Congress to pass a law for any territory which forbade a master to carry his slave there and hold him in bondage. But, if this were true, could a territorial legislature created by Congress do what Congress could not do? And, if so, what became of popular sovereignty, the right of the people of a territory to decide for themselves whether they would have freedom or slavery?

The Democrats of Illinois hesitated for a little as to what course they would pursue. Then Douglas came back from Washington and taught his followers the comforting doctrine that the decision buttressed popular sovereignty; for, without the positive police protection that a territorial legislature might give or deny the peculiar institution, slavery could not exist. The Republicans were in a more immediate quandary if not so deep a one. Their principle of free soil had been swept away by the work of the aged chief justice. They must gainsay the highest court of the land or admit that their most precious principle was unconstitutional. Lincoln, in answering Douglas at Springfield on June 26, 1857, promised for his party acquiescence in the decision for the time being but also an unalterable resolve that some day that decision should be reversed by the Court itself. Both parties waited upon the turn of events in Kansas and the decision of the voters of Illinois.

Douglas speedily found himself bearing the burden of obloquy earned for him by southern fire-eaters determined to win Kansas for slavery by fraud or force. In 1857 the infamous Lecompton Constitution, drawn by a proslavery-packed convention, was presented to Congress, the voters having been allowed to decide only whether they would have the constitution drawn in every line to protect slavery, "with slavery" or "without slavery." Such a travesty on popular sovereignty Douglas knew would alienate the majority of his Democratic following in Illinois. Anxious for his re-election as senator by the General Assembly to be selected in 1858, he appeared at the state fair in the fall of 1857 to sound public sentiment. At the next session of Congress he broke with Buchanan's administration and opposed the passage of the Lecompton Constitution.

"Mr. Douglas," said the President rising to his feet excitedly [so Douglas told the story of their final break] "I desire you to remember that no Democrat ever yet differed from an administration of his own choice without being crushed. Beware of the fate of Tallmadge and Rives." "Mr. President," rejoined Douglas also rising, "I wish you to remember that General Jackson is dead."[1]

Perhaps Buchanan may have remembered the days of 1838–39 when the party lash drove the Illinois congressmen into line for the subtreasury and may have hoped to repeat the triumph. But, as Douglas had reminded him, General Jackson was dead. Eastern Republicans, believing Douglas would carry with him but a handful of revolters, prepared to welcome him into the Republican ranks. Horace Greeley sent E. B. Washburne to Illinois to announce that Lincoln must not be run against Douglas for the senatorship. But western Republicans knew better. The stand taken by the "Little Giant" had awakened the enthusiasm of the remaining Democrats of Illinois save for a corporal's guard of office-holders. Every Democratic paper in the state approved his course. Buchanan, to defeat Douglas, mustered his small group of Lecompton office-holders and subsidized presses, strong in federal patronage and little else, led by worn-out politicians like John Reynolds and Sidney Breese, cringing from forty years of political meannesses. In moral stature and political honesty Douglas towered over such men.

Ostensibly the political contest of 1858 turned on the election of a state general assembly to choose a senator. Breese, the Buchanan or "Danite" candidate, had no chance of success, his only hope being to revenge Buchanan on Douglas for his revolt against the administration. Avowedly they planned to elect Lincoln rather than Douglas. "He [Dougherty] told Lincoln that

1. Allen Johnson, *Douglas*, p. 328.

ABRAHAM LINCOLN AS ILLINOIS KNEW HIM
Original in Library of Congress, Washington, D.C.

STEPHEN A. DOUGLAS (1813–61)
Courtesy of Illinois State Historical Library

the National Democracy intended 'to run in every county and District a National Democrat for each and every office.' " Lincoln replied to this by saying: "If you do this the thing is settled—the battle is fought."[2] Between Douglas and Lincoln was the race, the issues being which one was to speak Illinois' repudiation of the administration and the crime against Kansas, and whether that rebuke was to be couched in terms of moderation or of free soil. Both men were put forward by party conventions, the Republican convention declaring Lincoln its "first and only choice." In the famous "house divided against itself" speech, delivered the evening of his nomination, Lincoln indicated the principle of his campaign: that to oppose the proslavery excesses of the administration in Kansas as Douglas purposed was merely to apply palliatives to the evil; instead once and for all it must be decided whether slavery was to spread and strike new runners in free soil everywhere or whether, cut back stiffly to its present bounds, it was to exhaust the soil on which it grew, dwindle, and finally decay.

In the old frontier fashion Lincoln set out to ride the political circuit after Douglas. Finding himself reduced often to serve as a sort of anticlimax to audiences gathered for the "Little Giant," he challenged Douglas to a joint debate. Douglas agreed to debate with him once in each of the seven congressional districts he had yet to visit—at Ottawa, Freeport, Jonesboro, Charleston, Galesburg, Quincy, and Alton. Into the resulting debate was poured all the skill in handling, holding, and winning vast outdoor audiences developed in forty years of frontier stump-speaking, exemplified by two of its greatest masters. At the end neither could claim the victory.

The moral victory in the debate lay with Lincoln. Douglas, defending the principles of the old democracy, was compelled to expound them as insuring liberties to the white man only.

2. Herndon to Trumbull, July 8, 1858 (Trumbull Manuscripts, Library of Congress).

The solution of the territorial difficulty he offered was necessarily based on expediency and on fine-drawn constitutional quibbles. Trumbull, assisting Lincoln, had shown that Douglas in 1856 had cut out of a bill for the admission of Kansas a clause allowing a popular vote on the future state constitution. The commentary on popular sovereignty was an unpleasant one. At Freeport Lincoln drew his opponent into a restatement of the doctrine that unfriendly legislation by a territorial legislature was a legal and sufficient means to keep slavery out of the territory, the famous "Freeport Heresy." Lincoln rose to greater heights than pinning his shifty antagonist on a legal quibble that would gain him no favor in the South. In a moment of vision he announced the whole question as essentially a moral issue—the issue of the right or wrong of the oppression and exploitation of labor whether slave or free. The former Whig had ascended to the heights of the old Democratic doctrine.

That is the real issue. That is the issue that will continue in this country when these poor tongues of Judge Douglas and myself shall be silent. It is the eternal struggle between these two principles—right and wrong—throughout the world. They are the two principles that have stood face to face from the beginning of time, and will ever continue to struggle. The one is the common right of humanity, and the other the "divine right of kings." It is the same principle in whatever shape it develops itself. It is the same spirit that says, "You work and toil and earn bread, and I'll eat it." No matter in what shape it comes, whether from the mouth of a king who seeks to bestride the people of his own nation and live by the fruit of their labor, or from one race of men as an apology for enslaving another race, it is the same tyrannical principle.[3]

The moral victory was with Lincoln, but the senatorship fell to Douglas. Both Douglas and Lincoln had struggled for the old Whig vote in central Illinois, each claiming to be the true successor of Henry Clay; and Lincoln's success had been but par-

3. Alton Debate, in *Lincoln-Douglas Debates* (Sparks ed.), *Ill. Hist. Colls.*, vol. 3, p. 485.

tial. "Before us lies the field," wrote Herndon in 1858 after Lincoln's defeat. "It is in Sangamon—Morgan—Madison—Logan—Mason; in short it is a circle of counties reaching not more than 80 miles from the capitol. The people that live in that area must be somehow reached; and now. *Secondly* who are these people; they are from Kentucky, Tennessee, Virginia &c; and generally they are '*old-line*' whigs—timid—shrinking, but good, men."[4] In the popular vote Lincoln carried through to victory the Republican state candidates for treasurer and superintendent of public instruction. But since the state had been districted northern population had been pouring into Illinois. The "unterrified" democracy of "Egypt" elected more than its proportion of legislators, and, in spite of the Danites or Buchanan men, Douglas was re-elected by 54 votes to 41.

The election meant that the pivotal state of the Northwest, formerly its Democratic stronghold, had returned Douglas, in spite of administration intrigues and Republican strength, as a rebuke to Buchanan. The victory designated Douglas as the presidential candidate for whom the remaining Democrats of the Northwest would vote in 1860. But by that law of mass that teaches the tactician to oppose his main force to the main force of the enemy, the victory had designated also Abraham Lincoln as Douglas' opponent. On November 1, 1858, the *Olney Times* put the name of Lincoln at the head of its columns for President. By the next summer Lincoln was sweeping on in Illinois, and his strength was beginning to develop in surrounding states of the Northwest. His famous Cooper Union speech of February, 1860, introduced him to the East as well.

Many factors contributed to his progress. The outstanding Republican candidate was William H. Seward. But Illinois Republicans remembered that he and Greeley had tried to sidetrack Lincoln for Douglas in 1858.

4. Herndon to Trumbull, November 30, 1858 (Trumbull Manuscripts, Library of Congress).

Now that Seward, Greeley & Co. have contributed so much to our defeat, they may expect us in the true christian spirit to return good for evil—but in this I fear they will find themselves mistaken. If the vote of Illinois can nominate another than Seward—I hope it will be so cast. The coals of fire I would administer, will be designed to raise a severe blister.[5]

Seward's doctrine that there was a higher law than the Constitution injured him with the conservative Republicans. Of other candidates, Edward Bates of Missouri, favored by Browning because he could get old Whig votes that Lincoln could not, was displeasing to the Germans. The Republican state convention instructed the Illinois delegation for Lincoln.

Tremendously in Lincoln's favor was the fact that the national Republican convention was to be held in Chicago in the famous Wigwam on Lake Street. The local atmosphere was cleverly manipulated by Illinois Republican leaders, and delegation after delegation, by addresses, by persuasion, and by bargains, was won over to favor Lincoln's candidacy. The Wigwam, packed with Lincoln supporters in the galleries, at the name of Lincoln gave a "yawp" that put to shame the followers of Seward. The swing of anti-Seward votes to the candidate who seemed to have the best chance to defeat the New Yorker nominated Lincoln on the third ballot. In outward harmony the Republicans adjourned.

With the Democrats it was otherwise. After his re-election in 1859, Douglas had turned now this way, now that, seeking to conciliate both North and South. In spite of his concessions, in spite of his attempts to win southern sentiment and at the same time obtain a platform that would save the North, his party split. In the Democratic convention at Baltimore, Maryland, the Douglas men voted down resolutions which stated in Calhoun's old uncompromising style the right of slavery in the territories

5. Ebenezer Peck to Trumbull, November 30, 1858 (Trumbull Manuscripts, Library of Congress).

as a national institution; they offered the subservient platform of 1856 and acquiescence in the Dred Scott decision, but all to no purpose. The irreconcilables withdrew; and when Douglas was finally nominated at Richmond, John C. Breckinridge was set up by the southern Democrats to run against him, and John Bell, of Tennessee, appeared for a Whig following known as the Constitutional Unionists.

The campaign in Illinois was between Douglas and Lincoln, Republican and regular Democrat. The vote for Bell and Breckinridge was insignificant. Douglas threw himself desperately into the campaign, in defiance of precedent himself taking the stump. When the loss of Pennsylvania in October told him all hope was gone, he went South on a speaking tour, this time to endeavor to prevent the worst consequences. On the Illinois state ticket for the Republicans Richard Yates had obtained the nomination for governor over the better-known N. B. Judd. His Democratic opponent, James C. Allen, was nominated late, by a party jaded by the long struggle over Douglas' nomination. John T. Stuart, run by the Constitutional Union element, offered but little opposition. The Republicans carried the state by 12,000.

In those critical days of December, 1860, and January, 1861, the future chief magistrate of the nation was in the state capital of Illinois. The situation made Governor-elect Richard Yates in a sense the spokesman of the new national administration when in his inaugural he stood against any concession or compromise with the South. The Democrats, holding a convention at Springfield, professed themselves loyal to the Union but also in favor of attempts at compromise with the South. To a great extent public opinion was still with them on this, and reluctantly Lincoln and Yates sent an Illinois delegation to the peace convention called by Virginia at Washington.

State politics, too, were at cross-purposes. The General Assembly of 1859 had tried to gerrymander the state to continue the control of the legislature to the Democrats. Governor Bissell had vetoed the bill, and the Republicans, absenting themselves to break up a quorum, had prevented the passage of the gerrymander but also the passage of the appropriation bills. The General Assembly of 1861 passed an act districting the state on Republican lines and, as a sop to the Democrats, an act calling a constitutional convention. A bill for the reorganization of the state militia the Democrats would not submit to, and it was put aside at the end of the session.

The actual military participation of Illinois in the war will be taken up in a later chapter. Here the discussion of the attitude of the people to the administration, to the rebellion, and to slavery will be concluded.

The news of the firing on Fort Sumter and the vigorous measures by which Lincoln meant to deal with the rebellion threatened for the moment to break the commonwealth of Illinois into its component substances. Southern Illinois at first blazed with sympathy for the Confederacy. At Marion in Williamson County a meeting of southern Illinois men was held intended to be preparatory to setting up "Egypt" as a separate state and allying with the Confederacy. The evidence is debatable, but it points strongly to the fact that John A. Logan at first leaned toward the South. The least danger to be feared was that southern Illinois might be a recruiting ground for the Confederacy. Douglas flung himself into the breach. In Illinois he spent his last strength urging Democrats to put the nation before the party and to give support to the Black Republican President while he labored for the perpetuation of the Union. Speaking before the special session of the Illinois legislature, he urged on both parties the subordination of partisanship to patriotism. A life of political combat, the last seven years of it desperately fought, had sapped his vitality, and Douglas died on June 9, 1861. He had been the unconscious instrument to let loose the flood of civil war; but by his desperate efforts to stop it he had atoned for the error.

Douglas had won over most of the Democrats of southern Illinois. Logan and McClernand, the latter always a Union Democrat, led their section to the support of Yates's war policy and led the fighting men of their section to the battlefield. Southern Illinois was even to exceed northern Illinois in its quota of soldiers. Enthusiasm for the Union swept the whole state and put the seal of approval on the militia act and the other vigorous war measures of the special session of the legislature.

But difference of opinion still lay deep in the heterogeneous population of Illinois. Douglas had brought the mass of the democracy to support loyally the war for the Union; he had not tried to convert them to the Republican free-soil doctrine and thereby to stultify the record of his party for the last ten years. On the other hand, zealous Republicans preached a crusade against slavery and chafed bitterly at Lincoln's slowness to proclaim it. When General Frémont issued his proclamation, as commander of Missouri, freeing the slaves of rebels, and Lincoln disallowed it, there was deep discontent. When Lincoln removed him in November, there was an outcry, and a bitter one. "The repudiation by Mr. Lincoln of Frémont's Proclamation manumitting the slaves of Missouri rebels, gave more *'aid and comfort to the enemy'* in that state than if he had made the rebel commander, Sterling Price, a present of fifty pieces of rifled cannon."[6]

The much-tried President meanwhile was struggling with the problem of steering a course that would keep the support of the loyal men of the North. With radicals like Trumbull pressing for extreme measures and conservatives like Senator Orville H. Browning striving to confirm him in the paths of moderation, he was torn between forces diametrically opposed. When Trumbull pressed the drastic Second Confiscation Act on him in 1862, Browning warned him that he stood at the parting of the ways and that signing it he walked with the radicals to ruin.

6. John Russell to Trumbull, Bluffdale, December 17, 1861 (Trumbull Manuscripts, Library of Congress).

When Lincoln, at last believing that slavery should be cauterized, issued the First Emancipation Proclamation, Browning mourned over him. When he issued the second, Browning gave him up in despair.

The impossibility of Lincoln's waging the war to please both antislavery Republicans and Union Democrats for a time threw the state into the hands of the Democrats. In the constitutional convention elected in the fall of 1861 the Democrats outnumbered the Republicans two to one. In spite of the fact that Yates believed it honeycombed with secession, it contented itself with drawing up a constitution that sought to restore the old simple bankless rural Illinois that had passed never to return. Wentworth supported it, but it was beaten at the polls by a majority of 16,051.

The Emancipation Proclamation, and arbitrary arrests for disloyal utterances in 1862, so Browning believed, turned the state over to a rabidly Democratic legislature that elected William A. Richardson to succeed him in the Senate.[7] The Democrats, in defending the Black Laws of 1853, urged their necessity to save white labor in the state from competition with free Negroes. The flood of "contrabands" pouring in by way of Cairo gave point to their argument. They passed in the house resolutions for an armistice and a peace convention at Louisville; their apportionment bill was vetoed by Yates, and before they could pass it over his veto the governor prorogued the legislature.

On June 17 a Democratic mass convention of forty thousand denounced the arbitrary use of war powers and called for a national convention to negotiate peace. In local Copperhead movements and in the *Chicago Times*, suppressed for a day for disloyalty, the dissatisfaction with the war powers found vent. A plot was unearthed in November, 1864, to release the Confederate prisoners at Camp Douglas located in what is now the heart of the South Side of Chicago.

7. Browning had been appointed by Yates to fill out Douglas' term until an election by the General Assembly could take place.

Meanwhile the time approached for another presidential election. Lincoln in his middle course was still too timid and conservative for the radicals and too radical for the conservatives in his own party. For a time there was a real enthusiasm for Frémont among the out-and-outers, especially among the German Republicans. The party necessity for standing by the record, as embodied in the President, compelled the renomination of Lincoln; but Frémont was nominated independently.

The Democrats meanwhile were in a position less difficult at first sight, but still quite perplexing. They could not well denounce the war as a failure without alienating thousands of loyal war Democrats; of that General McClellan, their presidential candidate, was the first to remind them. Still their position even on the platform that the war was a failure was a strong one. But the military events of the fall of 1864 disproved their case. Farragut at Mobile, Sherman at Atlanta, and Sheridan in the Shenandoah were demonstrating that the war was not a failure— that the Confederacy was doomed. Frémont withdrew from the race. Logan aroused Illinois for Lincoln, and the election resulted in a majority for him of 30,736. Not three months later, on February 1, 1865, the Republican General Assembly ratified the Thirteenth Amendment forever abolishing slavery. At the same session the Black Laws were finally wiped off the Illinois statute-book.

Hardly eleven years had passed since Douglas had reopened the slavery question in the repeal of the Missouri Compromise. Since then the Whig party had disappeared, and the Democratic party had been torn by the secession of its best men. By 1864 it had sunk definitely in the state it had ruled for a generation to a minority party, good for little but an agency of rebuke to the Republicans. The Republican party had taken its place, for a time taking over the old Democratic doctrines of the rights of men but now seeking to combine them with the old Whig care for capital and vested interests. In the days of confusion men had changed sides fast. Old-time Whigs like Browning had become Republicans and, in dislike of the radical policies of Lincoln, shifted to the Democratic party. Zealous anti-Nebraska Democrats of 1854 like John Reynolds had in the days of the war walked very close to the edge of disloyalty. Democrats like John A. Logan, accused of advising men in 1861 to enlist in the southern army, were to become the most vehement prophets of Republicanism. Democrats like John M. Palmer, governed by principles rather than party allegiance, had been led by them to the Republican party in 1856 and ultimately were to follow them back to the Democratic group. Leaders and groups winnowed vigorously by the great days of 1854–65 were at length to find their places again in the Republican and Democratic ranks but in arrangements hardly to be foreseen from their previous associations.

The spring of 1865 came, and the Civil War was over; the United States flag was dramatically unfurled over Fort Sumter five years after the day on which Major Anderson had lowered it. Then came the assassination of Lincoln and the bearing-back of his body to its rest at Springfield. In his tomb was buried the enmity of those who had opposed him in life. Even the *Chicago Times,* his savage critic, added its tribute:

It is hard to conceive of the occurrence of any event which would be so shocking to the sensibilities of the country, occasion sorrow so profound, and create apprehensions and forebodings so painful, as the event which today absorbs all minds and agitates the public heart to its lowest depths. Since the 4th of March last a higher estimate has been put upon Mr. Lincoln's life, and more voices have ascended to Heaven that it might be spared, than before. Since that time all men have realized something of the magnitude of the concerns involved in his lease of existence, and have shuddered at the thought of the possibility of his death. It is not chiefly the manner of his death—awful as that was—that so moves the national mind. It is not this, but it is that at this present crisis of the country—more important and critical than any through which it has passed—the presidential mantle falls upon the shoulders of a man in whom nobody feels confidence....

CARICATURE OF STEPHEN A. DOUGLAS ADDRESSING AN AUDIENCE
Courtesy of the Illinois State Historical Library

STATUE OF LINCOLN, LINCOLN PARK, CHICAGO

There are not on this day mourners more sincere than the democracy of these northern states. Widely as they have differed with Mr. Lincoln—greatly as their confidence in him had been shaken—they yet saw in the indications of the last few days of his life that he might command their support in the close of the war, as he did in the beginning....[8]

Rare instances were reported of individuals who exulted at his death; in almost every case they met with private condemnation or public prosecution. The apotheosis of Lincoln was at hand.

Long since it has come to pass that the counsel of Abraham Lincoln is as if one inquired of the oracle of God. His writings are searched for sayings that may be used on either side of every question of public policy in the present day. As the historian, discarding present-day tradition, studies in the light of Lincoln's own day the character that has been accepted as the incarnation of democracy in peoples and nations of which he never heard, it becomes strangely complex. At first sight Lincoln appears a politician seeking by honorable means the advancement of his party and his individual welfare, in ways he thinks for his country's good. By the time he has reached the presidency he has learned to measure his course by the will of the people. While still he seeks that will, his contemporaries call him timorous and cowardly; when once he has found and executes it, they condemn him as ruthless; with small effect on him in either case. At times the politician and statesman seems possessed with a spirit, an oracle of the divine will; and there fall from his lips sayings of superhuman wisdom on liberty, democracy, the dignity of labor, the brotherhood of man, and mercy to the vanquished. Then politician and statesman are alike forgotten in the god.

The death of Lincoln marked the end of the heroic age of Illinois history. In the great struggle as to whether the United

8. *Chicago Times*, April 17, 1866.

States for the sake of union and democracy should temporize with slavery or should cast it out altogether, Illinois had furnished leaders and ideals in the persons of Douglas and Lincoln; in support of the man whom with his policy she had chosen, she had borne her full share in a mighty war that had taken terrible toll of her best. The enthusiasm for the ideal was to pass because human nature cannot as yet long sustain the ideal; and to it were to succeed the ages of bronze and of iron.

CHAPTER XII

The Civil War and Its Aftermath
1861–68

BETWEEN the second World War and the Civil War no comparison is possible. The first World War midway between the two may bear some comparison in scope to the contest of 1861–65. The Civil War was a far simpler affair; not a tithe, perhaps not a hundredth, of the expenditure in ordnance, ammunition, and equipment of 1917–18 was required to furnish forth the armies of 1861–65 for the battlefield. Illinois was just becoming industrial at the outbreak of the war; hence the burdens laid on her industry were trivial by comparison with those of 1918. In 1861–62 her wheat fields were important as contributing a share of the grain that Europe needed to supplement her crop failures and must secure from the United States at the price of neutrality; but the problem of helping to feed half-embattled Europe in 1918 was a far greater one. In manpower, however, her Civil War offering was far greater by proportion than that of the first World War. Counting enlistments of all lengths and re-enlistments, her total lay somewhere about 250,000. Of these, 5,857 were killed in action and 3,051 died of wounds and 19,934 of disease. The number came near that which she supplied from a far greater population in 1917–18; the number of casualties was far greater.

The troops for two years poured in by volunteering; only 3,538 men entered the service by the draft. Had the recruiting enthusiasm of the earlier years been left unchecked, even that small number might have been reduced. For it was the unfortunate policy of the War Department to discourage recruiting in earlier years and then have recourse to the draft. Illinois, too, made her mistake in not adopting a replacement system such as that of Wisconsin. She raised regiment after regiment by volunteering to the number of one hundred and fifty infantry, seventeen cavalry regiments, and thirty-three batteries; in most cases these units were sent under fire untrained, suffered heavy casualties, and then, instead of being filled up by recruits who would learn to be soldiers and acquire *esprit de corps* from the veterans, were kept as weak organizations, while new volunteer regiments were raised to afford commissions to inexperienced but ambitious officers. The toll in lives paid by this policy was a heavy one.

The share of Lincoln's first call of 75,000 allotted to the state was overfilled by five days' volunteering with six regiments. The legislature, meeting in special session, made appropriations to equip ten new regiments of infantry, one of cavalry, and four batteries. By June all were accepted by the government. Four additional cavalry regiments were raised before the disaster at Bull Run, sixteen more regiments after it. Recruiting was at floodtide. The War Department could not be induced to accept over a fourth of the companies offered; men enlisted in Missouri regiments. By October, Illinois had more regiments in the service than New York. In December she had 60,000 men in the army. During 1862 under the pressure of a state enrolment she more than doubled the number. It was perhaps unfortunate, for a system of enrolment and draft could have been used to fill old organizations; volunteering merely multiplied companies and regiments.

On March 3, 1863, Senator Trumbull's conscription act went into effect; but throughout 1863 volunteering went on so rapidly that on January 1, 1864, Illinois was far in excess of her quota of 145,000. In the summer of 1864 she was still in excess, and in many districts of the state a draft wheel never turned. The draft would undoubtedly have furnished a more efficient army; and there were unpleasant aspects to the workings of the system that actually obtained. The volunteering by companies which kept the state's quota ahead of the drafts often traded on the personal popularity of would-be officers totally unfit to command men in action; such companies were raised often by most liberal bounties and bonuses. Volunteers in Rockford in 1864 received as high a bounty as $400. Substitutes could be furnished for the draft, and at first exemption could be purchased for a payment of $300. Substitute brokers did their unsavory business in the West, and the man who enlisted as a substitute was quite likely to desert and earn another substituting fee. There were local insurance associations to insure men drafted of exemption through purchase of substitutes.

But the sordid nature of the service of a few men cannot detract from the devotion of hundreds of thousands. Illinois not only did her full duty in sending troops; she showed herself true in her historical mission as a political bond of union to men of divers sections and divers races. From the old South, from Kentucky and Tennessee, had come very many of her first settlers in the southern counties; and, after their first reaction of sympathy with the South had passed, their devotion to the Union put the northern elements in the state to shame. On October 1, 1863, the ten southern counties were credited with an excess of 50 per cent over their quota. Union County in eighteen months had furnished nineteen companies out of a voting population of 2,030, including but 157 Republicans. Allowing as much as possible for the enlistment of boys under twenty-one, one wonders how many able-bodied men under forty-five were left in the county. Throughout the state there was many an old man who perjured himself in swearing to his age on enlistment. Foreign-born citizens were no less loyal than the Democrats of "Egypt." Germans organized regiment after regiment officered by veterans of the "1848." There were Irish regiments, Scotch regiments, a regiment of schoolteachers mustered by President Hovey of Illinois State Normal, even an infantry company of young ministers.

The careers of the individual Illinois units it is impossible to follow in detail. In general, however, though they were found in every theater of the war, their main service was done in the West; for at the outbreak of hostilities the Mississippi and Ohio River boundaries of Illinois were in the zone of outposts. Southern Illinois, western Kentucky, and Missouri were factors in one military equation that would be solved according as they arrayed themselves for the Union or the Confederacy.

In the first days of the war a secession movement in southern Illinois was a danger to be reckoned with. The occupation of Cairo by Confederate forces would have made it infinitely greater; and Illinois' first duty was to garrison Cairo in sufficient strength. The next step was to throw her weight into the balance against secession in Missouri. The campaign of 1861 in Missouri was a haphazard affair of regiments operating independently. In spite of his poor leadership, Frémont during the period of his command in Missouri touched Illinois' imagination; and she groaned in spirit when he was removed. By his action at Belmont, in November, 1861, disastrous as it seemed, Grant prevented military co-operation between the Kentucky and Missouri Confederate forces. After 1861 Missouri was safe for the Union and became a less important field of action.

The military strength of Illinois was next turned upon the Confederates in western Kentucky. The Confederate defensive line resting on Forts Henry and Donelson on the Tennessee and Cumberland rivers was within a few miles of the Illinois border. Its reduction under General Grant largely with Illinois troops in February of 1862 assured the Union military control of western Kentucky. In establishing the allegiance of the border states to the Union, the influence of Illinois was paramount. It is so easily taken for granted that we usually ignore the other possibility of 1861 that secessionists in Kentucky and Missouri might have made southern Illinois a seat of war.

Though after 1861 war never even approached Illinois save in the form of guerrilla raids, her military contributions to victory on more distant fields were great. At Shiloh, at Vicksburg, at Chattanooga, Illinois troops were a decisive factor. Seventy Illinois regiments were in the army with which Sherman made the Georgia campaign of 1864. In the western armies the Illinois troops had their most important part; but in all the great battles of the East they were present.

Among many brilliant feats of arms of Illinois regiments there stands out as one of the great exploits of horse cavalry the mission of the Sixth and Seventh Illinois and the Second Iowa Cavalry, known as Grierson's Raid. Riding night and day, dodging or baffling pursuing Confederate cavalry, destroying bridges, remounting from horses commandeered or captured en route, Grierson's brigade rode through the western Confederate lines, entering them in Tennessee and coming out at the Federal outposts at Baton Rouge above New Orleans. The raid destroyed needed Confederate supplies and communications; above all, it blinded the Confederates as to the first moves of Grant's Vicksburg campaign.[1]

The war produced for Illinois a generation of statesman-generals. The small regular army of the United States of 1861 was for its size an admirable force, but its officers, however well they might understand their duties and the art of war in its tactical phases, could not supply enough men with the natural ability to control large affairs or the knowledge of human nature, outside the few special types that enlisted in the old army necessary to lead great masses of men fresh from civil life, who

---

1. For a brilliantly written account of the raid by a participant, Professor Stephen A. Forbes, see *Transactions of Illinois State Historical Society, 1907*, pp. 99–130.

came ready to sacrifice themselves for an ideal. So long as American life remains what it is, great citizen armies drawn from civilian life must be treated differently from small professional armies; and enthusiasm, genuine natural ability, and sound common sense in an amateur officer can often atone for much lack of information about the fine points of formal guard-mounting or court-martial procedure. It was not surprising that the period should have looked to its political leaders to supply men with the intelligence and leadership needed to lead the new armies; and the results were probably as good as could have been obtained by men drawn from any other walk of life, including the regular army.

Of the numerous generals credited to Illinois, the service of a few is typical. General McClernand was in the actions of Belmont, Fort Donelson, Shiloh, and Vicksburg and later served in Louisiana and Texas. John M. Palmer served in Missouri in 1861, at New Madrid, at Corinth, at Stone's River and Chickamauga, and in Sherman's Atlanta campaign, latterly in command of the Fourteenth Army Corps. Later he served as department commander in Kentucky. General John Pope earned at New Madrid and Corinth the reputation which gave him the command of the Army of the Potomac in 1862. His defeat at the Second Battle of Bull Run ended his active career. Stephen A. Hurlbut fought as a brigadier at Shiloh, and as a major general commanded at Memphis and in the Department of the Gulf. Elon H. Farnsworth rose to be a brigadier general on June 29, 1863. Four days later he fell in a desperate cavalry charge at Gettysburg. Richard Oglesby fought at Donelson and at Corinth, rising to the rank of major general. He was severely wounded at Corinth and in 1864 resigned to seek the governorship on the Union ticket.

Major General John A. Logan well earned the title of the typical volunteer soldier and general of the war. At Belmont, at Donelson, where he was wounded, at Vicksburg and Resaca, at

Dallas, where he was wounded again, he fought gallantly and commanded skilfully. On the death of General McPherson he succeeded to the command of the Army of the Tennessee. Because of General George H. Thomas' dislike for Logan, Thomas being the commander of the Army of the Cumberland, Sherman feared the two men could not co-operate and replaced Logan by Howard in command of the Army of the Tennessee. Without complaint Logan asked only to return to the command of his Fifteenth Army Corps in the campaign before Atlanta. Later dispatched by Sherman to relieve Thomas in command at Nashville, he generously allowed Thomas to retain the command and to fight the battle that annihilated Hood's army. It is easy to understand why in later years with his old soldiers Logan's military career cloaked any and every defect in his civil record.

One man whom Illinois claims as her contribution to the Civil War was to go farther than any of these men in military success and political rewards. Ulysses S. Grant had entered West Point from Ohio, had fought in the Mexican War with a good record, had left the service under a cloud as the result of intemperance in a lonely station on the Pacific Coast, and had lived for some years in a cabin on the outskirts of St. Louis, cast off by his father's family, supporting his wife and children by hauling cordwood into town. Forgiven by his father and taken into the family leather business at Galena in Illinois, soon after the outbreak of war he had found his way to Springfield, where his knowledge of the forms of the old regular army made him valuable to the military amateurs around Governor Yates who were engaged in mustering the state forces. Put in command of an undisciplined regiment, he had speedily reduced it to order. His record around Cairo in the fall of 1861 insured his command of the army that captured Forts Henry and Donelson and launched him in his career. The unraveling of the riddle of his military success, whether it was genius, stolidity in the face of reverses, ability to gain the confidence of his men, or the guidance of some clever staff officer, is a question for the historian of the Civil War to decide.

Of the other military leaders of the war, McClernand's race in politics was run. John Pope was not to be a major figure in Illinois politics. John A. Logan, his flirting with secession in 1861 condoned or forgotten, was to stand as the beau ideal of the Grand Army of the Republic for long years of political service. Oglesby, returning wounded to be elected governor in 1864, was thenceforth the darling of Illinois politics. Palmer was later to be governor, senator, and candidate for the presidency, a man whose career rings true on the note not of party but of principle. Among civilians Richard Yates was endeared to future generations as the war governor of the state. He had stood for the utmost effort in the carrying-on of the war, had loyally supported the administration throughout, and, after Fort Donelson in 1862, had organized the Illinois Sanitary Commission, which thereafter functioned as the Red Cross did in the first and second World Wars. He shared the popularity of the veteran generals—Logan, Oglesby, and Palmer—and was to be their competitor for high office.

The first issues that these men and that Illinois had to meet in succeeding years were the national issues of reconstruction. What was the constitutional status of the former Confederate states? Conquered provinces or states whose lawful governments had been temporarily unseated by the rebellious Confederacy? Did they have rights that they could demand under the Constitution, or was it for the loyal states to dictate the terms of their forgiveness? What were those terms to be, and how far was it just, how far expedient, to grant the Negroes citizenship in the seceded states and exclude ex-Confederates from it?

At the first many radicals, convinced that Abraham Lincoln would be too merciful to rebels, regarded as a dispensation of

ULYSSES S. GRANT IN JULY, 1864
Courtesy of Illinois State Historical Library

GALENA, ILLINOIS

From William Franklin Wells, *Western Scenery* (1851)

Providence his taking-off and the succession to the presidency of Andrew Johnson, the Vice-President, a Tennessee Democrat, illiterate, plebian, but loving the Union and hating the aristocratic southern planter rebels. If Lincoln had been unwilling to chastise the rebels with whips, surely Johnson would chastise them with scorpions. When Johnson in December, 1865, announced a liberal presidential policy of reconstruction, they were undeceived; and radical men in Congress set themselves to wrest out of the President's hand the power of reconstructing the southern states and to do it themselves by limiting southern representation to voting population, organizing the Negroes into a Republican political machine, and setting up military rule over defiant southern majorities.

As late as December, 1865, however, the Republicans of Illinois were still not definitely decided to drop Johnson, and the Democrats resolved to take him up. However, his veto of the Civil Rights and Freedman's Bureau bills of Senator Trumbull, embodying the congressional reconstruction policy, made his conduct an issue in the campaign of 1866. Some former Illinois Republicans like O. H. Browning, soon to be his secretary of the interior, gathered around him. The Democratic state convention of 1866 adopted Johnson and his measures and nominated a ticket of war Democrats, including Colonel T. Lyle Dickey for congressman-at-large. The Republicans had previously nominated a ticket largely made up of war veterans headed by John A. Logan. The contest between Logan and Dickey was a savage one. Logan's doubtful course in 1861 was dragged to the light; but all in vain. The reconstruction issue was the main one; and Illinois, led by her military heroes, her voting list filled with veterans of the war, was in no mood to listen to the expediency of mercy to the South. The eight-hour day and greenback issues advanced by the Democrats could not counteract the other issue. Logan was elected by a majority of 50,000.

The General Assembly of 1867 had the task of electing a

senator. Palmer, with the support of Logan and Oglesby, contested Trumbull's re-election. But Trumbull's record from the outset of the war was the exemplification of what the Republicans had stood for in the election of 1866. After the state at their behest had rebuked Johnson for vetoing the Civil Rights and Freedman's Bureau bills, they could not turn away from the author of these measures, and Trumbull was re-elected.

This was, however, the closing triumph of Trumbull's career. When Johnson's opposition to the congressional policy of reconstruction led in 1868 to the attempt to impeach him, Trumbull voted for his acquittal. With the Republican party united on the congressional reconstruction policy and the Democrats hopelessly in the minority, there was no place for him in Illinois politics; and the official career of Trumbull, second in importance in the critical years only to those of Lincoln and Douglas, came to an honorable end.

Apart from the question of reconstruction the issues that came to the front in Illinois in 1868 were protection and the currency. Illinois was still predominantly rural and opposed continued protection by the high revenue tariffs of the Civil War. The failure of the Republicans to put a tariff clause in the platform helped them in the state. There was something inviting, on the other hand, in the "Ohio idea" of Pendleton, espoused by the Illinois Democrats, that the way to get rid of the war debts and supply the scarcity of currency in the West was to pay the bonds off in greenbacks. In spite of the fact that the Democratic national convention had nominated Horatio Seymour, a hardmoney man, the Illinois Democrats made the best of the greenback clause in the platform.

The issues of the war, however, could not be put aside.

In the present contest, the Republicans unite in demanding peace upon the basis of accomplished facts, and in consonance with lawfully-enacted statutes, and in requiring the payment of the public debt with "the utmost good faith" to all: while the Democracy sound the tocsin of insurrection and threaten repudiation in one form or another. He who prefers a pacific and an honorable national policy will vote for Grant and Colfax: he who prefers internecine war and bankruptcy will vote for Seymour and Blair.[2]

A national ticket headed by General Grant and a state ticket by John M. Palmer could not be opposed by Horatio Seymour and John R. Eden. Again by a majority of fifty thousand the Republicans were successful. The men of the Civil War had entered finally into their own.

2. *Chicago Tribune*, August 4, 1868.

CHAPTER XIII

Economic and Social Readjustment

THE rural prairie commonwealth between 1870 and 1893 underwent changes that dwarf those of the preceding twenty years. Population and industry developed according to the trend taken in 1850, it is true, but at an accelerated rate. From the early period of her statehood Continental Europeans had found their way to Illinois as the land of promise; but now their coming was to be measured not in thousands but in hundred thousands, and not only the old nationalities but others whose former habitat was as strange to the provincial westerner as their tongue. The first feeble beginnings of manufactures developed by the demands of the Civil War were turning into mightier and mightier industries; for some products Illinois was becoming a world source of supply. The farmer, even though learning new methods, was to find himself distanced in the race for production by the newer lands to the west. As Illinois strode toward supremacy in industry, she saw a competitor or two overtake her in agriculture. A new population, the necessity of adjusting an industrial world to organized labor, the farmer's aspirations toward better things—all contributed to make the period one of mighty change and profound unrest. These conditions the party politicians, intent on their old game, sought to turn to their own account.

A part of the change in population in the seventies and eighties was the tendency of native-born population to drift into the state during one generation and out in the next. In 1870, 41.7 per cent of the native-born in Illinois came from other states, 31.5 per cent in 1880, 25.7 per cent in 1890. In 1870 one-fifth of the persons born in Illinois lived outside the state, in 1880 one-fourth, in 1890 a little more. The same period in terms of rural and urban populations saw a movement toward Chicago. In 1870, 11.6 per cent of the state's population lived in Chicago; in 1880, 16.3 per cent; in 1890, 28.7 per cent. Meanwhile the percentage of population in smaller places above 2,500 in size grew from 13.5 to 18.6, the distinctively rural population falling from 76.6 to 55.3 per cent. Nor was this true in percentages only. After 1870 more and more the distinctively rural counties of the state tended to lose population. This continued until, between 1900 and 1910, one-half the counties of Illinois showed a decline in population. Kendall was the only one to do so before 1870, but by 1880 there were nine and by 1890 twenty-eight that had grown smaller.

The foreign-born population of Illinois showed the most remarkable development. In 1870 there were 515,198 foreign-born in the state, of whom almost 225,000 had been British subjects; 203,000 Germans, 45,000 Scandinavians, 4,180 Hollanders, and 8,980 Swiss were of Germanic blood. By 1890 the British element, including Irish, had grown only to 260,000, the German element had increased to 338,000, and the Scandinavian to 126,000. There were now 26,627 Bohemians, 3,126 Hungarians, 8,407 Russians, and 28,878 Poles in the grand total of 842,347. The absolute population of the state had measurably increased from 2,539,891 to 3,826,352.

The situation, of course, is only partially stated in the figures. The second generation of these races was often as deeply inlaid with distinctive characteristics as the first. Held aloof by the barrier of language, they clung together and were easily exploited by demagogues of their own race. In the seventies native Americans protested that the Chicago city offices were apportioned among the foreign groups. Some of them had brought with them not merely their language but doctrines of working-class solidarity, communism, socialism, anarchism; and in hard times they were not slow in teaching these to American fellow-laborers. Skilled workmen, many of them, in contradistinction to American-born labor, they early established trade-unions and engaged in industrial war to gain their share of the profits of the period of industrial development.

That industrial development was most amazing. The Civil War had given some encouragement to manufacture; in 1870 there were in the state thirty-four distinct industries, the annual value of whose products was over one million dollars. The seven with output above five million dollars are significant—flour- and gristmill, meat-packing, agricultural implements, distilled liquors, planed lumber, carriages and wagons, and clothing. With one exception they either prepared the products of the forest and farm for their first use or were subservient to agriculture.

The succeeding period saw other great industries develop—the manufacture of iron and steel, brick and clay products, cement, and the production of coal. Illinois coal production on a large scale was not developed until the seventies. Discovered at first on the edges of the Illinois basin or where rivers cut through, it was only slowly that coal came to be taken from the great interior fields of the basin. The Franklin and Williamson county fields have been developed since 1890.

The Illinois census of 1890 showed thirty-four industries with products exceeding five million dollars. By far the greatest was the packing industry; after it followed distilled liquors, foundry and machine products, flour- and gristmill, iron and steel, men's clothing, agricultural implements, lumber and carpentering—all above twenty million dollars. Cars, printing, furniture, and malt liquors followed. Since 1870 the average number of employees per establishment had increased from 6.5 to 15, the number of establishments from 12,597 to 20,482, the number of wage-earners from 82,979 to 312,198, and the net value of manufactured products from $78,020,595 to $379,621,191.

Statistics only unsatisfactorily convey the huge growth of the period. The little packing-houses, the little blacksmith shops, the carriage shops, and the gristmills of the frontier community were being replaced by modern factories, where the manufacturer was no longer master, teacher, and leader but the employer of hundreds of hands, with all the problems of labor, wages, strikes, railroad rates, rebates, and bank credits to consider as factors of success or failure.

First of all came the labor problem. The manufacturer of the seventies and eighties was probably no harder in pushing wages down as low as possible, making labor take its share promptly of of losses in a poor market, and exacting long hours of work, than the employer of a past generation had been. But then there had been the land to act as a safety valve for the enterprising, and there had been few laborers in a trade. Now with labor clustered in large cities, with the golden promise of the boundless continent already passing, above all with thousands of German and Scandinavian skilled workingmen, suspicious, restless, filled with the ideals of Lassalle and Karl Marx, conflict developed when wages were lowered by stress of hard times.

The change was first apparent in Chicago when the boom years of the Civil War period slumped into the Panic of 1873 and men were out of work. The red flag appeared on the streets, and in January, 1874, the Workingmen's party of Illinois was launched. Its demands at first were studiously moderate in hope of gaining the support of the farmers—the eight-hour day, no child labor, no prison labor save on public works, compulsory education, state management of means of transportation and savings banks, direct taxes, recall of public officers; but behind those demands was the extreme ideal of the Communist state.

The continual reduction of wages all through the period of 1873–77 only added fuel to the fire already kindled. In 1877 a strike of Michigan Central switchmen threatened to become general. Nineteen men were killed in contests with the police.

Defeat in the strike caused the radical group to turn again to political action; under the name of the Socialist Labor party they elected two aldermen in Chicago in the spring of 1878 and four members of the General Assembly in the fall. In the movement which had long since developed its own newspapers, most of them in German, the foreign element seemed generally to stand for direct action and communism in contrast to the more opportunist native Americans.

Meanwhile trade-unionism proper had been developing; its first form was that of craft unions among the skilled foreign workers, who led the way in this sort of organization. In 1877 Albert A. Parsons had been elected first president of the group of crafts unions that was finally to develop into the American Federation of Labor. By 1877 also the Knights of Labor had established their first locals in Illinois. A secret organization, its demands were the eight-hour day, weekly pay, mechanics' lien laws, arbitration, limitation of child labor and prison labor, equal pay for both sexes, and greenbackism. Like most labor unions of the type, it attracted the less skilled class of labor.

The trade-union movement soon became involved with anarchism. New economic and political doctrines, far removed from those the pioneer state had learned at the feet of John Adams and Thomas Jefferson, were being brought to her borders by her recent citizens. In 1881 there was organized the International Working People's Association, a branch of a London anarchist organization. It drew to itself more radical elements, aiming at the establishment by force of the ideal federation of producing communities. Its members used older associations for military drill; its newspaper began to print articles on the use of dynamite. Chicago had the distinction of being the center of the radical labor movement in the United States.

Between 1879 and 1882 a series of strikes for higher wages had taken place. The packers had struck in 1880 for recognition of their organization, had been defeated, and had not been re-

CYRUS H. McCORMICK (1809–84)
From a painting in the McCormick Agricultural Library, Chicago

JOHN PETER ALTGELD (1847–1902)
Courtesy of Illinois State Historical Library

stored to their jobs. In February, 1886, a struggle began at the McCormick works in Chicago over the principle of the closed shop. McCormick locked out its workingmen. The press, formerly inclined to favor the eight-hour day, now turned as the radical intent of the movement developed under the preaching of such papers as the *Arbeiter Zeitung*. There was a great riot at the McCormick plant on May 3. Hatred of the police and the Pinkerton detectives was at fever heat, and the Haymarket Riot was the result. A great meeting had been held in the old Haymarket of Chicago, where formerly the statue of a policeman, now in Union Park, commemorated the tragedy. A meeting addressed by Parsons and others was outwardly quiet. The police attempted to disperse it, and a bomb was thrown in their ranks, causing heavy loss of life.

The horror of the community at the outrage condoned measures against the anarchist leaders that overstepped the bounds of Anglo-Saxon liberty. For the eight men sentenced for the crime no direct connection with the throwing of the bomb or direct advice of its use could be established. All that could be proved was that their utterances were such as might be supposed to provoke violence. Parsons and three other men went to the gallows; three men sentenced to imprisonment were pardoned by Governor Altgeld.

The labor problem nevertheless had passed the worst stage. The development of the nineties was twofold. In the one direction moved the advocates of political action, the adherents of the various labor and socialist parties, and such labor unions as the Industrial Workers of the World. On the other hand, the skilled crafts, affiliated through national trade-unions with the American Federation of Labor, generally eschewed political action save to obtain the modification of laws and decisions calculated to prevent their use of the strike and the boycott to obtain shorter hours, higher wages, and better working conditions. However, the Chicago Federation of Labor always tended to be somewhat more radical than the national federation. Most of the demands that seemed extreme in the seventies and eighties have long since been adopted by the community by acquiescence or legislation.

The generation had its financial problem as well as its labor problem. The old state banking system, based on note issues secured by bonds, had passed away in the time of the Civil War. Its place had been taken partly by the new national banking system, partly by specially chartered banks and private banking corporations. The national system was under a certain degree of supervision, but not the state or private banks. Failures were numerous. Both national and state banks went down in the Panic of 1873. Four years later a group of savings banks failed through incompetence or fraud. In 1887 the state finally adopted a general banking law and forced the state banks in existence to accept its provisions; but a savings bank act passed in the same year was declared unconstitutional because it was not submitted to a vote of the people.

Among the poorer classes generally there was great distrust of banks and strong belief that the issue of bank-note currency was a profitable business that the government should take over itself by the issue of greenbacks. Accompanying the period of high prices there had been currency expansion by greenbacks in the days of the Civil War. Men looked back to it with regret in the period of falling prices after 1873. They ascribed the decline to the contraction of the currency at the behest of Wall Street financiers and eastern creditors, undertaken that the government and their western debtors might be compelled to pay in dollars growing dearer and dearer in purchasing power. Accordingly the debtors clamored for more money and cheaper money—the reversal of "the crime of '73," by which the silver dollar was alleged to have been demonetized: the issue of more greenbacks. Both demands appear in many reform and radical programs of the day.

Even more pressing than the problem of the banks and the currency was that of the railroads. The manufacturer who ordered his raw materials and delivered his products over them, the farmer who shipped his grain and hogs, the passenger who rode on them, the local taxpayer whose county had subscribed to their bonds, each and all had grievances and sought in one way or another to redress them.

Decade after decade had seen the railroad net woven closer across the state. From 1879 to 1884 it increased from 7,578 to 8,904 miles. By 1893 no land in the state was so much as twenty miles from a railroad; 85 per cent of the land was within four miles of one. From the beginning the co-operation of local communities had been enlisted in the building of railroads. This had been stimulated by the "tax grab" act of 1869, which allowed counties to deduct from the revenue increased by rising land values the interest due on their bond subsidies to the railroads which had presumably caused the increase. Probably twenty million dollars in such bonds were out. Many of them had fallen into the hands of speculators rather than railroad builders, and, when in 1874 the law was declared unconstitutional, the burden of the bonds fell on the communities that issued them. The roads had some fine palace, dining, sleeping, and chair cars for display; but at the beginning of the period we are considering unvestibuled trains light enough in tonnage to run over unballasted mud roadbeds on iron T rails were the usual thing. The state Railroad and Warehouse Commission established by the act of 1871—the first commission in the United States established to regulate warehouses, and the first after Massachusetts to regulate railroads—for years strove for ballasted tracks laid with steel rails, guarded crossings, flagmen, gates, and vestibule trains. By 1885 in these respects it had gained its ends.

Otherwise it had been less successful. Rates for passengers and freight were what the traffic would bear and no less. To competing points freight receipts were pooled. In 1876 a pool of lines to the East charged heavier rates from Chicago to the East than from Quincy and points in Wisconsin and Minnesota. The Wabash, the Chicago and Alton, and the Illinois Central had another pool for all competing points in the state; others paid enough to compensate. The railroads openly defied the rate regulations of the commission; cars filled with farmers, paying the legal fare, were cut out of trains and left on sidings; sometimes the farmers drew revolvers and knives on the trainmen. More than to passenger fares of course they objected to the charges for hauling produce. In 1873 C. B. Lawrence of the Illinois Supreme Court, on a rate regulation case, declared the act of 1871 contrary to the state constitution. The legislature re-enacted it; and the farmers, arising in wrath, deposed Judge Lawrence at the next election. The crux of the problem, however, was not the intrastate but the interstate rate; and that remained untouched until the federal Interstate Commerce Act of 1887.

The public turned to water competition to regulate railroad rates but had only partial success. Traffic on the Mississippi declined before railroad competition. In the seventies and eighties men looked to the Illinois and Michigan Canal and the Illinois River route as a possible means of keeping down railroad rates. To a certain extent it succeeded in doing so; but after 1880 the canal was run at a loss, and the Illinois River traffic steadily declined. The Hennepin Canal undertaken in this period to connect the Illinois at Hennepin with the Mississippi River, when finally opened in 1907, was practically worthless. The Great Lakes offered more competition. True the railroads secured most of the flour shipments to the East, but from 1870 to 1889 an increasing amount of wheat and corn was sent east from Chicago by boat. For many years the lumber schooner maintained her place on the lake; but before the end of the period Chicago had yielded her supremacy as a market and shipping point for both grain and lumber.

The warehouse offered still another type of problem. The warehousemen charged excessive rates for warehousing and were suspected of fraud in grading and weighing grain. The constitutionality of the state statute and of the regulations of the Railroad and Warehouse Commission was finally upheld in *Munn* v. *Illinois* in the United States Supreme Court in 1876—the first of the so-called "Granger" cases. The name may serve to introduce a study of farms and farmers in the state leading up to the state grange and cognate farmers' organizations.

The period has already been characterized as one in which the industry of the state was rising to the first rank in the Union and its agriculture slipping back from it. In 1870 more than one-half the employed population of the state was engaged in agriculture; in 1890, less than one-third, and this even though the farm area and the amount of cereals raised actually increased. In absolute amount, however, Illinois was compelled to yield to the Dakotas, Nebraska, and Kansas, and her production declined after 1881. Illinois' farming, however, improved. The primitive farm of the backwoods, distanced long since by competition, was beginning to develop. The farmer was buying machinery; he was demanding opportunities to market his produce that would give him his fair share of the comforts of life. The reaper, the binder, the hay tedder, and the grain drill were all increasing the production of Illinois farms, even though the proportion of labor was declining. Better brands of dairy and of beef cattle and of hogs were being used; sheep had reached their maximum number in the state in 1865—three million.

Tenant farming was on the increase. In 1880, 31.4 per cent of Illinois farms were operated by tenants; in 1890, 34 per cent. The possession of 211,000 acres of such farms by a British subject, William Scully, who introduced Irish methods of absentee landlordism and rack-renting, was responsible for the law of 1887 against alien land ownership.

The dissatisfaction and unrest among farmers in the age of

transition and change is illustrated by the formation of farmers' associations of one sort or another. Already the organization of the farmers of the state had been used by Jonathan B. Turner to secure the foundation of the agricultural colleges for their benefit under the Morrill Act. In 1867 at Washington, D.C., the organization known as the Patrons of Husbandry was formed. Organized into state and local granges, with degrees for both men and women, it came to Illinois in 1868 and flourished between 1872 and 1874. One of its purposes was to buy agricultural machinery for members at a discount. Montgomery Ward and Company of Chicago, establishing a Grange supply-house, was the first of the long line of mail-order houses. The well-to-do elements of the rural community were inclined to look on the Grangers with contempt, but they persisted. Naturally the farmers in their war on railroads and warehouses upheld the dicta of the state Railroad and Warehouse Commission. In 1874 they defeated the judges who threw out the commission's suits; in that same year an antimonopolist movement, begun among them under the leadership of Turner and John M. Palmer, elected a fusion superintendent of public instruction and nine independents to the legislature.

This for the present was the high-water mark of farmer activity. For a time thereafter the farmers realigned themselves in Republican, Democratic, and Greenback camps; but they had found a weapon and could use it again. In 1890 the Farmers Mutual Benefit Association elected fifty farmer assemblymen, both Republican and Democratic. Operating within the old parties, it could make its demands effective.

These were but a few of the greater aspects of the period; at every point the amazing development and change of the new commonwealth presented its problems to be mastered. Ever since the forties the state's educational system had been broadening. To the little colleges of the pioneer period Northwestern University had been added in 1851 and the old University of

Chicago in 1857. In the same years Jonathan B. Turner was gaining popular support for his ideal of an industrial university, where youth might secure technical and scientific training to turn to account in the development of agriculture and industry. The idea finally bore fruit in the Morrill Land Grant Act of 1862, which granted to each state lands in proportion to its representation in Congress for colleges of agriculture and the mechanic arts. The Illinois denominational colleges sought to divide the largess among themselves, but Turner won his fight for the endowment of a new institution. The Illinois Industrial University chartered by the legislature in 1867 was located at Urbana, thanks to adroit political manipulation on the part of the local assemblyman. Before 1870 its first regent, John Milton Gregory, had laid the foundation not merely of a technical school but of a college of liberal arts as well.

The Illinois Industrial University at first passed through troublous times. Its revenues were small; it was criticized keenly by the interests it was supposed to serve; it was almost overshadowed by some of the older denominational institutions such as Northwestern, Knox, and Illinois College. The change of name to the University of Illinois in 1885 seemed to help little. Not until the nineties did the series of state appropriations begin that has lifted the institution to the foremost rank of the western universities.

In primary- and secondary-school education progress from 1850 to 1893 was continuous. By 1850 men had come to regard as inadequate the old schools held for a few weeks, taught by men often fitted for nothing else, out of any and all books available, and enforcing their precepts with the rod. In the cities at least the little red schoolhouse was being replaced by the more modern school building and the haphazard teacher by the trained professional. School societies and school magazines appeared, pleading the cause of uniform and standardized education. The designating of the secretary of state as superintendent of public instruction in 1845 and the creation of an independent officer in 1854 had been earnests that a state system would soon come. The first superintendent, Ninian W. Edwards, drew up a comprehensive free-school bill providing for the support of schools by state-wide taxation; it passed in 1855. The normal school appeared in 1857. By 1870 the first public high schools could stand comparison with the best private academies. Their opponents in vain raised the cry of extravagance and the education of a select few at public expense.

The school problems of the seventies and eighties revolved around the question of the parochial school. The convention of 1869–70 had omitted from the new constitution provisions for the reading of the Bible and religious instruction in the public schools of the state; it had expressly forbidden the deflection to parochial schools of a part of the school funds. Although this last was urged as an act of justice to those who paid school tax but whose consciences compelled them to send their children to schools where religious instruction was given, the idea of the public nonreligious school prevailed. In 1883 and 1887 were passed the state's first compulsory education laws.

In other ways the intellectual development of the state became marked. In 1850 there were 33 public libraries in Illinois; in 1870 there were 3,705, with 924,000 volumes—more than any other state except New York or Pennsylvania. The Chicago Historical Society was established in 1856. Within a year it had a collection of 11,000 volumes; with other treasures, its priceless collection went up in the Chicago Fire. The Society, undaunted, began the construction of a building walled in massive granite and furnished throughout with iron, and under these protections began the accumulation of a new collection; its impressiveness was tempered only by the recollection of the irreplaceable materials lost in 1871.

The Chicago slums and the city's foreign-born dwellers inspired the setting-up in 1889, 1891, and 1894 of three philanthropic institutions—Hull House, the Northwestern University Settlement, and Chicago Commons. The first of these was the creation of Jane Addams, born at Cedarville, Illinois, a graduate of Rockford College, sharer of the Nobel Peace Prize in 1931, and perhaps the outstanding woman in the United States of her day. The goal that she set at Hull House was not merely to place before the less privileged the ideal of better living; it was to persuade the Illinois citizen of foreign extraction to preserve whatever was fine and valid in the intellectual and cultural heritage of his race as a contribution to the enrichment of his adopted country.

As to the fine arts, development throughout the nineteenth century was generally imitative. Concerned with the immediate tasks of getting a living and of establishing an agricultural and industrial commonwealth in the wilderness, inhabitants of the state put the best of their minds to their concrete problems and in literature, painting, and sculpture were content to copy and adapt, however ably, from more leisured societies. One conspicuous exception was the functional development of innovations in architecture due to the immediate urgency of Chicago's location and of the problems it produced.[1]

Situated as it was at a strategic point in the natural route of travel from the Lakes to the Gulf, the necessary focus of east-and-west lines of communication that passed around the southern end of Lake Michigan, the original site of Chicago was sand, dune, and marsh. One immediate artificial alteration in its site was the digging of a new outlet for the Chicago River to Lake Michigan, which carried it due east and eliminated the southward bend which formerly left its mouth near the foot of the present Madison Street. The rush of population in the 1830's at Chicago, as at numerous other towns of the frontier, called for

1. Anyone acquainted with Thomas E. Tallmadge's *Architecture in Old Chicago* will at once perceive the extent of my indebtedness to a fascinating book which deserves a host of readers.

housing that could rapidly be run up by a few workmen. The demand about 1837 produced Chicago's first innovation in architecture, namely, the balloon frame type of construction. Hitherto the frame of each of the four sides of a wooden house had been constructed of large and solid beams, sometimes pegged together on the ground and then raised to an upright position by the willing hands of neighbors. But in 1837 a Chicago architect hit on the device of laying four crossbeams as a foundation, nailing to those beams two-by-four uprights, joining those uprights at the top with other two-by-fours, and crossing them with diagonals, all made fast by unlimited use of nails. Here was a frame house built by a few days' labor by two or three carpenters. Only by such a time-saving device could the necessary housing for the millions who came flocking westward in the next two generations have been secured.

For more pretentious buildings, such as churches, homes, and courthouses, the pioneer architects copied the simple classical forms of the so-called "Greek Revival." These were quite sufficient for erecting on the original site of Chicago the one-, two-, and three-story homes, stores, warehouses, and office buildings that it required.

With the coming of the railroads in the 1850's, Chicago had taken on a greater degree of pretentiousness. As a packing center it drew meat animals from a constantly enlarging area around the city. It became an important grain market of the western country. It distributed to a constantly increasing rural population rudimentary manufactures and consumption goods. At the same time it manufactured and supplied agricultural machinery of constantly increasing complexity.

To satisfy the demands of business for space on which to operate, to supply housing for transients who visited the city on business, the decade of the fifties and sixties demanded pretentious five- and six-story buildings of brick and stone. These, in general, were poor imitations of the lavish and sophisticated ornamentation in vogue in the Paris of Napoleon III and the London of Victoria. The homes of the well-to-do citizens who were continually growing richer were designed in similar styles with similar ostentation and poor taste.

The city was just reaching the climax of this period of its development when the Chicago Fire of October 9, 1871, laid it low. This fire was, in a great part, the result of the haste with which the city had been constructed and of the inflammable qualities inherent in balloon construction. A hot, dry summer and fall had left the frame portions of the city like tinder, and strong southwest winds swept the fire over an area of approximately three and one-half square miles, leaving some ninety thousand people homeless.

In some of the later construction men had endeavored to take thought and to construct fireproof buildings. The method which they had employed was the erecting of strong outer walls of stone and brick with the interior floors of the building supported on cast-iron pillars, only to see the Chicago Fire reach such an intensity that the pillars themselves melted and sent the floors they supported crashing one after the other into the basements.

Here a second innovation came to fruition. An English architect, Edward Johnson, devised the method of surrounding the cast-iron supports of the buildings with baked tile and brick which protected them against the most extreme temperatures. On these theories iron skeleton construction thenceforth proceeded.

But as Chicago leaped forward to greater and greater growth after the disaster of 1871, new problems demanded solutions. The very railroads that had created Chicago now threatened to stifle her. Immediately to the west of the business district railroad rights-of-way running north and south hampered the westward development of the city. To the south a narrow bottleneck two blocks wide was all the room for expansion available between the south-bound lines of half-a-dozen railroads. To the north expansion was increasingly narrowed by the westward curvature of the lake shore and the northward-running railroad lines. Necessarily, therefore, higher and higher office buildings in the Loop to accommodate the increasing numbers of business middlemen, lawyers, and others were essential. By the 1880's office buildings ten stories or more in height, served by elevators, were in demand. The problem of basing adequate foundations for them on the sand and marsh of the Loop area of Chicago caused the architects of the period to devise the floating foundation, a wide network of iron set in concrete upon which the footings of the building could safely rest.

Necessarily, as buildings grew taller and heavier, stronger foundations and walls on the lower floors were required to sustain the increasing weight of the superstructure. At the same time the renter of offices was clamoring for more and more light. Between 1884 and 1887 this problem was solved in two of the earliest Chicago skyscrapers, the Home Insurance Building and the Tacoma Building. To Major William Jenney, architect of the former, is ascribed the idea of making the essential core of the building a network of iron or steel uprights and girders which not merely supported the upper floors of the building but which also buttressed the outer walls. The outer walls, in effect hung upon the steel skeleton, could be reduced to a mere skin and the window space made as great in proportion to the wall space as possible. The skyscraper of this type was distinctly a Chicago invention. The foreign architects visiting the Chicago World's Fair in 1893 turned aside from the lavishly ornamented lath and plaster buildings that imitated the architectural styles of Paris to admire Chicago's real contribution to functional architecture.

While the skyscraper was solving one of Chicago's needs, Chicago architects were applying with success to the more ornamental buildings the Romanesque architecture of the Boston architect, H. H. Richardson. The essential principle of the Romanesque style was derived from the lofty arches and high interiors with which the law courts and the baths of imperial Rome were constructed. Round-topped arches could be carried up with harmonious detail through a half-a-dozen stories and beautiful façades constructed. Among the Romanesque buildings of Chicago, Richardson's own masterpiece, the Marshall Field wholesale building on Wells Street, was torn down in 1930. The Chicago Auditorium, modeled after Richardson's ideals by Louis Sullivan, still stands as one of the great buildings of the Middle West.

With the 1890's the final step in the development of the skyscraper was taken, and caissons going down ninety feet to the limestone strata below Chicago became the foundations for newer skyscrapers towering twenty or thirty stories in the air representing the supreme achievement of the type.

A pupil of Louis Sullivan, Frank Lloyd Wright, began his career with the designing of seemingly grotesque and fantastic dwellings and churches in Oak Park and elsewhere in the Chicago area, evolving an architectural principle of fitting a structure harmoniously into its site, with every detail planned for the ease and comfort and efficiency of those who occupy it. In his later years Wright stood for an architectural concept which would take advantage of the automobile and other advanced transportation to mingle the facilities of the city with the expanse and comfort in living of the countryside.

Chicago achieved the original and functional in architecture, but struggles with the problem of housing and transportation were less successful. By 1859 the city had expanded so far that public means of transportation were necessary to get the poorer citizens to their places of employment. The businessman of means living comfortably on the outskirts of the city relied upon his fast-trotting horses to drive him to work each morning. As the decades passed, the ordinary horse omnibus or horsecar was succeeded by the cablecar, and the cablecar in turn by the electric trolley. By the 1890's the electric trolley was supplemented by the elevated railroad, originally served by small steam locomotives, long since by electric power. Again and again these methods of transportation fell among thieves; the issue of inflated stocks and bonds based upon their supposed monopolies of transportation led to bankruptcy, to higher and higher fares, and to the indefinite postponement of any improvements in service.

As all these means of transportation operated aboveground, the transporting of people from one side to another of a metropolitan area measured in hundreds of square miles became an increasingly impossible task. Without the underlying rock foundations of New York, London, or Paris the subway on any extensive scale was a virtual impossibility. In the 1890's and 1900's your well-to-do citizen lived comfortably out of town in the suburbs, commuting back and forth to work on the railroad. Later he traveled by automobile, only again to be confronted by the impossible problem of parking areas in the business section of the city. Meanwhile, with a traction system more and more hopelessly inadequate, the fares for transportation and the discomforts of travel increased side by side.

In painting, a good craftsman, G. P. A. Healy, an Illinoisan by adoption, whose work still adorns the Newberry Library in Chicago, had early begun to teach his fellow-citizens the enjoyment to be won from it. In 1862 he set on foot a movement toward a free art gallery which was incorporated in 1865. The Academy of Design followed in 1868. In 1879 began the Art Institute, whose first building was undertaken in 1892. Thenceforth its galleries represented the developing artistic tastes of the Chicago millionaires who were the contributors to its collections. In the nineties they collected and donated the Dutch masters with their satisfying meticulous detail, the French sentimentalists like Millet, Jules Breton, and Rosa Bonheur, the pretty nudes of Bougereau, and the natty soldiers of the Franco-Prussian War by Meissonier and Detaille. They progressed through George Inness' later and mistier American landscapes to the great "Assumption" of El Greco, to Manet, Monet, Rousseau, and to the Italian, French, German, and Spanish primitives—as representative a collection as can be found in the Americas.

Great numbers of the foreign-born settlers in the state brought with them an appreciation of the finest in classical music. The state's first orchestra was established in 1857. Theodore Thomas, who came to the United States in 1845, first brought his orchestra to Chicago in 1869. In 1891 he became exclusively identified with Chicago, having been invited to conduct an orchestra which would have its expenses guaranteed by public-spirited citizens. Within a few weeks before his death in 1905 the Chicago Symphony Orchestra had established itself in its own building on the Lake Front. As early as 1855 Belleville boasted a *Sängerbund*. Twenty years later a three-day *Sängerfest* was held in Springfield by competing choruses. Conservatories of music arose at Jacksonville, at Galesburg, and at Evanston.

Public exhibitions evolved from the traveling juggler or acrobat to the circus—Barnum's Grand Colossal Museum and Menagerie toured Illinois in 1853. In two seasons five different circuses showed at Springfield. More conventional theatricals waited upon the existence of halls in which they could show. As soon as theaters were built, traveling companies appeared, with actors and actresses of wide reputation. In 1857 James H. McVicker built the first modern theater in Chicago, beginning a series that reached its architectural climax with Louis Sullivan's Auditorium in 1889, which became the original home of grand opera and of the Theodore Thomas orchestra.

In spectator sports Chicago had its first baseball club as early as 1856; a score of years later its team was a member of the original National League. On November 3, 1877, the *Chicago Tribune* gloomily remarked:

The disclosures contained in our columns this morning, of the rascality practiced by prominent members of some of the leading base-ball nines of the country can be accepted as unfailing evidence that the game of base-ball which for nearly ten years has enjoyed a remarkable popularity has virtually collapsed, so far as the maintenance of paid professional clubs is concerned. The Louisville and St. Louis Clubs are presumably not the only ones which have been corrupted by the gamblers into machines for swindling, and now that investigations are the order of the day they should not stop until a general exposure is brought about. If the dead game is to be buried in disgrace let all the assassins be buried with it.

Yet four years later, on August 28, 1881, the *Tribune* had to admit that Chicago was the principal supporter of the ball game:

The clubs from other places come here in order to share the receipts, or the "gate money," and from their earnings here eke out the scant receipts at the other towns. It is not an unusual thing to have 4,000 to 6,000 idlers at a game in Chicago; the number has reached 8,000, and rarely ever less than 2,000 or 3,000. At other places the number of visitors ranges from 300, to 1,000, the latter being a fair maximum outside of Chicago.

If the Great Fire ushered in the period with a challenge to Chicago's courage and inventiveness, the World's Columbian Exposition of 1893 closed it with a demonstration of her aggressive spirit and her imitative and adaptive capacity. For eight years Chicago organizations devoted themselves to the project of a fair to celebrate the four-hundredth anniversary of the landing of Columbus. Congressional support had to be engaged and other cities aspiring to hold the exposition maneuvered out of the running. A city subscription of ten million dollars assured her triumph. The fair was postponed to 1893, and then opened, a series of dazzling white buildings in which lath and plaster copied the elegances of *beaux-arts* design, with a few more somber and permanent erections scattered amid the lawns and lagoons of Jackson Park by the waters of the lake. In its scope, in the area it covered, in the volume of exhibits, and in the number of visitors it set new standards; and it left the city for a generation to come in the decaying classic loveliness of the old Field Museum in Jackson Park a nostalgic sense of lavish and appealing beauty.

In the field of writing, the existence in Illinois, and particularly in Chicago, of a distinctive group of literary craftsmen was coming to public notice. As early as January, 1869, there appeared the *Western Monthly*, which was "intended to be purely an institution of the West" and expected to "explore the fields of literature and gather the ripe fruits of . . . pioneer talent." Francis Fisher Browne acquired title to it and renamed it the *Lakeside Monthly* in January, 1871; during its three years of existence it raised considerable interest in midwestern authors and caused eastern publishers to seek their work. It was the forerunner of other publications. The *Dial*, a magazine of criticism, was begun in 1880; in 1894 the *Chap Book*, first of the miniature magazines, made its appearance. In 1912 Harriet Monroe began the publication of *Poetry*, devoted exclusively to poetry, paying its contributors and giving encouragement to new experiments in verse-writing. Margaret Anderson in 1914 began the *Little Review*, which remained in Chicago until 1917, when it was moved elsewhere. Development of these periodicals, interest in the World's Fair, and other conditions led to the formation of a literary group whose work began to be published. Probably the first of these in reputation was Theodore Dreiser, whose early novels are laid in the Chicago scene. His contemporaries rated most highly Henry B. Fuller, whose years of residence in Europe produced *The Chevalier of Pensieri-Vani*, but whose knowledge of Chicago provided the setting for his realistic novels, *The Cliff Dwellers* and *With the Procession*. Others writing in and about Chicago were Hamlin Garland; Frank Norris, in his novel of the wheat market, *The*

Pit; Robert Herrick, in the *Common Lot* and other novels; Sherwood Anderson; Edith Wyatt, whom William Dean Howells called an American Jane Austen; and others. William Vaughn Moody was perhaps best known of the poets; as a dramatist, too, his plays—notably *The Great Divide*—had popular recognition. His wife, Harriet Tilden Moody, who under the spur of sudden poverty achieved a notable business career, for years maintained their home as a center for all writers, musicians, and artists.

The Chicago newspapers developed special writers and columnists, a series of compounders of matchless trivia that are occasionally genius. First among them were Eugene Field, who found a medium in the *Daily News* for his "Sharps and Flats," and Bert Leston Taylor, originator of the column "A Line o' Type or Two," in the *Chicago Tribune*. Both writers brought a solid and appreciative background in the classics and literature and a close connection with daily life of their readers. Also noteworthy were Finley Peter Dunn, the recorder of Mr. Dooley on the affairs of the universe, and George Ade and the cartoonist John T. McCutcheon, whose joint production of *Fables in Slang* struck with precision in word and picture at the heart of midwestern life and thought.

Downstate Illinois produced two men in the period who expressed the life around them in poetry: Vachel Lindsay, who forever fashioned songs which he hoped an unexpressive democracy might be taught to sing, and Edgar Lee Masters, whose epitaphs of the Illinois pioneers sometimes smell of the charnel-house and sometimes of lilies. The expansive Carl Sandburg of Galesburg, of Chicago, and of the United States ranges from song to history. All this literary activity in Illinois was cited by H. L. Mencken in 1920 in the *London Nation* when he declared that there had been scarcely a literary movement in the United States in twenty or thirty years that had not originated in the shadow of the stockyards.

CHAPTER XIV

Politics from Grant to Wilson

THE politics of 1870–90 seem remote from the real questions of the period. While the state was struggling with a series of problems caused by its growth, political parties were contending on issues of the Civil War and reconstruction, appealing to old partisan loyalties, parading enthusiasm to certain striking personalities, and using the vital state issues only as stalking horses. Only occasionally does a man like Palmer appear, with an appreciation of the deeper questions of the time; and necessarily he walks athwart regular party lines in his course.

The Republican party of 1870 was not by any means the Republican party of 1854, of 1856, or even of 1860. Democratic converts like Logan had entered it to outdo in vehemence the founders and make them feel out of place. Because a man had the type of mind that sensed danger from an aggressive slave power in 1856, he was not necessarily disposed in 1870 to make the beaten South pay to the uttermost farthing. Such men could see too many unclean spirits that had fattened off the blood of the men who had given their lives to the Union clustering around the party for protection. Tariff-protected manufacturers, financial manipulators who had grown rich during the Civil War, were shouting the most lustily for the ideals of 1860, although, when those ideals had been at stake, other men had struggled and sacrificed for them. The liberal Republican movement represented a protest for cleaner politics and for freeing the party from the big businessmen and protectionists who dominated it.

The election of 1870 passed without much comment. The disaffected Republicans supported the Democrat, S. S. Hayes, for congressman-at-large against John L. Beveridge; but Beveridge won handily by twenty thousand. The senatorial election of 1870 resolved itself into a contest between two Civil War heroes, popular, lovable, and beloved men both, Richard J. Oglesby and John A. Logan, in which Logan was successful. Logan, the "Black Eagle," had atoned for his earlier democracy and copperheadism by his gallantry in the war; he was the ideal of the old soldier. To be told that John A. Logan needed his vote would bring a Negro or old soldier voter out under any circumstance. That Logan was accused of spoils politics and was vehement rather than statesman-like made no difference to his admirers.

There were men in his party who saw him in a different and less favorable light. The *Chicago Tribune* of January 22, 1879, wrote:

Logan is a sort of Republican Voorhees. A demagogue originally of the same breezy, primitive Western type, though by reason of being a Republican demagogue under the restraint of the somewhat more intelligent opinion of his party, in a section which it must be confessed is not distinguished among the nations of the earth by a high grade of popular intelligence, with the physical traits and bearing which romancers are fond of attributing to their heroes, the swarthy, long-haired, and black-eyed political General and martial politician—who still carries on the War against the Rebellion in full regimentals at the head of his corps in the politics of Illinois—impresses the popular imagination of the Suckers more as a fine martial figure sustaining intimate and patriotic relations with the American Eagle than by his intellectual qualities or his value as a political leader. He is a half-educated, distinguished-looking humbug, with a gift of meretricious glibness on the stump, whose smooth and sonorous inconsequences pass for eloquence and wisdom with the popular audiences. . . .

There was widespread dissatisfaction with the national administration under Grant, the gold ring, the whiskey ring, the various other scandals developing, the appointments of members of Grant's family to office, the abrogation of the civil service principle. Even the *Chicago Tribune* became independent. A general revolt against the Grant administration impended, led by John M. Palmer, Lyman Trumbull, John Wentworth, Jesse W. Fell, and Judge David Davis. Palmer had already crossed blades with Grant in behalf of the dignity of the state when the President at the time of the Chicago Fire had sent troops to Chicago without their being requested by the governor. At the Cincinnati Liberal Republican convention Davis and Trumbull both claimed the support of the Illinois delegation. The delegation split its vote between them; then, because it hesitated too long in turning to Charles Francis Adams of Massachusetts, the nomination fell to Horace Greeley. There was little chance of carrying the Republicans of the West, dissatisfied with Republican high tariffs, for an ardent protectionist like Greeley. The Democrats in Illinois as elsewhere indorsed the ticket in spite of Greeley's long Whig and Republican record, but without enthusiasm.

In the state race Oglesby and Beveridge ran on the Republican ticket for governor and lieutenant-governor. To oppose Oglesby, Liberal Republican and Democratic conventions, meeting in Springfield and working in harmony, nominated Gustavus Koerner. This placated the Germans; but the farmers, the discontented element in which alone lay the chance of Liberal Republican success, did not expect more of their desired legislation from Democrats than from Republicans, and the convention platform evaded the tariff issue. Oglesby won on the state and Grant on the national ticket, Grant's vote running 241,936 to 184,884. The result showed the state was still Republican, tariff and all.

Oglesby in 1873 accepted election to the Senate, leaving Beveridge to fill out his term as governor; "the quiet-mannered and wonderfully astute graybeard now rattling around in the

Governor's chair," the *Cairo Bulletin* called him. In 1876, however, Beveridge lost the nomination for governor to Shelby M. Cullom. The Democrats indorsed the Greenback candidates for governor and auditor, Lewis Steward and John Hise, and nominated their own men for other offices; greenbackism was the thing they had to trust now to break the Republican strength as they had trusted liberal republicanism four years before. The Greenback movement offered a strong appeal to the state. Farmers, vainly seeking loans, pressed to find interest to pay on mortgages, readily listened to asseverations that there was not enough money in the country. Wage-earners, counting their few dollars' pay, were reminded of the flush days of the sixties when greenbacks flourished and apparently wages were high. So strong was the demand for inflation that Democrats began to have hope of success, especially with an anti-temperance campaign to draw the German vote from the Republicans.

In the end Cullom and Hayes carried the state by a narrow margin. Cullom had but seven thousand majority, not an eighth of what Grant had had four years before. In the Illinois legislature the Greenback group held the balance of power. Palmer and Logan contested the senatorship; but eventually the Democrats turned to David Davis, electing him with the help of the independents. Meanwhile Illinois, like the nation, during the contested election between Hayes and Tilden had reached a pitch of political excitement that almost threatened civil war. That the Democrats acquiesced in the decisions of the electoral commission, in spite of the fact that those decisions are now questioned by impartial students, was a triumph for orderly government.

In the years that followed 1876 the Democrats forgot their new-found affection for the Greenback movement—the "rag baby" of Republican orators. With the Greenbackers drifting off toward the Knights of Labor and more radical labor reform, the Democrats were willing to make a place for both Greenback and anti-Greenback men in their ranks. Both parties were inclined to sneer at the demands of the labor enthusiasts for the eight-hour day and the abolition of child labor. And to satisfy the cry of the workingman and farmer for cheap money a new and more respectable inflationist scheme had arisen—the re-monetization of silver.

For sixty years before 1853 the United States had been trying to keep silver and gold on such a ratio to each other in the coinage that both would stay in circulation. First one and then the other felt the unfavorable ratios and disappeared. From 1853 the United States had tacitly dropped the attempt at bimetallism, the holding of silver equal with gold as the standard. In 1873 a coinage act had omitted the silver dollar from the list of coins to be struck—the famous "crime of '73." For a generation free-silver orators expatiated on the plot of British capital to subject the United States to slavery to British gold or told the man of religion that Congress had wickedly defied God by excluding from the coinage a metal mentioned in his holy word. The silver-mine owner added his enthusiasm; and in the West at first practically all men, Republican and Democratic alike, favored the Bland-Allison silver measure of 1878. Not until the nineties did the western Republicans develop a change of heart on the subject of free silver.

Meanwhile Logan, defying protests against boss rule, was supreme in the Republican party. In 1879 a Republican legislature elected him senator over Oglesby, who came up for re-election. Logan especially lent his influence to the movement to nominate Grant for a third term in 1880. In spite of Republican protests at Logan's domination, the Grant men controlled the state convention and instructed the delegation for him. In the national Republican convention, however, Garfield was un-expectedly put up as a compromise candidate, running against Weaver for the Greenbacks and Hancock for the Democrats. Hancock's declaration that the tariff was a local issue took the heart out of the Democrats, who might still have capitalized the state's dislike of protection. Cullom, the Republican nominee for re-election as governor, was easily successful over Lyman Trumbull, the Democratic candidate, the Greenback candidate holding the balance between them. In 1882 Cullom in his turn left the governor's chair to accept a senatorship, and his thirty years' service in the Senate began. The lieutenant-governor, John M. Hamilton, took his place.

Eighteen eighty-four was a Democratic year in the nation. In Illinois, Oglesby was nominated for governor over Hamilton to contest the election with the elder Carter Harrison, the famous mayor of Chicago. Both sides had now indorsed the demands of labor, the Democrats declaring for the eight-hour day and the right of labor to organize. Logan was indorsed by the state convention for the presidency but ultimately had to accept the vice-presidential nomination on the ticket with Blaine. The Republicans, though successful in the state, lost the national election. The Illinois legislature was closely divided, and one of the most thrilling political contests in the state's history began.

The senate of the General Assembly that convened at Springfield in January, 1885, consisted of twenty-six Republicans, twenty-five Democrats, and one Greenbacker. The house contained seventy-six Republicans, seventy-seven Democrats, and an "independent," E. M. Haines of Lake County. First came the difficulty of organization. Haines was chosen temporary speaker as a compliment. He then blandly with the help of his friend Sittig, a Republican, attempted to retain the office on the ground that the constitution of the state knew but one speaker, the permanent one. After much disorder the Democrats gave way and elected him speaker. Even more serious was the contest over the senatorship, for the sum of the members of both houses on joint ballot, including one doubtful vote on each side, was 102 Democrats and 102 Republicans. The Republicans selected

Logan as their candidate, agreeing to support him to the end. The Democrats, divided between William R. Morrison and Carter Harrison, finally adopted Morrison, and the long contest began. The session dragged on indefinitely; the people of the state became indignant at the farce of the seemingly interminable party struggle.

Twice during the earlier part of the session members had died. On both occasions the members had been replaced by others of similar politics; and on the death of Representative Shaw of the Thirtieth Senatorial District—the counties of Cass, Mason, Schuyler, and Menard—it seemed certain that the same thing would happen, for the district was Democratic by 1,800 or 2,000 majority. To a certain Henry Craske, however, occurred the idea of a "gumshoe" campaign to get the Republican vote out without alarming the Democrats until too late. Logan gave his consent, though skeptical of success. The Republicans put forward no candidate, but a secret campaign through the district warned the Republican voters to turn out to the polls late on the day of the election. Two days before election, men posing as cattle buyers passed through the district distributing to the precincts Republican ballots for William H. Weaver for assemblyman. The Democrats were not alarmed until too late to get out their vote, and Weaver won by a few hundred. He was immediately seated, and Logan was elected to the senate.

The state election of 1888 resolved itself into a contest between "Private Joe" Fifer, the Republican candidate, an old soldier who, in an age of political generals, enjoyed the distinction indicated by his nickname, and John M. Palmer. Palmer once more took a decidedly prolabor point of view. He had the clear-sightedness to lay a part of the trouble of 1886 in Chicago to the Pinkertons and the police. But Illinois was now a normally Republican state, and Fifer as well as Benjamin Harrison on the national ticket was duly elected; two years later, however, the fifty farmer-members elected by the Farmers' Mutual Benefit Association held the balance of power in the house, and, in a three-cornered battle for the senatorship between Palmer and Republican and farmer candidates, Palmer was elected on March 12, 1891.

In 1892 Fifer was again the logical candidate of the Republicans; his Democratic opponent was the remarkable John P. Altgeld, German by birth, a man rich by his own exertions, social and political reformer, labor sympathizer, and radical by nature, whose motives were pronounced by his best friends a strange medley of high ideals and personal prejudices, a man in whom intellect and emotion were strangely mixed. As Palmer had done in 1888, Altgeld strove to keep out of Illinois gubernatorial elections the old Republican issues of Civil War and reconstruction and to pin the canvas to the questions of legislative and social reform that directly concerned the state. He adopted the public and parochial school issue as his main platform; both the state and the national Democratic candidates were successful.

With 1893 opened the first Democratic state administration since the Civil War under Governor Altgeld. A tremendous dissatisfaction with the Republican party had carried into power a political liberal who in turn roused discontent. Men grew tired of the high hopes of the idealist which hardly comported with defalcations that took place under him, and in 1896 the Democrats went out of office to stay out for four terms. William Jennings Bryan, then in the first flush of youthful enthusiasm, was preaching the cause of the masses against the classes on the old issue of cheap money, this time in the form of free silver. In 1896 and again in 1900 on this issue he lost the state to McKinley. In those years, respectively, John A. Tanner and Richard Yates, son of the war governor, were elected to the governorship over Altgeld and Samuel Alschuler. The Republican vote mounted, Alschuler, the most successful of the Democrats, falling 60,000 behind his opponent. In 1904 the Republican majority for President and governor rose to 300,000. It was the "Roosevelt" year when Charles S. Deneen, nominated for governor after a hard convention struggle, ran against Lawrence B. Stringer. In 1908, however, with Deneen running against Adlai E. Stevenson, former Vice-President with Cleveland, this majority was cut to 23,000; but Taft beat Bryan in the state by 179,000.

In these years the political composition of the congressional delegation had fluctuated. For the Congress elected in 1890 under dissatisfaction with the McKinley tariff it numbered six Republicans and fourteen Democrats. In 1892 the Democrats had to be content with one-half the delegation. In 1896 they could elect but four out of twenty-two. In 1894 they had not a single member. After the Roosevelt landslide of 1904 they had but one.

The general assemblies showed smaller fluctuations; the principle of minority representation assured the minority party a respectable strength in the house, however weak it might be in the senate.

Briefly, the bipartisan wars of Republican and Democrat were interrupted by the meteoric course of the Progressive movement of 1912-16. Liberals of all shades from Theodore Roosevelt to Jane Addams met in harmony, ignoring the fundamental difference of their views of the universe, to push a program of liberal reform, political, legal, and social. The term "social justice" was vague and meant many different things; but the enthusiasm of a crusade for righteousness swept through the country and Illinois as well. Point had been given to it in Illinois by the unseating of William Lorimer in 1912 by the United States Senate on the ground that corrupt interests had brought about his election through bribery of the state legislature in 1909.

It was at Chicago in the Republican national convention that the Progressive movement began. The contest between Taft and Roosevelt for the control of the convention and the nomination had led to a series of contesting delegations; alleging votes were unjustly taken from Roosevelt by the national committee, the revolting Roosevelt forces refused to vote on the nomination, assailing the presiding officer with jeers when their delegations were called. After the convention had renominated Taft and adjourned, the Roosevelt forces met at Orchestra Hall to launch the movement that became the Progressive party and put Roosevelt in the field as a third candidate against Taft and Wilson. For a time there was doubt as to whether a candidate for governor should be run against Deneen, who had supported Roosevelt up to the point of revolting from the party; the decision was made, however, to run Frank Funk. With the state Republican party divided on both governor and President, the election of Woodrow Wilson, liberal enough to hold the Democrats in line, and of Judge Edward F. Dunne as governor was assured. In the General Assembly elected in 1912 the Democrats had ninety-six votes in joint ballot, the Republicans seventy-seven, and the Progressives twenty-eight. A coalition of Democrats and Republicans elected L. Y. Sherman, Republican, and James Hamilton Lewis, Democrat, United States senators.

In Illinois the Progressive movement sank away a little more slowly than it arose. The liberalism of Wilson's administration carried away some of it, the rest under the issues of the war was reabsorbed in the Republican party by the election of 1916. In that year the normal Republican majority in Illinois reasserted itself, and Frank O. Lowden was elected governor over Dunne, the state electoral vote going to Hughes as against Wilson. In 1920 the Republicans swept the state for both governor and President, in spite of the fact that the nomination of their candidate, Len Small, had come about after a bitter contest with the faction headed by Lowden; the two groups warred on each other savagely during the whole course of Small's administration.

The Spanish-American War fell in the period we are considering. Save for the wave of patriotic enthusiasm it called out, it did not affect Illinois deeply. Nine regiments of infantry, one of cavalry, and a battery of artillery were the state's quota. Of these, the First Infantry served in the Santiago campaign, the Third and the battery in Puerto Rico, the Sixth in Cuba and Puerto Rico, and the Eighth and Ninth in Cuba.

From the point of view of government the history of the period is better studied with regard to certain movements for change in political organization. Chief among these was the demand for constitutional amendment or revision. The constitution of 1870, ably framed for the Illinois of its day, an agricultural community with one large city, was quite inadequate for a commonwealth as much interested in manufacture and commerce as in agriculture and containing a world metropolis. The framers of the constitution, satisfied with the work of their hands, had made amendment difficult; an amendment must be submitted by two-thirds of each house of the General Assembly and ratified by a majority of those voting at the next election; amendments could be submitted to but one article at a time; and no two for the same article could be submitted within four years. Before the State Ballot Act of 1891 amendment was easier, because in the ballots furnished by political parties before that year amendments were usually submitted as affirmative propositions, and all votes not cast specifically against them were counted for them. After 1891, unless a voter on the official ballot expressed his opinion specifically for the proposition, his vote was counted against it. Lack of interest on the part of voters thenceforth would insure the defeat of an amendment.

After 1891, too, it became increasingly difficult to secure a two-thirds majority of the legislature for any proposed amendment. Sectional interests, Chicago versus downstate, financial interests, and privileged interests generally were likely to be engaged pro or con on any given amendment; and it was not difficult in a legislature with houses chosen on fundamentally different principles to secure a dissenting one-third in one or the other house. Worse than this, rival amendments contended at session after session to be the one the Assembly was permitted to submit; and the groups supporting them worked each for its own and against the others. The so-called "gateway" amendment to amend the amending clause, offered session after session, was always sidetracked in the Assembly or defeated at the polls. Three times in thirty years attempts were made to call a convention to frame a new constitution; in 1893 and in 1901 resolutions were voted down in the Assembly. In 1917, however, a convention resolution passed the Assembly and eighteen months later was adopted by the voters. The convention met in 1920, carried on its work intermittently for two years, and finally submitted a complete constitution to the people. Much could be said against it on various points, and strong groups and classes of the electorate were mustered in opposition; it was overwhelmingly defeated.

The defects in the constitution of 1870 were numerous. Many technical objections could be alleged to the judicial clauses. Its revenue article providing for a uniform tax on all property, fair enough in the agricultural commonwealth of 1870, allowed vast amounts of intangible personal property to escape. Its restrictions on municipalities and their debts prevented a thoroughgoing development of Chicago. The system of minority representation permitted each voter to cast three votes for members of the house of representatives of the General Assembly for one, two, or three candidates. Accordingly, under any circumstances one-third the voters might insure the election of one assemblyman. In practice a much smaller fraction might often do it. The system was one of vicious minority overrepresentation. The constitution left no opening for improvements on republican government such as the initiative and referendum, the latest political fashion in the earlier twentieth century. It pretended to achieve democracy by setting the voters in state and local elections to fill a long list of offices, supremely ignorant as to their functions, or as to how far the men for whom they voted

STARVED ROCK

Site of Fort St. Louis under La Salle and Tonty, 1682–91, is now an Illinois State Park

Courtesy of Illinois Department of Conservation

ARGONNE NATIONAL LABORATORY, ARGONNE, ILLINOIS

Courtesy of Argonne National Laboratory

were qualified to perform them. Every four years it set voters to pass on the qualifications of a secretary of state with whose office they had come in contact merely to apply for automobile licenses and an auditor of public accounts with whose office they had probably had no relation at all.

Meanwhile for a half century after the constitution of 1870 was adopted the administrative system of the state grew more and more cumbersome. The constitution provided a simple list of administrative officers: governor, lieutenant-governor, secretary of state, auditor of public accounts, treasurer, superintendent of public instruction, attorney-general. But, as one private activity after another required regulation, additional professions and occupations had to be licensed, more special industries and public utilities had to be supervised, special officers, boards, paid and unpaid, were heaped up until the number reached over a hundred. Every regulating statute created its board to administer it.

The situation finally stood revealed in all its absurdity in the report of the Efficiency and Economy Commission of 1913–15. In large measure based on this report was the Consolidation Act of 1917. This act, leaving untouched the older constitutional offices—secretary of state, auditor, superintendent of public instruction, attorney-general—until a constitutional convention could deal with them, set beside them new departments, the heads to hold office for four years by appointment of governor and senate. Of these departments, that of finance was intrusted with a state budget; agriculture, labor, mines and minerals, trade and commerce, and public health had the functions implied by their names. Registration and education took over the license examinations for physicians, pharmacists, and others and maintained a general supervision of the normal schools and scientific surveys. The Department of Public Works had control of buildings, highways, parks, state printing, and the purchase of supplies.

The state's charitable institutions had been under the advisory control of a state board of charities since 1869; in 1909 a state charities' commission with powers of visitation was linked with a state board of administration to replace all local boards. The Department of Public Welfare was given responsibility for all charitable hospital and penal institutions, as well as for pardons and paroles. Under the various departments were grouped the few surviving separate boards in more or less dependent relations. The act was a long step toward a modern scientific state government, but unfortunately the constitutional convention failed to adjust it to the older offices, leaving them to function as before.

By 1920 Illinois had finally achieved a good state civil service organization. The history of civil service reform in Illinois begins with the act of 1895 allowing the adoption of the system in cities. It was so adopted by Chicago, Evanston, Springfield, and Waukegan. Naturally the system was most important with respect to Chicago, where it has remained in a precarious situation, continually invalidated by the use of sixty-day permits to keep in office persons without due qualifications. In 1901 the Cook County Civil Service Commission was convicted of malfeasance in office. In 1911 the Cook County civil service system was extended to all county employees; but the act was declared unconstitutional as unduly passed. State civil service came more slowly but surely. In 1905 it was applied to all charitable institutions. In 1910 the question of a state-wide civil service was carried in a popular public policy vote; and in 1911 an act was passed. It secured their positions to all incumbents, but provided for competitive examinations which in the case of certain scientific posts were "unassembled," consisting of questions as to training and experience. For the first six years of the act employees could be removed only by charges and trial. After 1917 the appointing authority could remove, subject to appeal that the removal was due to religious, racial, or political reasons.

Reforms between 1890 and 1920 revolutionized the suffrage

of the state. Before the Australian Ballot Act of 1891, parties supplied their own ballots and made nominations independent of any legal control. With 1891 the state began to recognize in law the party system that had existed since 1834 in practice. An official ballot was provided on which candidates were to be listed under their party labels; and a system of nominating conventions was prescribed.

The defects of the nominating convention and the possibility of packing it caused an agitation for direct primaries to choose party tickets. Primary acts passed in 1905, 1906, 1908, were declared unconstitutional by the state supreme court. An act passed in 1910 stood the test; but it could not be applied to judicial nominations, which, with the drawing-up of party platforms, was still performed by nominating conventions. In 1901 provision was made for the submission to the voters, on petition of 10 per cent of the voters of the state or 25 per cent of those of any district, questions of public policy not more than three in number on a ballot; but there was no compulsion on the legislature to pass measures corresponding in case of an affirmative vote.

The period saw the establishment of woman suffrage. In 1891 women were allowed to vote in school elections. In 1909 they were permitted to be candidates for all school offices from which they were not barred by constitutional provision. In 1913 they were allowed to vote for all political offices not constitutional in their origin, the most important being presidential elector. Since the ratification of the Nineteenth Amendment to the federal Constitution they have been permitted to vote for all offices.

An early effect of their franchise was to extend the prohibition area over the state. In 1907 a law permitting votes on local option in villages, towns, etc., was passed; dry areas spread steadily, increasing greatly in the election of 1913, with the women voting for the first time. The federal Volstead Act of 1919 and a state enforcement act almost as rigid made the sale or manufacture for consumption of alcoholic liquors generally unlawful. For years the state Antisaloon League campaigned for the defeat of "wet" and the election of "dry" candidates; and in the state General Assembly the designation of "wet" and "dry" cut across parties and factions alike.

In some respects the most remarkable part of Illinois's legislative record during the period was labor legislation. The beginnings had been made earlier. The first regulation of mines and mining, early recognized as a dangerous occupation, was enacted in 1872. In 1883 a board of examiners of mining and state mining inspectors was established. In 1899, 1910, and 1913 the law was further expanded and codified. In 1891 the state's first child labor law was passed, setting the age limit at thirteen; it remained a dead letter, but by act of 1893 a department of factories and workshops was created to enforce it; the age limit was raised to fourteen, with supervision of children of fourteen to sixteen. In 1903 the act was made still more stringent, limiting employment during school sessions and in certain places and occupations. In 1904 child labor in Illinois mines came to an end.

An eight-hour clause for women in the act of 1893 was declared unconstitutional, but ten-hour laws for women were passed in 1909 and 1911. A law providing all possible safeguards against occupational diseases passed in 1911, and workmen's compensation laws in 1911, 1913, and 1917. Even earlier, in 1899 free state employment agencies had been created. Generally by 1920 Illinois ranked high among the states in its labor legislation.

The thirty years after 1893 saw great masses of legislation passed compared with the meager output of 1872–93. This was done chiefly in the comparatively narrow biennial legislative sessions between the first week in January and the last week in June. Necessarily the influence of individual members on legislation declined as that of committees and of the steering organizations of the house and senate increased. Since 1937 the Legislative Council, with ten representatives from each house and a permanent staff, has served as an interim organization to make factual studies of matters of legislative concern.

Two outside influences had increasing weight in legislation. The Illinois Supreme Court, as appears by the foregoing narrative, exercised freely its power of declaring laws unconstitutional. Between 1870 and 1913 it decided against the constitutionality of laws in 257 out of 789 cases. The governor too, since 1884 possessed of the power to veto separate items of appropriation, has exercised an increasing influence. Passage of acts or items over his veto became impossible as the great mass of legislation was passed only on the eve of the June adjournment. Further, the system of minority representation rendered it practically impossible for any party even to approach a two-thirds majority in the house of representatives; and the danger of an overwhelming majority becoming undisciplined or rebellious did not exist. At the close of the first hundred years of its statehood, the Illinois General Assembly was in a state of relative subordination to governor and supreme court, almost the reverse of its commanding position in 1818.

CHAPTER XV

The First World War

IN A sense the story of Illinois as a distinct social and economic entity may be said to end with the first World War. The organization of the United States for victory in 1917–18 necessitated vast extensions of federal agencies in regions hitherto left to the state, to the municipality, or to individual enterprise. The day when a citizen might live a normal life without ever coming in contact with any federal agency except the post office passed, never to return. The depression beginning in 1929 and the measures of the New Deal to counteract it resulted in so overwhelming an extension of federal control over the economic activities of the individual that the state became merely one segment of a vast amorphous mass. Although in World War II part of the machinery of World War I was copied, its working was altogether different. The military as well as the civilian contribution of the state was swallowed up in anonymity.

There can be no question but that the deciding factor of the first World War was the weight in soldiers, munitions, money, foodstuffs, and above all in intelligence and moral enthusiasm contributed by the United States in 1917–18. In this contribution the state of Illinois was of supreme importance, far greater than her relative mass in the nation would indicate. Situated as she was at the heart of the Mississippi Valley, almost the first in the Union in agriculture, third in manufacturing, with one of the largest foreign and especially German populations, everything depended on her attitude. Were she to "fight backwardly" as Kentucky and Maryland had done in 1861–65, were her allegiance divided, the resources of the nation would be disastrously crippled at the start. Possibly a part of those resources would have to be diverted to hold her neuter in the struggle. When she outdid herself in contribution, victory was assured. The way of her contribution and the measure of it are here to be told.

The moral issues involved in World War I cannot be adequately appraised until future historians have finally come to an agreement as to the causes that in August, 1914, sent three hundred and fifty million Europeans at one another's throats and eventually drew into the whirlpool well-nigh all the peoples of the earth save Spanish South America and a few of the lesser states of Europe. But the people of Illinois and the Union from the first passed moral judgments as to the origin of the conflict; they were far from unanimous in them. The mass of the people of Illinois condemned Germany from the beginning for the violation of Belgium, for the lurid tales of atrocities inflicted deliberately on civilian populations, and for the schemes of world conquest ascribed to the German militarists.

The Americans of German extraction, on the other hand, insisted bitterly that the Fatherland was striving desperately to free itself from the insidious encircling web of diplomacy woven by Isvolsky, Poincaré, and Sir Edward Grey; they decried the tales of atrocity and maintained the invasion of Belgium to have been a commonplace of European military theory for twenty years. The difference passed beyond argument to emotion. On the one hand were those of German blood, on the other those whose racial antecedents led to England, Italy, Russia, and the subject peoples of the Dual Monarchy.

The weapons of war employed by Germany only deepened the hostility of her American opponents. The introduction of poison gas and of submarine attacks on merchant vessels seemed brutal, lawless, and violent compared with Great Britain's aggressions on neutral commerce and her blockade of neutral Continental ports. The sinking of the "Lusitania" in 1915 and the loss of American citizens on board swept the country to the verge of war. The President attempted by diplomatic means to obtain reparation and security for the future. A pledge was finally obtained in 1916. But the conviction that all government in Germany was subordinated to a ruthless, headstrong, military group gained headway when the limitations on submarine warfare were denounced by Germany in January, 1917. In spite of the fact that in 1916 Woodrow Wilson had been re-elected on the slogan "He kept us out of war," the President could no longer hold back the tide that was sweeping us in.

The greater part of the American people would doubtless have been content to air their moral condemnation of Germany without actual resort to war. Most intelligent people regarded the declaration of war of April 6, 1917, as merely a gesture of support for the winning side, until the Allied missions revealed the fact that the submarine blockade was fearfully effective, that Russia, beaten again and again in the field, had at last disintegrated in a radical revolution, and that the whole strength of the United States was required to avert a crushing defeat.

The necessities now seemed clear. There could be no question that the triumph of Germany would leave a militarist clique in charge of the destinies of Europe. In Germany there seemed to be no hands able to hold them back if they won. Wilson therefore sounded in his war message and in other state papers the call to a crusade for democracy against militarism, the war to end war. Assured that Armageddon was at hand, the American people rallied at his call for the conflict.

There was a minority of opposition stronger in Illinois than elsewhere to this program. Five of the fifty congressmen who voted against war were from Illinois. The vast mass of Germans by birth and descent acquiesced loyally in the war; but a small minority took up the trade of the spy and sower of sedition. Many genuine pacifists like Jane Addams and Jenkin Lloyd Jones, himself a veteran of the Civil War, believed the war unnecessary. The Socialists opposed it, as did the Industrial Workers of the World, the radical labor group whose national headquarters were in Chicago. The then mayor of Chicago was reluctant, doubtful alike of the draft and of the dispatch of American troops to Europe. And the meeting of the People's Council in Chicago in September, 1917, to insist on a statement of terms of peace, dissolved only under a threat of military action by the governor.

These elements of dissent were silenced sooner or later. The American Protective League, a volunteer secret service organization, originated in Chicago and at one time had thirteen thousand operatives in the city who ran down one hundred thousand cases of suspects for disloyalty and draft evasion. German aliens were registered on February 4 and June 17, 1918, and were barred from certain zones save with special permit. A widespread refusal to register for the draft at Rockford was dealt with by prosecutions. The Department of Justice from July to September, 1917, checked the activities of the Socialists, suppressing their newspaper; the headquarters of the IWW were raided in September, 1917; and in 1918 numerous convictions of radical leaders were obtained on indictments for disloyalty. In some of these proceedings there is no question that judicial agencies overstepped the bounds of free speech and freedom of the press; but in modern war all are combatants, and among civilians and soldiers alike uniformity of thought on the war becomes a military necessity. Practical unanimity of expression in the form of support of the war was one way or another attained.

A very important part in the organization of Illinois for war was played by Governor Frank O. Lowden. When early in February diplomatic relations with Germany were broken, he appeared before the General Assembly to urge united support of the President. In large measure he was responsible for the creation of the State Council of Defense by act approved May 2, 1917. The council so created consisted of fifteen members, representing capital, labor, and all the large interests of the state, and itself organized all the state's resources for victory. Under it functioned the whole improvised civilian war organization of the state. It had to complain that federal agencies instead of using the organization sought to supersede it; but that was remedied by executive order in August, 1918.

It would require a volume to cover adequately the manifold activities in which the State Council of Defense engaged or the organizations created by it or affiliated to it to carry on its work. It co-operated with the Red Cross, the U.S. Treasury Department, the Federal Food and Fuel Administration, the National Security League, a "preparedness" organization antedating the war, and the Four-Minute Men, the last being an organization of four-minute speakers at theaters, churches, and lodges who week by week explained the government policy and invoked support of enlistment, Liberty Loans, Red Cross, and other war activities. The State Council of Defense created county auxiliary committees to function as its executives throughout the counties. Affiliated with it was a woman's committee whose activities may be measured by its subcommittees of Allied relief, Americanization, child welfare, training women for special work, food conservation, publicity, speakers, war information, and women and children in industry. On September 2–15, 1918, the State Council of Defense held a great war government exposition at Chicago, the proceeds of which went into the coffers of the federal department of publicity.

Among the first problems that confronted it were those of food and fuel. War industries were sure to demand vast amounts of coal; the railroads, crippled in equipment and burdened with extraordinary demands for transportation, foresaw difficulty in the winter. Coal prices went up. The operators, anxious to keep them up, repudiated an agreement to arbitrate them, hoping for higher prices from the federal fuel administration; and the governor considered taking over the mines in the state as a war measure. A conference of councils of defense of the thirteen northwestern states interested in the western coal fields was held with a view to concerted action, which was abandoned only on learning that a federal fuel administration was to be installed. Thenceforth in Illinois as elsewhere coal of various grades was rationed at fixed prices according to the relative importance of the industries that used it. Even so there were fuel shortage and suffering, lightless nights and heatless days, during the bitterly cold winter of 1918.

Food was an even more serious problem. Food production in the Allied and neutral countries of Europe had been falling short. Crops of 1917 were below average, and the United States was confronted with the problem of feeding Europe at the same time that it drew great armies from the harvest fields. The problem presented itself from two different angles, conservation and economy in the use of foods, especially wheat, sugar, beef, and pork, and increased production.

To economize in the use of food a direct campaign was launched at the housewife, teaching her the necessity of avoiding waste and using substitutes for the crucial foods. That such an appeal should have been so effective would have seemed almost unbelievable before 1917. In no European country would it have succeeded. Eight hundred and fifty thousand pledge cards were signed in Illinois guaranteeing co-operation with the Federal Food Administration. Wheatless days and meatless days were thus enforced in restaurant and home alike. The Federal Food Administration in Illinois was further engaged in rationing to dealers wheat flours and sugar and proceeding against violators of the regulations in this class.

More important than this was the positive campaign for the increase of food production. Even with the lure of high prices, the mighty shift by which Illinois in a year changed her main crop from corn to wheat is an amazing example of the triumph of organization and propaganda. The wheat crop of Illinois increased 100 per cent from 1917 to 1918, while her corn crop fell off from 418,000,000 to 344,350,000 bushels. The steering of a course between producer and consumer in regulating prices was not always easy, and the producers complained of a disposition to recede from prices fairly fixed; but even at that the results in increase of food production would before the war have seemed impossible.

This was done, too, in the face of the withdrawal of labor for the armies. The draft regulations, it is true, granted deferred classification to those engaged in agriculture; but they were not always enforced and at the best subtracted much labor. Some of this was accounted for by putting city boys to work on the farms as a patriotic duty; a woman's land movement was little more than a gesture, and the greatest part of the result was ascribable to the more efficient manipulation of experienced labor already available.

The State Council of Defense was responsible in March, 1918, for initiating a movement to direct to western factories a part of the vast flood of government war contracts. Already before 1917 Allied nations had placed contracts in Illinois for wheeled transportation, shell cases, shell forgings, and cartridges. Now a flood of government orders of all imaginable sorts taxed factories to their capacities. In some cases the government itself provided firms with additional factory and housing space to deal with its orders. Statistics are fragmentary, but, of orders exceeding $100,000 in amount, $890,000,000 was placed in Illinois by the War Department exclusive of $26,000,000 spent in camp construction. The navy alone expended $20,000,000 on additional construction in the state.

An important phase of the state's war activity was the floating of the five Liberty Loans. The organizations for these were developed on the basis of the two Federal Reserve districts, the Seventh, or Chicago, and the Eighth, or St. Louis, within which the state lies. Within each of these the ramifications reached down to the county organizations, which attempted to equal or exceed set quotas based on population, wealth, banking assets, and other criteria. Starting with a rudimentary organization for the first loan, the organization became more and more elaborate for successive loans as the quotas increased. It became advisable to get as many purchasers as possible in order to encourage thrift and to prevent demands for luxuries from diverting industry from the filling of government war contracts.

To this end campaigns were launched with posters, competitions, speaking, every imaginable advertising device to force home on the individual the duty of purchasing. In many places individual quotas were set and the individual expected to subscribe accordingly. The banks made arrangements to carry purchasers on partial payments. The result is told by the figures. In the northern part of the state, included in the Seventh District, the sales run from $195,685,200 in the first loan subscribed by 280,000 persons, to $250,000,000 on the second and 661,104 subscribers, $247,662,250 on the third with 1,417,131 subscribers, $424,112,000 on the fourth from 1,866,064 subscribers, and $332,323,200 on the fifth from 1,130,854 subscribers. Not all these sums were actually allotted.

The Eighth District with the southern counties of the state fell short of its quota on the first loan but subscribed to the remaining four a total of some $130,000,000. The number of subscribers increased from 54,125 in the second to 190,430 in the third, 258,282 on the fourth, and 73,768 on the fifth.

As a further incentive to economy, war savings stamps were put on sale in December, 1917; thrift stamps at twenty-five cents, war savings stamps at $4.12 to $4.25 were sold in Illinois to the amount of $73,000,000.

To the colorful civilian Illinois of the war days, noisy with bands, eloquent with four-minute and noonday speakers urging this and that cause or conservation, glowing with posters adjuring to every patriotic duty from enlistment to buying war savings stamps, the organization charged with the welfare of our own fighting forces and those of the Allies added their appeal. The Red Cross in membership campaigns of December, 1917 and 1918, gained paid annual memberships of 1,298,111 and 1,194,472, respectively. In drives for funds in June, 1917, and May, 1918, it acquired $5,638,074 and $10,524,422. Its functions in Illinois included relief to soldiers' families, instruction clinics, preparation of dressings, garments for refugees, and the enrolment of trained nurses.

The Young Men's Christian Association took over the maintenance of canteen service and recreation and amusement at the Great Lakes Naval Training Station, Camp Grant, Fort Sheridan, and other camps. The Knights of Columbus, the Jewish Welfare Board, and the Salvation Army carried on similar duties on a smaller scale. The Young Women's Christian Association maintained hostess houses at the camps and looked after women engaged in war work. The American Library Association collected and bought books and provided libraries for the books in this country and in France. These organizations combined in the latter part of 1918 to raise money in a United War Work campaign, to be divided pro rata among their organizations. The quota of Illinois was $12,719,700, collection on it $13,250,364, and this in spite of the fact that the armistice diminished enthusiasm. Besides these, dozens of organizations devoted to relief to one or another of the Allies functioned in smaller groups, collecting money and needed supplies.

The Illinois citizen at the climax of the war in November, 1918, had been made a peculiarly useful cog in a war machine. Elaborate organizations and methods of propaganda existed to tell him what was expected of him in subscriptions, to spur him on to accomplishment, and to key up his loyalty to the government. That a reaction came from the mood of exaltation so produced was not surprising.

A consideration of the military activity of Illinois has been left to the last. In view of the numerous slogans such as "Food Will Win the War," the reminder of Theodore Roosevelt that, while such things might help to win the war, it would be won as wars in the past, by fighting men, was timely. The military participation of the state is hard to define in terms of battles. Reacting from the Civil War method of regiments organized from neighborhoods, the War Department used a replacement system that shuffled men from localities and states. Even National Guard companies raised in a single town in 1916–17, by March, 1919, could show representatives of forty different states. Comparatively few units that saw actual fighting can be classified as predominently of Illinois men.

The Selective Service System was the method by which most Illinois citizens entered the service. In the three respective registrations of June 5, 1917 (men 21–30), June 5 and August 4, 1918 (men 21 since the first registration), and September 12, 1918 (men 18–45), Illinois registered 653,587, 54,375, and 866,-915, respectively. The determining of eligibility from the first was placed in the hands of local boards, of which there were 227. Eight district boards in the state acted upon appeals for exemption or deferred classification. After December 15, 1917, a system of classification was adopted as to eligibility to service. The Illinois figures are: Class I, 397,171, Classes II-IV, 534,465, Class V, 252,033, and not classified (men 37–45), 391,208. There were numerous delinquents in registration, as might have been expected in a floating population: 40,000 were rounded up in Chicago in July, 1918. The total number inducted by draft during the war was 193,338.

The draft, while the largest, was not the most effective source of manpower. In the year ending June 30, 1917, there were 30,000 applicants for enlistment in the army, of whom 16,000 were accepted. The precise number of Illinoisans who enlisted first and last is difficult to establish. The Navy in 1917–18 enlisted 9,600 out of 31,000 applicants. Between August 5 and 11, 1917, the whole National Guard of the state was federalized with a strength of 590 officers and 18,029 enlisted men. Its place was taken by a supplementary state militia. The naval militia of the state, 40 officers and 600 men, were inducted into the naval service. There were, in addition, 25,638 enlistments in the United States Naval Reserve Force.

The actual service and participation of Illinois men in the fighting is hard to estimate. Of the many Illinois men to go to France, but a minority were in organizations in which Illinois men predominated. The honors and service of some who served and merited best are merged in units not classified as belonging to Illinois. Of the National Army divisions in which Illinois men were an important factor, the Eighty-fourth, trained at Camp Taylor, Kentucky, was mainly used for replacements on its arrival in France, September–October, 1918. The Eighty-sixth Division, trained at Camp Grant, after losing thousands in replacements, arrived in France between September 21 and October 9. All the units except the field artillery brigade were broken up for replacements, and that was under training at the armistice. The Eighty-eighth Division, trained at Camp Dodge, Iowa, contained several units in which Illinois men predominated. It arrived in France, August–September, 1918, and was used on the front line in the Alsace sector.

The Thirteenth Regiment of Railroad Engineers, enlisted in May, 1917, sailed for France in July and was used in the operation of railroads behind the lines. The Three Hundred and Seventieth Infantry, the old Eighth Infantry of the Illinois National Guard, served with French units in the Oise-Aisne offensive of 1918.

The state's most distinctive unit was the Thirty-third Division, made up of its National Guard units excepting the Eighth Infantry, First Field Artillery, and the bands of the Fifth and Seventh infantry regiments. It was sent to Camp Logan, Texas, for training, where it met setbacks due to shortage of equipment and delay in sending supplemental drafts of national army men to fill its ranks. It sailed for France from May 8 to June 4 and on arrival, except for the artillery, was assigned to the British for training. While with them, detachments of two of its regiments were embodied in Australian companies in a minor operation at Hamel on July 4 that resulted in a gain of more than a mile. The One Hundred and Thirty-first Regiment assisted in the British offensive at Chipilly on August 9, 1918; members of the division were decorated by the king of Great Britain for their service. The division was then transferred to the Meuse sector, where it took part in the offensive of September 26, clearing the left bank of the Meuse. It was next used in a flanking attack across the Meuse and saw some hard fighting in the struggle to clear the heights to the east of the river. Finally it was relieved and transferred to the Troyon sector, where it was advancing at the armistice.

The Thirty-third enjoys the distinction of being the only American division to serve under British, French, and American command. It suffered 8,279 casualties, of whom 785 were killed in action. It captured 3,987 prisoners, was fourth among the divisions of the American Expeditionary Forces in prisoners taken, ninth in the number of kilometers advanced, twelfth in number of casualties, and twentieth in number killed in action. After the armistice it was held in Luxemburg until its return to the United States in May, 1919.

The Illinois unit with the most brilliant military record is the One Hundred and Forty-ninth Field Artillery, of the Forty-second, or Rainbow, Division, so called because it was made of select units from the National Guard of twenty-six states. The Illinois First Field Artillery was mustered into service on July 20, 1917, and after a brief training at Fort Sheridan was sent to France, arriving on October 31, 1917. Following a long period of training it occupied the Lunéville sector, February 21– March 23, 1918, the Baccarat sector, March 31–June 21, and the

Esperance Souain sector, July 4–14. It took part in what is officially known as the Champagne-Marne defensive, July 15–17, helping to smother Ludendorff's last offensive. It served brilliantly in the Aisne-Marne offensive that swept the Germans out of the Château-Thierry pocket, July 25–August 6, 1918. It served in the Saint-Mihiel offensive, the first undertaken by the American army, September 12–16, and is credited with occupation of the Essey Pannes sector, September 17–30. It took part twice in the Meuse-Argonne offensive, October 7–November 1 and November 5–November 9. It formed a part of the Army of Occupation, being stationed on the left bank of the Rhine, returned to the United States, and was mustered out in May, 1919.

The recognition by the state of the services of its soldiers was generously given. Special arrangements for the welcome of the returning units were made, most of the Thirty-third Division units being greeted by the governor on their arrival in New York and parading in Chicago before discharge at Camp Grant. Special civil service privileges were awarded all veterans of the war; distinctive medals were authorized. A history of the Thirty-third Division was published by the state and distributed to members of the division. In 1921 the General Assembly passed an act for a service compensation to soldiers and sailors with a maximum of $300. The necessary bond issue was approved by the voters in 1922, was declared constitutional by the supreme court of the state in April, 1923, and payment of claims was begun in July, 1923.

Certain military and naval posts in the state were important factors in training the enlarged war forces of the nation. Great Lakes Naval Training Station, established on the lake shore thirty miles north of Chicago, had been founded in 1904 for training naval recruits. It was enlarged repeatedly after 1917 to take care of the war enlistments and drafts. During the war it sent out 71,440 trained men. Its schools trained seamen, petty, warrant, and commissioned officers, actively co-operating with training ships and schools at Chicago.

Fort Sheridan, since 1893 a regular army post, was used in 1917 for two successive three-month officers' training camps. The first camp included men from Wisconsin, Michigan, and Illinois, and the second those from other states of the farther West as well. Four thousand officers were commissioned in the first camp and three thousand in the second. In 1918 Fort Sheridan was turned into a rehabilitation hospital, but later was restored to a regular army post. Two flying fields were established in Illinois in June and July of 1917, Scott Field near Belleville and Chanute Field at Rantoul, the latter co-operating with the School for Military Aeronautics at Urbana, from which 2,691 men were graduated.

A post for the training of a National Army Division was built at Rockford, June–December, 1917, and named Camp Grant. It was the place of training of the Eighty-sixth, or Black Hawk, Division, but was also used as depot and remount station. In 1921 it was abandoned as a post.

In this connection should be mentioned the units of the Student Army Training Corps established in colleges and technical schools of the state to take advantage of their facilities for training officers, noncommissioned officers, and specialists. All told, there were thirty such units in Illinois, the most important being those at the University of Illinois with 3,000 enrollees, Northwestern with 1,839, and the University of Chicago with 1,500. This was only a part of the service rendered by the specialists of those universities in all capacities from increasing the yield of the state's cornfields to advising on the terms of the peace.

If the citizens of Illinois showed themselves appreciative of the service of their men in the war, their reaction to the war as a whole was more mixed. The last act of the war, the Treaty of Versailles, came to the people tired with the strain of moral exaltation and self-sacrifice and weary of being urged on grounds of patriotism to submit to every piece of bureaucratic directive that emanated from Washington. The treaty and the League of Nations seemed to commit the United States to expend her blood and treasure in European quarrels yet unforeseen and at the bidding of others. Half-sensed was the looming danger of militarism in France and Japan only less dangerous than that crushed in Germany. To reason was added the instinctive reaction against the party that, while in control of the war government, had had to serve as a hard taskmaster. And in the election of 1920 the governed turned on their government. By a vote of 1,420,480 to 534,395 Illinois repudiated in a measure the policies, but still more the government, of Wilson. The new policy of the United States was to be felt out by opportunists and not imagined by a theorist.

CHAPTER XVI

Prosperity, Depression, and War

L IKE the rest of the nation in the 1920's, Illinois rode serene-
ly upward toward a golden plateau of permanent prosperity presided over by the Republican party as fairy god-
mother. A series of Republican senators represented the state.
Medill McCormick succeeded the red-whiskered Democrat, J.
Hamilton Lewis, in 1919; William B. McKinley, a local utility
magnate of Champaign, followed the Republican veteran Lawrence Y. Sherman in 1921. Charles S. Deneen, governor of the
state between 1904 and 1912 and chief of one of the Republican
factions of that era, followed McCormick in 1925. Frank L.
Smith, elected to succeed McKinley in 1927, was unseated by
the Senate, and Otis F. Glenn filled out his term from 1928 to
1933. Congressional delegations followed the same pattern. In
the Sixty-seventh Congress (1921–23), the Illinois delegation
consisted of twenty-four Republicans and three Democrats.
The Democrats gained four seats in the Sixty-eighth Congress,
lost two in the Sixty-ninth, recovered them in the Seventieth,
and had six of the twenty-seven seats in the Seventy-first. In
1931 the state legislature passed an act reapportioning congressional districts, only to have it declared unconstitutional by
the state supreme court. The congressional delegation, therefore, continued to be elected from the twenty-five districts
into which the state had been divided in 1901; the two additional members were chosen at large on a state-wide ballot.

In state politics the Republican control continued despite
bitter factional warfare. Len Small was elected governor in

1920 and re-elected in 1924 despite extremely vocal criticism within the party, which considered his machine methods of party politics the summation of political inequity. Specifically accused of retaining interest on public funds in his charge during a previous term as state treasurer, he was brought to trial during his second term only to be acquitted by a jury. In 1928, however, he lost the Republican nomination to Louis L. Emmerson, who, with Herbert Hoover running for President, carried the state by four hundred thousand votes. This was to be the last Republican state triumph for a decade.

The causes of the stock-market crash in 1929, of the lessened consumer demand that followed, and of the unemployment resulting from and in turn accentuating lessened consumer demand need no special analysis here. We may content ourselves with considering some of the special contributive factors in Illinois.

Here, as in other agricultural states, the skyrocketing prices for agricultural produce in 1917 had inspired small farmers to buy large quantities of land on mortgage and at inflated prices. The demand for wheat to win the war in 1917–18 had put in tillage inferior lands which could not produce at a profit under normal conditions. As demand and prices steadily declined through the 1920's, foreclosures by insurance companies and banks beggared overoptimistic mortgagors and loaded up mortgagees with slow assets of dubious value.

In any case, the banking structure of the state was none too sound. Some six hundred private banks had been forced out of business by legislative enactments of 1917 and 1919; many of these had traded on the financial ignorance of members of foreign-language groups. In 1920 there were 484 national banks in the state with combined capital and surplus of $156 million, or an average of $344,000 each; and 1,018 state banks with a capital of nearly $117 million. When the capital and surplus of a few very large banks are subtracted, these figures indicate a great number of very small banks. Since both state and federal law prohibited branch banking, this was inevitable; but there simply were not enough persons of sound financial judgment available to direct fifteen hundred banks. Unwise loans encumbering small banks with slow or depreciated assets caused a steady stream of bank closings and bank failures from the 1920's onward. At first consequences were averted by the stronger banks taking over the insolvent ones; this weakened the stronger banks as it weakened public faith in them. Runs on banks grew more and more frequent. At the time of the moratorium of March, 1933, only a few of the strongest remained in operation.

Indications of unemployment and dependency on a disastrous scale had been visible in 1930—in Chicago alone from April, 1930, to January, 1931, the number of unemployed increased 168 per cent. Downstate, where the coal-mining industry had been declining since the 1920's, distress grew for years, and local governments responsible for relief had in many cases exhausted their resources. A governor's commission, operating through local committees, was appointed to raise funds to supplement the public revenues of local tax units and sums raised by established charitable agencies. The millions subscribed were quickly exhausted. Finally, late in 1931 the governor called the first of three special sessions which by enactments of February 6, 1932, created the Illinois Emergency Relief Commission. Immediate funds were made available by an appropriation of $20 million, a general tax levy of $25 million, and authorization of a state bond issue of $20 million to run twenty years, subject to the voters' approval in November. These state funds were exhausted within six months, but when, in July, 1932, federal loans were available through the Reconstruction Finance Corporation, the governor acted promptly. The Illinois Emergency Relief Corporation, in August, 1932, transformed into the (federal) IERC with the addition of three state officials, became the governor's agent. Eventually $43,-

191,721 to the state, with $12,250,000 going to Cook County, was secured from this source.

At this point control of the state as well as of the nation passed to the Democratic party. The year 1930 had seen Deneen replaced in the Senate by J. Hamilton Lewis. In 1933 the Democrat W. H. Dieterich replaced Glenn. The congressional delegation in the Seventy-second Congress consisted of twelve Democrats and fifteen Republicans. The Illinois General Assembly of 1931–32 had in the senate eighteen Democrats and thirty-three Republicans; in the house seventy-two Democrats and eighty-one Republicans.

In the election of 1932 the Democrats scored a clean sweep. Franklin D. Roosevelt carried the state by a plurality of almost 450,000, and Henry Horner defeated Len Small for governor by 566,000. The state delegation in Congress included eight Republicans and nineteen Democrats. In the General Assembly the Democrats controlled the senate 33 to 18; in the house, 80 to 73. Democratic control continued in 1936 when Roosevelt once more carried the state, Horner was re-elected governor, and Lewis re-elected to the Senate. Democratic power in the state was based on gains in both the urban and the rural vote. The Negro vote, heavily Republican until 1932, largely shifted to the Democratic side. The Democrats retained their hold on their old constituencies in southern Illinois and in addition captured one after another of the formerly prosperous agricultural sections in the central part of the state, which were won over in great part by the national administration policy of guaranteed returns to the farmer.

Archaic revenue clauses of the Illinois constitution of 1870 were a great handicap to the General Assembly in finding new tax sources for the continued needs of unemployment relief. The general property tax, thoroughly out-of-date in principle, taxed men according to their real and personal property, with the result that intangible personal property such as stocks, bonds, etc., completely escaped and such consumptive goods as watches, jewelry, and automobiles were undervalued or ignored. The whole weight of taxation fell on land, buildings, and farm equipment. The decay of income from these sources produced in Illinois, as in other similarly burdened states, a taxpayers' strike. Taxes were not paid, and no one could be found to bid on forfeited property at tax sales.

The General Assembly, seeking new tax sources for the continued needs of unemployment relief, struggled to get around the archaic revenue provisions of the Illinois state constitution. Several enactments were thrown out as unconstitutional before a 2 per cent sales tax was passed in 1933 in a form acceptable to the courts—an occupational tax levied on the retailer which he was at liberty to pass on to his customers. All sorts of arguments were urged against the sales tax: it was regressive, exacting a higher proportion of income from the lower-income groups; it was a tax on necessities; as levied by retailers, it took a larger share out of purchases of from ten to thirty-three cents than from higher amounts. But it raised funds and was not unconstitutional. The tax was raised to 3 per cent in 1935, and in 1937 it was supplemented by a 3 per cent tax on public-utility sales. In 1939 sales and utility taxes were the most important items among the state's sources of revenue, affording almost one-third of the total receipts. One-third of the sales tax and all the utility tax went to emergency relief; two-thirds of the income from the sales tax was designated for other forms of public assistance and various school and university funds. The gasoline tax of three cents per gallon and the motor-vehicle license tax, next in amount of revenue, supported the public roads. The state liquor taxes, levied on the repeal of prohibition and third in importance, went into the General Revenue Fund. After 1932, except for delinquencies arising before that date, the general property tax was left to local governments as their main source of revenue.

Federal assistance in the work of general relief was first afforded by grants-in-aid from the Federal Emergency Relief Administration to supplement funds from state and local sources. Beginning in 1935 this assistance was shifted from direct contribution to the general relief fund to the institution of a works program through several agencies designed to give work to the unemployed and to reduce the general relief rolls. With the creation of the Federal Emergency Relief Administration in May, 1933, grants to the state became available on the basis of need, and through December, 1935, Illinois was given $205,218,475 from that source. In 1935, however, federal aid was gradually shifted from direct grants to the institution of a works program. Through several agencies the works program gave employment in projects ranging from construction of public works to the writing of state guide books. Set up in Illinois in August, by November it began to effect a reduction of the relief rolls.

In 1936, having promptly qualified for participation in this provision of the 1935 Social Security Act, Illinois began to pay old-age pensions to needy persons sixty-five years old or over; costs were met jointly by state and federal governments. Administration was vested in the Department of Public Welfare, working through its counterparts in each county. At the same time the counties were made increasingly responsible for their financial share of the direct relief program. In order to share state funds, they were obliged to make the maximum poor relief levy.

Though supplemented by federal employment on Public Works Administration (PWA) and Works Progress Administration (WPA) projects and other aids, the state's burden remained a heavy one. In March, 1935, unemployment relief had reached a peak with grants to 1,183,340 persons. In June,

1936, general relief was given to 428,378 persons, with 160,062 on the WPA rolls; a year later to 427,427 persons, with 120,998 on the WPA rolls and 115,500 receiving old-age pensions. The figure was higher in 1938, and through 1939 an average of 1,226,686 persons in Illinois were receiving public assistance through general relief, WPA, old-age pensions, and pensions to needy mothers and to blind persons for which payments were made jointly by state and county. In 1939 a total of $67,022,222 was spent for general relief, of which the state paid $48,388, 592, local governments $18,589,572, and the federal government $44,058, with an average monthly payment from all assistance programs of $17,682,904.

A change came with the onset of war in Europe in 1939 and with rearmament in America in 1940. By September the number of persons dependent on public assistance had been reduced to 952,015. In 1941 there was a tremendous increase in all forms of economic activity within the state, and the end of the year saw four million persons at work in Illinois, a greater number than at any time in the state's history and a gain of nearly six hundred thousand in the year. The income of the state's citizens rose to more than $6 billion, almost equaling that of 1929. As a result the number of public-assistance recipients fell to the lowest on record—645,000— the decrease taking place within the employable groups. A system of county re-employment committees was organized to help relief recipients to re-enter industry and business. The end of 1942, America's first year of war, saw the termination of the WPA and CCC programs, and the number of all-benefit recipients was reduced to 328,192. A further reduction of 20 per cent took place in 1943, and increased employment reduced even the rolls of old-age assistance recipients, numbering, in December, 143,726. The year 1943 also marked a reorganization whereby the Illinois Public Aid Commission, which had succeeded the Illinois Emergency Relief Commission in 1941, had all benefit programs under its jurisdiction, including the new aid to dependent children and blind assistance.

In 1944 with surplus funds from the sales tax mounting in the treasury, the state expended $74 million on relief and finished paying off the 1932 relief bond issue of $20 million. In August, 1945, the public-aid rolls drifted to an all-time low of 214,712, and expenditure of all benefits amounted to $6,165,148. Three years later the monthly program in July, 1948, was benefiting 268,879 persons, at an expenditure of $9,643,875. In addition to these aids, payment under the Illinois Unemployment Compensation Act had in 1948 been made for nine years, and for the year ending March 31 had totaled $5.5 million. The state of Illinois was now well advanced in a reorganized program of social welfare, of which the appointment of the IERC was the forerunner. State and federal governments would henceforth move in the direction of increased responsibility for the well-being of their citizens.

In 1940 the political balance of the state once more shifted to the Republican party. In 1938 Democrats elected Scott Lucas senator and eleven of the twenty-one members of the House of Representatives. Governor Horner was incapacitated by illness after October, 1938, and John Stelle as lieutenant-governor took his place. Horner's death on October 6, 1940, left Stelle, who had been defeated in the April primaries, to fill out his term.

In the elections of November, 1940, Roosevelt carried the state against Wendell Wilkie but the Republicans elected Dwight H. Green governor, C. Wayland Brooks to fill the Senate seat left vacant by the death of Lewis, and nineteen of the twenty-six congressmen. The Republicans controlled both houses of the General Assembly. In 1944 Roosevelt, running for the last time, carried the state, and Scott H. Lucas, Democrat, was elected to the Senate. The state officers, however, with Green as governor, were Republicans except for the secretary of state, and the legislature remained Republican.

As a part of the national defense program Illinois was being activated for war participation many months before the attack on Pearl Harbor.[1] The first units of the Thirty-third Division of the Illinois National Guard were inducted into the federal service late in 1940; others were inducted in March, 1941, and served throughout the war at home and in the European and Pacific theaters. Through the Illinois National Guard more than fourteen thousand men served in the armed forces. The Illinois Naval Reserve, made up of eleven divisions, was also ordered into the federal service in 1940–41, all organizations serving at sea in various types of navy ships.

To replace the National Guard, the Illinois National Militia was organized at once, and its authorized strength of six thousand was increased to ten thousand on the declaration of war. Units which included an air corps were assigned to protect bridges, airports, and war plants, and to help in fires, explosions, and tornadoes; especially in the heavy floods of 1943 and 1944 were their services important in saving lives, crops, and property. When the militia was mustered out on April 1, 1947, more than thirty thousand officers and men had served, many of whom entered the federal service.

The defense program effected an enormous increase in size in the military and naval training centers in the state. At Chanute Field, Rantoul, training was given to Air Corps technicians, and courses in weather observation and forecasting were organized; for a year, 1942–43, training was given to bomber pilots. Scott Field at East St. Louis specialized in radio and communications courses; its graduates were commissioned second lieutenants in the Army Air Corps. Camp Grant was

1. For a full account of Illinois' wartime activities see Mary Watters, *Illinois in the Second World War* (2 vols.; Springfield: Illinois State Historical Library, 1951–52).

redeveloped as a recruit-reception center and medical-department replacement center. Fort Sheridan, also a reception center, became the hub of the Sixth Army Corps special services. Camp Ellis was added to these older centers in April, 1943. Built on the site of little Bernadotte, near Galesburg, with a capacity of thirty-five thousand, it trained service units for combined operations. Great Lakes Naval Training Station, with greatly expanded facilities soon was training a large share of the enlisted personnel of the Navy. In addition the Naval Reserve Aviation Base at Glenview was giving preliminary training to men qualified as naval aviation cadets through the selective service, and at George Field, near Lawrenceville, instruction was given in advanced flying.

Illinois was beforehand in setting up a state-wide organization to direct civilian war activity. An Emergency Council of Defense was named by Governor Stelle in December, 1940, and the Illinois State Council of Defense was appointed by Governor Green in April, 1941; in scope of activities and organization it followed the state pattern of the First World War. Renamed the Illinois War Council in July, 1943, it directed 652 local councils with committees on civil protection, agricultural resources and production, adjustment of business to war conditions, industry, housing, public health, war bonds and stamps, and many others. Through the local councils thousands of volunteers salvaged fats, tin, silk, and nylon, grew victory gardens, conducted fund drives, and gave clerical service to rationing boards and other wartime agencies.

By 1941 Illinois manufacturing was fully geared to a colossal war effort. With the United States Arsenal at Rock Island already retooling and expanding production, new government ordnance plants were developed at Wilmington, Kankakee, Elwood, and Crab Orchard Lake; a depot and proving ground were established at Savanna. Plants by the thousands were built or adapted to war production until by the end of 1943 the Chicago area was second only to Detroit in war production; from 1940 to October, 1943, the state had produced approximately one-tenth of the national total. The peacetime diversity of Illinois manufactures produced a like range of products for war use. Caterpillar tractors, uniquely an Illinois product, became indispensable for building airports, roads, and harbors, establishing beachheads, clearing rubble, destroying land mines, even attacking pillboxes. There were many cases of industries converting their product to war needs: two firms manufacturing printing presses won top achievement honors ("E" awards with six and five stars, respectively) for gun mounts and for gun sights and rockets. At Seneca, on the Illinois River, was produced "The Trojan Horse"—a landing barge designed to carry tanks with tank and repair crews. Cargo vessels and naval craft of various types were also produced in Chicago, Quincy, and East St. Louis. More than eight hundred Illinois plants were manufacturing aircraft and aircraft parts.

As well as war material, Illinois was equipped for a record production of food for the armed services. Food processors supplied meat, eggs, milk, vegetables, flour, corn products, and candy, to provide a balanced diet even when taken in K-ration cans. Illinois farmers, numbering more than two hundred thousand, put into operation the greatest program in the state's history. High school boys and girls were trained for farm work in the summer, and young businesswomen from the cities were enrolled to detassel corn during their vacations as a part of the program to supply needed farm labor. Victory gardens to the number of 1,151,000 were planted in 1943, with the object of reducing demands on farm products.

Illinois citizens participated in every variety of special service required of civilians during the wartime emergency. Investments in war-savings bonds and stamps exceeded quotas. From the inception of the sales program through October 31,

1946, Illinois had bought bonds amounting to $4,434,176,000, ranking fourth among the states in purchases. Contributions were made to many wartime causes, but communities in the state outdid themselves in providing for the comfort, recreation, lodging, and feeding of the men in the armed services. Chicago won a golden reputation from the men who traveled through or visited the city on weekend passes; it offered lodging, meals, and entertainment free of cost to any man in uniform. Other communities near service installations carried on similar services, usually through the United Service Organizations (the U.S.O.), a co-operative agency made up of the YMCA, YWCA, National Catholic Community Service, Jewish Welfare Board, and National Travelers Aid Association. Elsewhere servicemen enroute to new stations were given canteen service at railroad and bus stations.

The state's specific contribution to manpower can be told only in general figures. Selective service, re-established in September, 1940, became the channel through which the majority of Illinoisans entered military service. The state organization under a director (closely following the 1917 pattern) consisted of three appeal boards and 361 local boards. More than a million men registered in the state on October 16, 1940, and the first quota was levied on November 18. Six registrations by December 31, 1945, (not including the fourth—men forty-five or over, not liable to induction) brought the state's total to 1,954,674, of whom 615,973 men were inducted. Of these 504,875 served in the Army, 95,682 in the Navy, 14,168 in the Marine Corps, and 1,248 in the Coast Guard. Enlistments (to September 1, 1945) added 293,527, bringing the total to nearly a million Illinois men and women in the four services. Women (as of June 30, 1945) numbered 18,782; 10,605 (4,073 officers) in the Army, 6,305 in the Navy (1,384 officers), 1,297 in the Marine Corps (68 officers), 575

(45 officers) in the Coast Guard. Casualties in the line of duty published in June, 1946, listed a total of 18,601 from Illinois: killed in action, 10,921; died of wounds, 1,568; died of injuries, 57; died, non-battle, 4,830; legally declared dead, 1,151; missing, 74.

Compulsory re-employment of the returning veteran had been made a part of the selective service law, and state and local boards found Illinois employers co-operative; few cases had to be adjudicated. The federal government, through the "G.I. Bill of Rights" enacted in 1944, guaranteed loans to veterans for specific purposes and provided funds for school, college, and numerous training programs. Early in 1943 the state inaugurated the Governor's Committee on Veterans' Rehabilitation and Employment, and in 1945 the General Assembly created the Illinois Veterans' Commission. Branches were set up in every county to acquaint the veteran with his rights and benefits under state and federal programs; in 1949 these were reduced to sixty-six field offices, with headquarters in Springfield and a branch office in Chicago. In 1946 a state bonus was voted by the General Assembly and ratified by the voters; it was paid at the rate of ten dollars a month for service in the United States and fifteen dollars a month for service overseas. Approximately 915,000 veterans were eligible for payment, and according to the final report of the Service Recognition Board 889,255 claims were paid, 862,976 to living veterans.

Activities of the Illinois Veterans' Commission have continued to the present, as have those of the Selective Service organization, except for a few months in 1947–48. From the outbreak of the Korean War to September 30, 1953, Illinois inducted 102,526 into the armed forces through selective service. More than half of the units of the Illinois National Guard, some 12,000 officers and men, were again federalized from 1950 to 1952, including all of the new Forty-fourth Division made up of downstate units; many of the officers and men were sent to European and Pacific theaters.

The federal government in 1952 extended to the Korean veteran the same benefits accorded the World War II veteran; in Illinois the 1959 legislature voted a cash bonus of $100 to each man who had served in the combat area and $1,000 to the next of kin of men who died in service. The Illinois Veterans' Commission, responsible for administration of the act, reported early in 1964 that claims had been paid to 1,825 beneficiaries and to 94,318 living veterans.

The first postwar state election of 1946 was a victory, if short lived, for the Republicans. For Congress the representative for the state at large, four members from the Chicago area, and all downstate members save one—twenty in all—were Republican, leaving six districts represented by Democrats. For the General Assembly thirty-eight Republicans and thirteen Democrats were elected to the senate, eighty-eight Republicans and sixty-five Democrats to the house. In the 1948 election the Democrats swept the state for national and state offices. Truman led Dewey by a small plurality of 33,612, but Adlai E. Stevenson, grandson of Cleveland's vice-president, was victor over Green by 572,067, and Paul H. Douglas was elected to the Senate, defeating C. Wayland Brooks, senator since 1940. For Congress fourteen Republicans and twelve Democrats were elected. In the General Assembly the Republicans controlled the senate, with thirty-two members to the Democrats' eighteen, with one vacancy; in the house there were eighty-one Democrats and seventy-two Republicans.

Meantime in specialized form the state confronts the general postwar problems of the nation.

CHAPTER XVII

The State's Economy

ILLINOIS' population, predominantly rural until 1900, was rated 80-per-cent urban by the 1960 census which gave the state 10,081,158 residents. Communities of more than 2,500 population numbered 327, where there had been none listed until 1840. In addition to Chicago, now having a population of 3,550,404, the state had two cities over 100,000, Rockford and Peoria, and 12 others over 50,000. Although both the 1950 and 1960 censuses reflected a substantial growth of most Illinois cities, in 1960 Chicago, Peoria, LaSalle, and East St. Louis showed a loss representing a shift of population from the city proper to suburban communities around them. Thirty-four of these communities, ranging from 10,000 to 20,000 in population, grew more than 100 per cent in the years 1950–60. Cahokia Village (population 15,829) had an increase of 1893.6 per cent. Carpentersville, Kane County (17,424), increased 1044.1 per cent. Eight metropolitan areas covering fifteen counties were designated in 1960 by the Bureau of the Census; these areas represented 96 per cent of the state's growth in 1950–60. In density of population Illinois ranks eleventh among the states with 180.2 persons per square mile of land area.

Half of the 102 counties gained, while the other half lost in population in 1960; at the extremes DuPage County gained 103 per cent, Pope County lost 30 per cent. The county gains and losses for 1950–60 followed a general pattern seen in 1940–50—gains in the northern tier, central and east central sections, losses in the south and west. Natural increase (excess of births

over deaths) accounted for 89.5 per cent of state's growth
in the period 1950–60, immigration into the state for 10.5
per cent. A heavy immigration of non-whites from the southern states has been taking place since 1940; from 1940 to 1960
the white population of Illinois increased 20.1 per cent, non-
white 170.5 per cent. The Negro population in 1960 was
1,037,470, of which 890,154 live in Chicago. Foreign-born residents number 686,098.

Nevertheless Illinois remains one of the great agricultural
states; in spite of recent land diversions to subdivisions, highways, landing fields, parks, and other uses, more than 30 million acres, about 85 per cent of the state's total area, remain
in farms. With a diversity of soil and climate capable of producing a wide range of commodities, the Illinois farm land
value of $8.9 billion in 1960 was outranked only by California
and Texas; in value per acre, $294, Illinois ranked second.
Values are highest in the Chicago metropolitan area, with its
urban and industrial composition, and in eight fertile agricultural counties in the heart of east central Illinois. Southern
Illinois showed the greatest proportional gain in land value
outside Chicago in the years 1954–59; this area which had a
very high proportion of low-income farms in 1950 so successfully adopted new technological methods that land values in
the southern thirty-six counties increased 47 per cent in the
five years.

While agricultural acreage has been reduced only slightly,
the number of Illinois farms has decreased steadily since 1920,
when there were 237,181 farms to 138,641 in 1963. Mechanization of farms has been rapid during this period. Rural elec-
trification has made possible milking machines, brooders, re-
frigerators, and other equipment for farm and domestic use;
tractors, trucks, and other machinery have virtually eliminated
the mule and work horse and have so reduced the need for
farm labor that an estimated 750,000 persons have moved from

the farms in the past forty years. The modern farm represents a heavy investment in land and equipment, but technology has so multiplied farm output in both field crops and livestock that unit production has greatly increased. Moreover the farmer has ready access to the results of continuing research of state and federal agencies and he makes use of them promptly. About 40 per cent of Illinois farms are operated by owners and 33.5 per cent by tenants but those farms include 58 per cent of the land under cultivation. About one-third of the land is farmed by men who own part, rent part of their acreage. At present tenant farming is not increasing as popularly supposed, but a growing number of professional farm managers operate farms for owners. While the median farm ranges from 70 to 259 acres, there has been a gradual increase in farms of more than 1,000 acres.

Illinois staple products continue to be cattle, hogs, corn, and soybeans; dairy products, wheat, eggs, oats, and other commodities make up the balance of which the value in 1963 was over $2 billion. Illinois was second only to California in the production of agricultural products. Corn yields averaging 85 bushels an acre and soybeans averaging 29.5 bushels both exceeded records set in 1962. The breeding and feeding of beef cattle is the project which brings the greatest cash return to the Illinois farm on the basis of investment. The number of hogs raised on 60 per cent of Illinois farms made the state second in production. Marketing livestock in Illinois has undergone changes in recent years with the removal from Chicago and East St. Louis of the large meat-processing plants. Less than half the sales in the state are now made at the old terminal markets of Chicago, East St. Louis, Springfield, Peoria, and Bushnell; the rest are sold directly from farmer to buyer at some 180 stations and most of this stock is then sent to out-of-state processors. Quantities of Illinois beef and hogs, as well as grain, poultry, fruit, and vegetables, are a source of supply for food processing plants in the state; since the farmer in turn is a customer for machinery, fertilizer, pesticides, motor fuel, building materials, and numerous services, the farm-based industries added to agriculture make a heavy contribution to the state's economy.

Illinois farmers have participated in federal agricultural control programs chiefly in conservation and feed grain programs, but to a lesser extent in soil bank and wheat control. In 1962, when cash receipts from Illinois farm marketing totaled $2,197,473,000, total support payments were $109,251,000, thereby ranking Illinois third behind Texas and Iowa.

Illinois possesses great mineral wealth in the form of coal, oil, and gas, lead and zinc, glass sand, stone, clay, and other industrial materials. The state's production maintains a consistently high place nationally, and in 1962 the value of its products reached an all-time high of $631 million. Fuel products accounted for nearly 68 per cent, with crude oil at present of more value than coal. Bituminous coal underlies more than half the area of the state, but is mined chiefly in the southern third. Though approximately 3.7 billion tons have already been mined, the state's mineable reserves are estimated at more than 136 billion tons. The industry took some years to recover from the low levels of production in the 1920's and 1930's when railroads, manufacturers, and domestic consumers were turning to the use of oil and gas. Labor troubles were added to technological changes, and southern Illinois, an area of one big industry, began to experience the depression some years before it spread over the rest of the state. Recent years have shown an annual gain in production owing chiefly to the increased use of Illinois coal by electrical utilities, as well as other uses being developed by the research of the Illinois Geological Survey. Strip mines have increased in the past twenty-five years, and in 1963 these produced more than half of the state's output. Both strip mines and underground mines are highly mechanized; in 1963 employees numbered 9,202, a decline from 11,400 in 1958. Illinois held fourth place in national production of bituminous coal in 1962, mining 11.5 per cent of the country's total; the total output was 48,353,913 tons, valued at $186,646,104.

Crude oil, the state's most valuable mineral, in 1962 yielded 78.8 million barrels valued at about $237 million, and an additional estimated 24 billion cubic feet of natural gas, of which Illinois produces only a fraction of what it consumes. Though oil is found in forty-one counties roughly to the south and east of Springfield, the heaviest production comes from five counties. Exploration and drilling are continually under way, resulting in new pools and extensions each year; oil was found recently in DeWitt County twenty-five miles north of any other wells. Scientific methods of recovering oil from existing wells—water flooding and hydraulic fracturing—are an important factor in present production. About two-thirds of Illinois crude oil is shipped to refineries out of the state, but the great refinery areas at Wood River–Roxanna, Chicago–Indiana, and southeastern Illinois process some two and one-half times the Illinois output, including oil imported from the west and the Gulf states. Here the oil is converted to gasoline, kerosene, distillates, and residual fuel oil and is shipped by rail and tank cars, barge or pipe line.

The petroleum industry in Illinois currently employs some 60,000 people. These are engaged in the production of the output of 32,000 wells, processing at 14 refineries and 18 petrochemical plants, distribution by pipe line and truck, marketing at wholesale and retail. Primary service stations employ about 25,000 people.

Other Illinois minerals, small in contrast with fuels, are important contributions to industry: stone products valued in 1962 at $52,313,571; sand $11,943,268; gravel $15,040,907; special sands—bonded molding and silica—$12,026,071; clay products, $56,495,460; cement, $31,500,000; fluorspar (64.5 per cent of the amount produced in the United States and 20 per cent of the amount consumed), $6,304,990; zinc and lead, $6,969,230.

Illinois manufacturing continued its expansion into the postwar years; in 1958 in value added by manufacture the state's total product was $11,664,070,000, and this was exceeded only in New York, California, and Pennsylvania. In 1961 the figure increased to $12,752,785,000. A wartime shifting in the relative importance of Illinois industries has persisted. Machinery in 1960 was the top-ranking product measured by numbers of employees and amount of payroll: electrical machinery, including household appliances, radio, television, and other communications equipment and electronic components; non-electrical machinery for farming and construction—the great earth-moving machines and caterpillar tractors, also machinery for metal working. Fabricated metal products and primary metals were next in importance.

In 1960 food products ranked first in value added by manufacture but fourth in employees and payrolls. Although the big packers have abandoned their plants in Chicago and East St. Louis, meat products in 1961 were valued at $183,113,000, and required 20,804 employees. Total value of food products was $1,872,000,000. Printing and publishing is second only to New York in value of product, and in the state ranks fifth in all categories—employees, payrolls, and value added by manufacture. Three of the largest commercial job printing firms in the country are located in Chicago; they print directories, catalogs, and encyclopedias, as well as magazines and other items. A great diversity of other goods is produced in which the state ranks high nationally: furniture, musical instruments, academic apparel, pharmaceuticals, cosmetics, fabricated plastics, glass.

Non-manufacturing activities in the state now have a greater total employment than manufacturing, and are expected to increase in the immediate future, primarily in the fields of services, employment in government, federal, state, and local, and in wholesale trade. By June, 1964, the state's civilian labor force was estimated at 4,531,800, of which 3.6 per cent were unemployed. Of the 4,361,600 employed, those in non-manufacturing occupations (2,440,500) outnumbered those in manufacturing nearly two to one. Those in service and miscellaneous occupations totaled 537,900; the 470,800 persons in government positions include those in the field of public education.

Illinois' importance as the center of the nation's transportation system has been magnified in recent years by new and expanded facilities. Railroads have declined in relative importance since the First World War because of the competition from other carriers and rising costs of operation. Conversion to diesel engines and mechanization of many operations have lowered costs but raised a host of labor problems involving firemen in freight and yard services whose jobs were being eliminated.

The resultant dispute was more than four years old on August 28, 1963, when a nation-wide strike was averted by joint resolution of Congress, which imposed the first peacetime compulsory arbitration of the two main issues, and barred a strike for 180 days. The decision of the arbitration board on November 26 ruled that jobs of 90 per cent of the firemen in freight and yard services be eliminated, but that crew "consist" be decided on the local level; the decision was to be binding for two years. Another strike was threatened over issues not decided and on April 8, 1964, some seven thousand on-train employees of the Illinois Central walked out over a four-state area, abandoning passengers and freight trains in transit. A fifteen-day truce halting the Illinois Central strike and the spread to other lines was accepted on President Johnson's proposal; on April 22 terms were reached as to holidays, wage structure, pay, and road and yard crews.

Illinois' 32 railroads and 25 switching and terminal companies operate over some 11,000 miles of track. Coal, sand, gravel, manufacturers' goods and agricultural products are the principal freight cargoes, which in 1960 amounted to 87 million tons originating in the state, and 96 million tons terminating there. Innovations in equipment and handling have been introduced to increase freight service but many communities on railroad lines have greatly reduced passenger service. Along with communities not on railroads these are served by intercity buslines which cover the state, and at various key interchanges offer transcontinental connections. Similarly, motor truck carriers are reaching some twelve hundred points in the state with no other freight service. More than 2,500 trucklines have headquarters in Chicago, and others are located throughout the state.

A good highway system is essential to such transportation services, as well as to the needs of several million Illinois passenger vehicles. Later than many other states, by 1914 Illinois had begun the construction of hard roads by a system of state aid to county highway departments, and by 1918 had authorized a $60 million road bond issue which qualified it for federal aid, first made available in 1916. A primary paved road system of 4,800 miles was laid out linking the principal cities by 47 routes, and in 1924 with a second bond issue of $100 million this was extended to 9,800 miles. The Division of Highways of the Department of Public Works and Buildings created in 1917 has the responsibility of constructing and maintaining the state highways, construction being done by contract and maintenance by state employees. With rapidly increasing traffic and higher powered motors, the first narrow pavements at once became inadequate and the reconstruction of old roads as well as the building of new routes has been continuous.

Revenue for highway appropriations is derived from motor and operator license fees and from the motor fuel tax, part of which is paid back to counties and municipalities for roads and streets under their jurisdiction. Federal aid of 50 per cent of construction is available when the roadway is part of the federal primary system or approved extension of the federal secondary system. Toll roads, first successfully revived in Pennsylvania and other states, seemed to provide a means of dealing with expensive costs of operation and maintenance. An Illinois Toll Commission was authorized by the General Assembly in 1953 to build and operate roads in Illinois, financed by self-liquidating bonds. An initial network of 193 miles was laid out and a $415 million bond issue was authorized, only to run into a year's delay in the courts. Bonds were sold and work was begun near Rockford in 1956; in 1958 the first section, the Northwest Tollway, was opened, from the Wisconsin line near Beloit to O'Hare Field. Three routes integrated with the metropolitan expressway system of Chicago and with tollway systems of adjacent Indiana and Wisconsin are now in use, and in 1961, during the third year of operation, revenue began to exceed cost of operation and use. When the revenue bonds have been retired the roads will revert to the state.

The federal-aid highway act of 1956 however ended interest in the further construction of tollroads. A 41,000 mile network of interstate and defense highways at a cost of $41 billion is to be built by 1972. Illinois has been assigned approximately 1,600 miles for which 90 per cent of the construction is paid by the federal government; the state's 10 per cent share of the cost is estimated at $150 million. Tollways may be incorporated in the system, but tollway additions may not be made with federal funds. Half of the state's allotment of mileage was in use by 1964.

Illinois had more than 100,000 miles of surfaced roads by the end of 1962, including primary, secondary, county, city, and township highways; new construction that year was 2,802.40 miles. In 1962 a total of $430,440,797.67 from state and federal funds was spent on Illinois highway construction.

Air facilities in Illinois were expanded rapidly in the postwar years when the Federal Airports Act of 1946 made grants for airport construction available to local authorities. Projects and plans required the approval of the State Department of Aeronautics, established in 1945. Many small airports used principally in giving flight training under the G.I. Bill have since been closed, but in 1963 there were 125 airports, 71 heliports, and nearly 500 private landing fields for restricted and emergency use. Some 28 commercial air lines schedule service which is focused on Chicago; passenger, mail, express, and freight service is available, and 16 air lines schedule international flights. Midway Airport in Chicago, which handled 7 million passengers in 1956, was superseded by O'Hare International Airport when jet flights were inaugurated. Called the world's busiest airport, in 1963 it was used by more than 16 million passengers. An international terminal was completed at O'Hare in 1963, and facilities are still being expanded. However, Midway Airport was reactivated on July 4, 1964, no passenger flights having touched down in nearly two years; one line has scheduled jet inter-city service.

The Illinois Department of Aeronautics in addition to working with local airport authorities has various regulatory and educational functions, and maintains safety and civil defense programs. One project aided some thousands of farmers to observe from the air the results of various conservation practices. The department also sponsored the writing of a history of aviation in Illinois, published in 1957.

The expansion of water-borne traffic by the completion in 1933 of the Illinois Waterway, modern successor to the Illinois-Michigan canal, and by the opening of the St. Lawrence Seaway in 1959 has been the most recent development in the state's transportation system. Chicago's location at the portage between two water routes providing ocean-to-gulf navigation has been utilized since the days of the French explorers, and modern facilities now multiply its advantages. The waterway provides a toll-free route of 326 miles from the Mississippi River to Lake Michigan, where barges, moved by tow boats singly or in multiple groups, transport coal, sand, gravel, oil and oil products, iron, steel, and grain. Navigational aids developed in the war—sonar, radar, gyroscopic stabilizers, nuclear power— have been adopted on the river with great effect. The U.S. Army Corps of Engineers maintains and operates the waterway but the State Division of Waterways maintains the fixed and movable bridges. This division also operates the Brussels and Kampsville ferries over the Illinois River. These are needed for the motor transportation of residents of Calhoun County where there are no railroads.

Negotiations for the joint construction of the St. Lawrence Seaway by the United States and Canada had been the occasion for airing Canada's longstanding grievance against Chicago for diverting water from Lake Michigan to flush sewage down the Chicago Ship and Sanitary Canal, completed by the Sanitary District in 1900 to avoid the pollution of the lake as a source of the city's water supply. In 1901 at a time of high lake levels, the Secretary of War issued a permit for the diversion of 4,167 cubic feet per second. By 1907 when lake levels were declining the Great Lakes States and Canada joined in bitter protests and court proceedings were started. The Sanitary District nevertheless had further increased its intake to 10,000 cfs. when in 1925 the Secretary of War allowed the withdrawing of 8,500 cfs., stipulating that a ten-year construction program for sewage treatment be started. More suits were filed, and in 1929 the United States Supreme Court ordered that the Sanitary District gradually reduce the intake to 1,500 cfs. by December 31, 1938, though in 1930 it decided Chicago need not return domestic-use water to Lake Michigan. Efforts were made to increase the amount of intake through acts of Congress while Canada continued to plead with the State Department and the Great Lakes States filed more suits. Bills allowing increased diversion were vetoed by President Eisenhower. In 1959 the United States Supreme Court finally agreed to review its earlier decisions and appointed a special master to review testimony. Hearings were still being held in 1964, a year when Lake Michigan fell to its lowest level in a century, with serious damage to navigation, recreation, and property. At several joint conferences held during the summer the Canadians were disposed to recognize natural causes rather than Chicago diversion as a source of their common problem. The International Joint Commission set up in 1909 by the United States and Canada will make a long-term study of measures to control the lakes, considering the problems of pollution, domestic water, sanitation, navigation, and other needs. Meantime negotiations between the United States and Canada allowed construction of the Seaway to begin in 1954.

Even before the construction of the Seaway Chicago had become an ocean port with ocean liner service operating on a regular schedule between Chicago and European ports since 1933. In 1952 there were over one hundred sailings between Chicago, Europe, and North Africa with six companies operating some forty ships especially designed for the Great-Lakes-to-Europe trade. The Seaway, with deeper channels and bigger locks, permits the passage of vessels up to twenty-five thousand tons, about 51 per cent of the world's ocean fleet. In anticipation of the increased traffic, additional waterway and harbor improvements were planned and started by government and private agencies at both Chicago ports, Chicago Harbor at Navy Pier, and Calumet Harbor at the foot of Lake Michigan. At Chicago Harbor the city, financed by a $9 million bond issue, dredged the harbor area to twenty-nine feet, and built warehouses and modernized docks capable of berthing six ocean vessels at a time. Further expansion will be possible when the University of Illinois vacates Navy Pier. The Chicago Regional Port District, created by the General Assembly in 1951 to plan and make harbor and port improvements in Cook County south of 87th Street and in the southeast portion of Du Page County and authorized to issue bonds, began a $24 million program at Lake Calumet. This included twin grain elevators, docks for bulk and oil cargoes, roads, tracks, warehouses, sheds. The United States Army Corps of Engineers widened and deepened the Little Calumet and the Cal-Sag Channel to adapt the waterway to the increased traffic to Calumet Harbor. Although the formal opening of the Seaway was celebrated by visits from President Eisenhower and Queen Elizabeth and Prince Philip to Chicago in July, 1959, in May a 353-foot Dutch vessel was the first to arrive at Chicago Harbor where it was given a festive welcome. Experts warned that seaway benefits would be acquired gradually and that some domestic production would be harmed by increased imports. The annual seaway traffic has been below expectations. Nevertheless water-borne exports from Chicago in 1959 increased 170 per cent over 1958, and imports 117 per cent, and 1,148,000 tons were loaded or unloaded in Chicago. In 1963 tonnage handled rose to 1,325,428 over the seven and one-half month season, the ratio of exports to imports being about two to one. The Chicago Regional Port District has begun a second project of $25 million to provide more warehouses, wharves, and cargo sheds designed to permit winter storage and early shipment when navigation opens. After five seasons of shipping serious bottlenecks still exist in the Calumet River, where five bridges must be replaced and one improved. Completion is scheduled for 1966.

Illinois has made effective use of a wealth of natural resources—location, fertile lands, water and transportation facilities, and industrial potential—evidence of which is found in a rising per capita income, $2,844 in 1962, a record high for Illinois, placing it sixth in the country. In net personal income Illinois ranked third. A growing problem of unemployment is nevertheless a matter of public concern. That considerable part of unemployment in Illinois is preventable is the conclusion of the Governor's Committee on Unemployment reporting in January, 1963; this is true specifically among the unskilled or those with obsolescent skills, and also among the young, uneducated, and non-white workers. Earlier state, local, and private planning agencies had emphasized the importance of public works and new industries in areas of high unemployment. The first State Planning Commission was established in 1931 after an inventory of state resources had been taken by the Civic Development Committee of the Illinois Chamber of Commerce. This functioned chiefly as a sponsor of WPA projects and terminated in 1942. The Illinois Post-War Planning Commission, in existence from 1943 to 1949, with state and federal funds promoted the construction of public works to prevent unemployment. It also published an *Atlas of Illinois Resources* in 1944 to serve as a basis for future planning. This useful volume was the forerunner of a series issued by various state agencies, of which six had appeared by 1964.

Southern Illinois, which continued into the postwar years as an area of high and permanent unemployment, was the focus of several special studies. The Executive Committee on Southern Illinois, representing the University of Illinois, Southern Illinois University, the State Geological, Natural History, and Water Surveys, published a report in 1949 on the resources and potential of the sixteen southernmost counties which had experienced the worst of the depression. A *Pilot Study of Southern Illinois* by Charles M. Colby, published in 1956, covered a study of the thirty-two southernmost counties. Area development projects have been launched by the state and federal government, Southern Illinois University, and the University of Illinois, and a volunteer agency known as Southern Illinois, Incorporated, has been an effective continuing action group.

In 1961 the General Assembly established the Board of Economic Development to publicize the advantages of locations in Illinois to industrial enterprises. At the same time it created an Industrial Development Authority to give financial aid to communities in attracting new industry which was soon declared unconstitutional. Illinois communities, however, had access to federal funds through the Area Redevelopment Administration and twenty-three southern counties, with persistently high industrial employment, and nine rural counties were designated as eligible for federal loans. The State Board of Economic Development drew up an over-all program, local agencies acted, and various projects have been approved by the ARA. The largest of these is a $35 million project to dam the Big Muddy River between Mount Vernon and Benton, creating 25,000-acre Rend Lake, with recreation area and facilities for an industrial complex similar to the Crab Orchard Lake project developed in the 1930's.

The Manpower Development and Training Act of 1962 provides federal support for instruction to train unemployed workers in skills for which there is a demand. The Illinois State Employment Service makes the skill surveys and certifies trainees to job-training programs set up by the State Board of Vocational Education. On the completion of the course, the trainee may be found a job through the Employment Service.

Among the specific measurers for alleviating the problem of unemployment, the expansion of educational opportunities is basic. "The State's educational enrollment is its most effective tool in achieving a high level of prosperity for its people. This is true at the highest level of scientific research and development and is equally true in the broad regions of intermediate and elementary education." In support of this conclusion, the

Governor's Committee on Unemployment called for an increase in the state's resources allocated to education.

Education and training on all levels to meet new technological needs for skilled workers and professional leadership placed great demands on the state's public school system in the postwar years, when it was also necessary to cope with heavier enrollments and a shortage of teachers and classroom facilities. The consolidation of school districts, made possible by the laws of 1945 and 1947, finally cancelled Illinois' unenviable national record for the most school districts, 12,000, and one-room schools; by the fall term of 1963 these had been reduced to 1,430, which included 375 unit, 834 elementary, and 221 secondary school districts. A postwar construction program for new school buildings and additions to older schools by 1956 amounted to more than $700 million, but the arrears of the depression and war years were not yet met. In 1961 the State Superintendent of Public Instruction reported classroom shortages were causing 39,634 students to attend class less than a full day. A School Problems Commission appointed by the General Assembly as an interim commission in 1947, but made a continuing state agency in 1957, is responsible for annual recommendations of which a high proportion has been enacted by the legislature. Salaries, which had been so low that many teachers were leaving the profession and few were being recruited, were raised so that by 1956–57 with an average teacher's salary of $4,725 Illinois ranked seventh instead of ninth as in 1943–44 when the average was $2,018. In 1962 the average salary for elementary school teachers was $5,450, for high school teachers $6,350. Standards were raised for teachers' certificates, a bachelor's degree being required of all who are certified.

State appropriations for education have grown from $54,929,816 for the first postwar biennium 1945–47, to $361 million for 1959–61; these sums however represent only a fraction of the total costs. The chief support of the public schools is borne by the local school district; state aid is paid on the basis of a flat grant of $47 for each elementary school pupil, and $32 for each high school pupil. In addition, to equalize school opportunities in all districts where specified levies are met, a sum is paid which brings the total to $252 per pupil.

The high enrollment anticipated from the increased wartime birth rate has now materialized. From a total of 1,159,164 pupils for 1947–48, the figure increased to 1,880,664 in 1963–64. Of these 1,292,818 are in elementary schools, 687,846 in high schools. The importance of retaining the maximum number of pupils enrolled through the twelve grades, and keeping to a minimum school drop outs who swell the ranks of the unskilled for whom there is little or no employment has been recognized by adding guidance counseling services in the schools, as well as tests to determine aptitudes. Federal aid for agricultural, trade, and industrial programs in the public schools under the direction of the State Board for Vocational Education has been available since 1917. In addition to training offered as part of the high school curriculum along with academic courses, programs are also available as evening and part-time extension courses to journeymen apprentices and other adult workers. Criticism of the present system has been made on the ground that it does not offer instruction in occupations in which there are major labor shortages, such as repair services of all kinds, skilled crafts, public services, and other white-collar rather than blue-collar jobs. The Superintendent of Public Instruction commissioned a two-year study completed in 1960, which recommended regional consolidation of vocational schools on the high-school level and greatly increased facilities for technical training in junior colleges.

The problem of junior colleges is one of many considered by a permanent co-ordinating and planning agency for higher education in Illinois, created in 1961 by the General Assembly and organized with a permanent director and staff. Preceded by several earlier study commissions from 1943 to 1957, this Board for Higher Education was by statute required to make a master plan with recommendations to be presented to the General Assembly in 1965, the board then to continue its studies and recommend continuing changes.

The public institutions of higher education are headed by the University of Illinois at Urbana and Chicago, five state universities at Normal, DeKalb, Carbondale, Charleston, and Macomb, with a combined enrolment of 76,702 in 1963–64, up from the 31,847 in 1953–54. Additional public institutions are the Chicago Teachers College and 23 junior colleges. The non-public institutions include 9 universities, 31 colleges, and 5 two-year colleges. Some 45 other specialized institutions, a few very small, offer college work. Enrolment in the non-public institutions has grown from 79,181 resident students in 1953 to 114,118 in 1963, a rate of increase much lower than for state institutions. The total state enrolment of 114,118 is expected to become 499,000 in 1975, the outcome of the high birth rate of the 1940's and 1950's, and the rising rates of college attendance, which in Illinois in 1960 had been about the same as the national average of 37 per cent, and was excelled by 22 other states.

The master plan published in March, 1964, made recommendations as to students, faculty, curricula, expanded programs, a state-wide system of junior colleges, physical facilities, and over-all organization. The three existing governing boards of the state universities were retained and, in addition, an Illinois junior college board was recommended. The minimum costs for construction from 1965 to 1971 alone are estimated at $285.6 million. The plan was given wide publicity and public hearings were held in a number of cities before the board drafted its final report to the 1965 legislature.

UNIVERSITY OF ILLINOIS, URBANA-CHAMPAIGN

Looking south from Illinois Field, quadrangle is center, stadium and assembly hall, upper left, university farms lie beyond

UNIVERSITY OF CHICAGO

The Midway crosses the right-hand part of the picture; University buildings surround the quadrangle. Rocke-
feller Chapel appears in upper left.

A bond issue voted in 1960 made possible the beginning of enlarged construction programs for the six state universities, adding needed housing, laboratories, classrooms, and service facilities. The University of Illinois schools of Medicine, Pharmacy, and Dentistry are located in Chicago, and since the end of World War II the University has been operating a two-year undergraduate program in temporary quarters on Chicago's Navy Pier. Demands for a permanent center were met in 1961 by the choice of a site at Chicago Circle, the juncture of the Eisenhower, Dan Ryan, and Kennedy expressways, and a construction program in three parts calls for sixteen buildings to be ready in 1965. The architecture will be contemporary, with buildings designed for purpose—lectures, laboratories, and offices. The famous Hull House, founded by Jane Addams, lies within the area, and its activities have had to be relocated. The house will be restored to its original dimensions and the Student Union will be located nearby. Plans call for the early enrolment of some nine thousand students in four degree-granting colleges and two two-year divisions.

In addition to its programs at three campus locations, the University of Illinois in 1963 had 10,000 students enrolled in courses offered in 97 cities throughout the state. Of these enrolments one-third each were for graduate and undergraduate credit; others were for no credit. Some 3,000 students were also enrolled in correspondence study courses. In common with other institutions in Illinois, the university receives contracts for research and development projects from government, business, industrial, and private sources. Currently these total about $35 million, and for the most part cover research in agriculture, engineering, life sciences, and the physical sciences. Services in the areas of social, economic, and governmental problems are carried out by the Institutes of Government and Public Affairs, Labor and Industrial Relations, the three Bureaus of Economic and Business Research, Educational Research and Community Planning, and the Department of City Planning and Landscape Architecture.

Other state universities, all sharing bond issue allocations, have constructed new facilities and have enlarged educational programs. Two have installed off-campus centers. Northern Illinois State University at De Kalb maintains the Lorado Taft Field Campus at Oregon as a project in outdoor-teacher education. Southern Illinois University has located off-campus centers at Alton and East St. Louis, and has built new facilities to be known as Southwestern Campus at Edwardsville. Through its Division of Area Services, Southern Illinois University has worked with some sixty communities since its organization in 1953, and has published several studies on regional development.

Of Illinois' forty-five non-public institutions of full collegiate rank, the University of Chicago and Northwestern University are outstanding among the great institutions of the country. The University of Chicago, which opened its doors under the leadership of William Rainey Harper, set as its ideal the union of collegiate life with graduate instruction then to be found in but one or two institutions in the country. Since its founding graduate schools have multiplied, but the University of Chicago has maintained its distinguished rank. The University now has the College, four divisions, seven professional schools, and a downtown adult education division; it also includes the Oriental Institute, the Yerkes Astronomical Observatory at Williams Bay, Wisconsin, the Institute for the Study of Metals, and the Institute for Nuclear Studies named for Enrico Fermi, who with his colleagues at the University on December 2, 1942, inaugurated the atomic age by setting off the first controlled nuclear chain reaction.

In 1946 the University of Chicago was given the first contract to build and operate the Argonne National Laboratory under the Atomic Energy Commission for the purpose of conducting research into the peaceful uses of atomic energy. This community of thirty-seven hundred acres lies twenty-five miles southwest of Chicago; the personnel of the laboratory in 1963 included forty-eight hundred men and women, of whom twelve hundred were professional scientists and engineers. Only about 1 per cent of Argonne's work is secret. Scientific divisions include biological and medical research, chemical engineering, high energy physics, and reactor engineering. A reorganization of the Argonne Laboratory ordered by the AEC in October, 1964, will place policy management in a non-profit corporation to be made up of a group of midwestern universities. The University of Chicago will remain in control of operations.

Northwestern University, established in Evanston in 1851 when Chicago had a population of thirty thousand, has trained generations of Chicago leaders. Organized with a College of Liberal Arts, the Graduate School, and the Schools of Education, Journalism, Music, Speech, and Business, at Evanston, with its professional schools—Medicine, Dentistry, Law—in downtown Chicago, it also operates a full-scale evening division on both campuses. The Evanston campus at present is being enlarged by a gigantic lake-fill project which will provide some seventy-four acres for a dozen buildings. On the tip of the new campus will be the Lindheimer Astronomical Research Center with a forty-inch reflecting telescope; graduate training for astronomical scientists will be its chief purpose. A faculty planning committee with a ten-year program is giving direction to Northwestern's course of action; meantime a six-year medical program for students of highest competence, and research in solid state physics, industrial engineering, and computer science are areas of special achievement.

Along with the three large universities the Illinois Institute of Technology must be noted as a distinguished center for undergraduate and graduate training and research. It was formed in 1940 by the merger of Armour Institute of Technology and Lewis Institute. With its two affiliates, the IIT Research Institute and the Institute of Gas Technology, the American Railroad Research Center, and the John Crerar Library, it fills a 115-acre campus on the near South Side of Chicago. Adjacent to the campus is being developed an industrial research park.

Construction to meet the Illinois housing shortage in the postwar years can be measured by 1960 United States census figures: from 1940–49 296,241 housing units were built throughout the state; from 1950 to March, 1960, a total of 721,844 units was added. To meet the immediate needs of the thousands of returning veterans temporary housing was provided in many communities and on many college campuses. In Chicago a ten-year project supplied homes for families of some eight thousand servicemen; quonsets, demountables, and trailers were located on some twenty-two city and county-owned sites which were restored in 1956 when the last structure was demolished. Long-term loans from the Federal Housing Administration and the Veterans Administration made possible building a home with minimum down payments. Twenty years after the passage of the "G.I. Bill of Rights," it was reported that more than 237,000 veterans bought homes in Illinois with $2,299,979,342 in mortgages guaranteed by the Veterans Administration.

A state-wide program of housing construction was nevertheless in progress after 1932 when local governments were authorized to set up housing authorities and thus secure federal aid for the construction and maintenance of low-income housing units.

Chicago's public housing construction had its origin in the PWA program which in 1935 broke ground for the Jane Addams project, first of four thousand units constructed under the program. The Chicago Housing Authority, created in 1937 to build and manage low-rent public housing, in 1948 moved from a strictly federal-aid program to one participated in by state and local government. Through the Chicago Land Clearance Commission, which in 1962 merged into the Department of Urban Renewal, the city's blighted areas are cleared and made available for housing, institutional or industrial redevelopment; as an essential step displaced persons are first relocated. At the end of 1962 more than 28,000 units providing housing for some 45,000 adults and 90,000 children had been erected on 830 acres of land in scattered sites; additional projects with 1,449 units for families with children have been planned for 1967. Private as well as public agencies became active in developing housing projects. The New York Life Insurance Company built Lake Meadows, a 101-acre development and the first non-public project in a slum area. A successful integrated project, it led to the building of higher-cost units. Housing for elderly families of middle incomes is being developed by the Chicago Dwellings Association, a non-profit agency operating with state-grant funds.

The focus is now shifting to urban renewal where conservation areas or neighborhoods are designated in which some sites are cleared and community facilities improved but the rehabilitation of individual buildings by private property owners is emphasized. The elimination of all slum and blighted areas in the near future is the object of the program. In 1963 the program covered ten conservation areas. The Hyde Park–Kenwood project in the neighborhood of the University of Chicago aimed to rehabilitate 80 per cent of its existing structures as well as to add to new housing and space for parks, playgrounds, and other facilities. Throughout the state some twenty cities in 1963 were undertaking urban renewal projects while others were in the planning stage.

Few American cities, declared the *Architectural Forum* in

its special Chicago issue of May, 1962, ever started with a better break in planning than did Chicago under the Daniel Burnham Plan adopted in 1909 and followed until the end of World War II, nor got a better start in clearing slums; and few, it concluded had greater need of a new plan and the will to execute it. The Department of City Planning, organized in 1957 and designated to work with the reconstructed Chicago Plan Commission, eventually in August, 1964, issued a 100-page report, "Basic Policies for the Comprehensive Plan of Chicago." Recognizing that Burnham's plan had shaped the city of today, it presented tentatively policies to control future use of land for homes, parks, libraries, schools, industry, business, and transportation. This report had been preceded by a number of area plans including the 1958 "Development Plan for the Central Area of Chicago," which has now reached the construction stage. At the north end of the area a new Civic Center uses the present City-County Building and the State of Illinois Building as a nucleus; a new thirty-one–story court and office building will face a civic plaza. At the south end of the La Salle–Dearborn Street axis the new thirty-story United States Court House is the first building to be constructed in the Federal Center; eventually the old domed United States Court House will be replaced by another building. A proposed transportation center, and redevelopment projects for the areas north, west, and south of the Loop, as well as new projects for the lake front, are included in the plan.

The completion of the forty-one story Prudential Building in 1955 and the announcement of the Central Area Plan began a building boom in the downtown district which it was hoped would check dispersal to the suburbs. Architects continued the tradition of the first Chicago School in producing functional designs and employing advanced technological methods and materials. New practices included the use of air

NORTHWESTERN UNIVERSITY, EVANSTON

Aerial view shows landfill project, future site of Lindheimer Astronomical Research Center, and other university buildings

ILLINOIS INSTITUTE OF TECHNOLOGY, CHICAGO

Campus lies between Thirty-first (*right*) and Thirty-fifth streets, State Street (*foreground*) and the New York

rights over railroads and the orientation of construction to the river and lake fronts. Marina City, called the most amazing building in Chicago since the Ferris wheel and about as popular, represents architect Bertrand Goldberg's idea of a building to be used 24 hours a day. Two round 60-story towers with petal-shaped balconies offer parking on ramps for 900 cars, 896 apartments, theater, shops, offices, bowling alleys, restaurants, and a marina for 700 small craft. Sponsored by the Service Employees International Union which invested $3 million, it secured one of the largest FHA mortgages ever negotiated, $17.8 million.

Thirty-nine buildings of Chicago were recently named by the Commission on Chicago Architectural Landmarks as masterpieces of modern architecture and include the work of Louis Sullivan, Dankmar Adler, Frank Lloyd Wright, William LeBaron Jenney, Daniel Burnham, John W. Root, and others. Also included are the works of Ludwig Mies van der Rohe, famous in Germany before he came to the United States in 1938. His plan for the new campus and buildings of the Illinois Institute of Technology, where he headed the Department of Architecture and City Planning until 1958, the "glass house" apartments on Lake Shore Drive together with the new U.S. Court House and the proposed federal office building make Chicago a greater showplace for his work than any other city.

Problems growing out of an excessive amount of migration into and out of Chicago during the 1950–60 decade have had serious impact on the city's school situation. The 1953–63 enrolment increase for the whole public school system was met with the addition of 260 new school buildings and additions, and by 1963 double shifts were dropped for the first time in 100 years. By 1960 the Negro population had grown to 812,637, nearly 30 per cent of the city's population of 3,550,404, and had settled chiefly in Chicago's south and west side areas. Protesting *de facto* segregation of public schools in those neighborhoods, civil rights groups organized demonstrations. Late in 1963 a one-day boycott was staged by some 225,000 pupils, the resignation of the superintendent of schools was demanded, and suits were filed by parents against the Board of Education in the United States District Court. The Board refused to accept the resignation of the superintendent and appointed a special panel to investigate the problem. A report by the panel headed by Professor Philip Hauser of the University of Chicago recommended wider choice of schools within an enlarged neighborhood district and a program of gradual but fundamental improvement of facilities. While the report was being studied the superintendent of schools proposed that pupils above the fourth grade in congested schools might on application be transferred to others less crowded. "Sending" and "receiving" schools were designated, but a small proportion of those eligible for transfer made application in the autumn of 1964. A 500-page survey of education in the Chicago schools, in preparation for three years under the direction of Dr. Robert J. Havighurst of the University of Chicago, was submitted to the Board of Education in November, 1964. It urged greatly increased expenditures above present school costs, especially for disadvantaged children, and measures to achieve stable mixed neighborhoods.

CHAPTER XVIII

Politics and Administration

ILLINOIS at the end of the second World War, still functioning under the constitution of 1870, faced a critical need for an overhauling of its official structure. The governor, acting through his administrative code departments and commissions, was ranked high among the states as a strong head of the executive branch. The system of administrative code departments had proved effective and flexible in absorbing new services: to the original departments created in 1917 had been added Conservation (1925), Insurance, Public Safety (1941), Revenue (1943), and Aeronautics (1945). Trade and Commerce, one of the original code departments, was abolished in 1933 and its functions were distributed. Nevertheless new agencies were still being created with overlapping functions, and in 1949 the General Assembly set up the Commission To Study State Government, the "Shaefer" Commission, to make a broad study of the whole framework. Many of the commission's recommendations were incorporated in changes made by the General Assembly in the next ten years; some recommendations were adopted by department directors without legislative enactment. Recommendations were not made respecting problems growing out of the divided authority of the governor and other elected officers; constitutional amendments would be needed to effect changes in this area.

A new code Department of Personnel created by the legislature in 1955 provides a far-reaching reorganization of the Illinois civil service system established in 1905 and slowly extended to various state agencies. To the protective features of the old merit system have been added practices of modern employment administration—job classification, recruitment, and pay equalization studies. As yet the system applies chiefly to the agencies responsible to the governor, though certain provisions such as vacation, sick leave, etc., are generally applied.

Several new agencies were created in the general overhauling of the state's financial structure which resulted from the defalcations of the state auditor, reported in July, 1956, by a Chicago newspaper; the sum involved was more than $1.5 million. The governor promptly forced the auditor's resignation and appointed Lloyd Morey, emeritus president of the University of Illinois and formerly its comptroller, to serve out the term. A program of reorganization drawn up by Auditor Morey and Albert Jenner, Jr., chief investigator, by way of report to the Budgetary Commission, was given wide publicity; reform proposals were also made by other state officials and various private groups. Governor Stratton in his inaugural address, in January, 1957, indicated his own program, which included some of the Morey-Jenner proposals; in general the measures he favored were adopted. The auditor remained an elective officer though serious consideration was given to a "shorter ballot" amendment which would have eliminated the office. A Division of Administrative Services was added to the Department of Finance to administer a new purchasing act covering all state agencies; the Department of Finance was also authorized to make procedural audits of all state agencies. Post-audit control was to be exercised through a non-code Department of Audit, headed by an Auditor General, appointed by the Governor for six years, to make audit reports to the General Assembly, and by a Legislative Audit Commission acting as watchdog. A new code department, Department of Financial Institutions, was created to take over from the auditor the supervision of savings, loans, and other financial institutions. After a referendum in 1958, the new department also acquired supervision of state banks. From the general reorganization the auditor's office emerged with functions and patronage reduced; required to give a higher performance bond, the next incumbent was compensated by an increase in salary.

The Department of Public Health, created in 1917, was extensively reorganized in 1950 in line with recommendations the state had requested the U.S. Public Health Service to make. Five regional offices are located throughout the state. The department's specific health services include the administration of grants-in-aid to fulltime local health departments. Thirty counties and twenty communities now have such units.

Welfare and social services of the state, closely allied to those of public health, were reassigned by the General Assembly in 1961 and 1963. The Department of Public Welfare, made responsible in 1917 for all the state schools, homes, hospitals, and penal institutions, during the depression had acquired the administration of the public aid program; in 1943 the Illinois Public Aid Commission was created to direct that service. After a departmental reorganization in 1944 seven regions were set up in the state to make the welfare services more accessible to recipients. The administration of penal institutions and supervision of parolees had been transferred to the Department of Public Safety in 1941. In 1961 with 80 per cent of the budget going to the care and treatment of the mentally ill and retarded, the department was reconstituted as the Department of Mental Health. Six community-centered mental health clinics were set up in the state; essentially out-patient centers, each would have some beds for adults. A bond issue approved in the election of 1960 made possible the construction of new hospitals and improvements to older institutions.

Two more code departments created in 1963 bring the total to seventeen reporting to the governor; in addition in 1962 some sixty-six permanent and eighteen temporary non-department boards and commissions performed specific functions. Services continue to be reassigned and functions of independent commissions are at times absorbed in the various departments. The new Department of Public Assistance took over the functions of the Illinois Public Aid Commission. The Department of Children and Family Services completed reassignment of duties of the Department of Public Welfare; it will provide social services to children and their families, operate the children's institutions, and provide rehabilitative care.

Strong sentiment for a reduction in the number of the state's elective officers has been expressed in recent years; with the removal from the ballot of the auditor, treasurer, superintendent of public instruction, and members of the Board of Trustees of the University of Illinois these offices could be filled by appointment. The necessary constitutional changes involved would now be much easier because of the passage of the Gateway Amendment by the voters in November, 1950. Henceforth at any session the General Assembly may propose amendments to as many as three different articles of the constitution, instead of only one. Moreover an amendment may be adopted by a majority of the persons voting at the election, or by two-thirds of those voting on the amendment. Under the old provisions for amendment only nineteen proposals had been placed before the voters from 1870 to 1950 and of these twelve failed; in the years 1950–64, fourteen amendments have been proposed and seven adopted.

The census of 1950 reduced the state's delegation in Congress from 26 to 25 members and in 1951 the General Assembly laid out the lines of the new congressional districts. This re-apportionment was made just four years after the redistricting of 1947, the first since 1901 and the result of a long bitter fight through many sessions of the legislature. In 1901, when Illinois had attained 25 representatives in the U. S. House of Representatives, 25 districts were drawn, 10 in Chicago and Cook County, 15 downstate. Illinois acquired two more members in 1910; these were elected at large until the 1940 census reduced the number to 26, with one representative to be elected at large. The 1947 act drew lines for 26 districts, 13 for Cook and Lake counties, 13 downstate. In the Eighty-second Congress elected in 1950, the last under the 1947 apportionment, the Illinois delegation was 8 Democrats, 18 Republicans; representatives elected in 1952 to the Eighty-third Congress were 9 Democrats, 16 Republicans. Everett Dirksen, Republican, had been elected to the Senate in 1950, winning over Scott Lucas by nearly 300,000 votes. After the 1960 census the Illinois delegation again lost one member, and the 1961 General Assembly designated 24 congressional districts divided equally between Chicago, Cook County, and downstate. The 1962 election returned 12 Democrats, 12 Republicans.

Remapping the legislative districts too had been ignored since 1901, despite a constitutional directive for redistricting every ten years. Reapportionment bills had been introduced into the General Assembly many times, and the proposed constitution of 1922 contained provisions for redistricting which contributed to its defeat; the courts were powerless to compel action and the urging of every governor for twenty years was unheeded. Reacting to accumulated pressure for action—and with the Gateway Amendment to ease the process—the voters in the 1954 election adopted an amendment requiring the General Assembly to redraw the representative districts in 1955, again in 1963, and every ten years thereafter. Provisions were made in case the General Assembly failed to carry out the terms of the amendment; all were necessary in 1963.

In 1955, however, the General Assembly achieved a remapping of the senatorial and representative districts. Instead of 51 districts, each with 1 senator and 3 representatives, 58 senatorial districts based on area, 59 representative districts based on population, were drawn. Cook County was given 24 senatorial districts (18 in Chicago, 6 outside), 30 legislative districts (23 in Chicago, 7 outside the corporate limits). Cumulative voting for representatives—each voter allowably casting his three votes for one, two, or three candidates—was continued for the assurance of minority representation.

In the presidential campaigns of 1952 and 1956, with Governor Adlai Stevenson as the Democratic candidate, the outcome of the election in Illinois was of first importance. Participation by a large non-partisan group of admirers of the governor, added to the party support, in 1952 was inadequate against General Dwight D. Eisenhower, who carried ninety-eight counties in the state with a plurality of 443,407. Republican candidate for governor, William Stratton, who had served two terms each as congressman-at-large and as state treasurer, defeated Democrat Sherwood Dixon.

In the 1956 primaries the Republican auditor, whose defalcations were later revealed, had been renominated to succeed himself; he was replaced as a candidate by State Senator Elbert Smith. Orville H. Hodge was brought to trial promptly, convicted and sentenced from twelve to fifteen years imprisonment. Another disclosure by a Chicago newspaper then reported that the Democratic candidate for governor, Herbert C. Paschen, Cook County treasurer, had a private employee welfare fund from banks holding county funds. On August 29 he resigned and was replaced by Richard B. Austin, judge of the Cook County Superior Court. Governor Stratton won a second term by a small plurality, though President Eisenhower carried the state over Adlai Stevenson by 847,645 votes. Republican Everett Dirksen was re-elected as senator; the congressional delegation composed 11 Democrats, 14 Republicans.

The Seventieth General Assembly, first elected under the new apportionment, had a Republican majority of 19 in the Senate, 11 in the House, A special session was called for June 16–20, 1958, to consider measures to alleviate the business recession; $15 million in relief was appropriated for the Public Aid Commission, and unemployment compensation was extended from 26 to 39 weeks.

The 1958 election gave the Democrats the lead in the state delegation to the Eighty-sixth Congress—14 Democrats, 11 Republicans; in the Seventy-first General Assembly the Republicans led by 4 seats, having a majority of 9 in the Senate while the Democrats led by 5 seats in the House. The Republicans led in both House and Senate in the legislature elected in 1960, with a majority of 5, but on the state ticket the party elected only Charles Carpentier as Secretary of State. Democratic candidate Otto Kerner, county judge of Cook County since 1954, defeated Governor Stratton by a 500,000 plurality, and Senator Paul Douglas, Democrat, was re-elected over Samuel W. Witwer by approximately the same vote. However, in the presidential race where thanks to television debates the voters had heard more speeches from the principal candidates than ever before, the vote for John F. Kennedy, Democrat, was 2,377,846, and for Richard Nixon, Republican, 2,368,988, a plurality of 8,858 votes. Election frauds were charged, and several hundred Chicago precinct election officials were indicted. Eventually all cases were dropped.

Measures to provide new sources and volume of revenue, as well as legislation for the social and economic welfare of Illinois citizens, have been called for in every general assembly of recent years. Increasing state services, co-operation with federal programs, and rising costs have increased the need for postwar revenue from $1,394,017,666 in 1947 to $3,526,695,336 in 1961 (biennial appropriations). A constitutional requirement that a tax be applied "with uniformity" as to the class upon which it is levied has caused various new tax laws to be thrown out by the courts. The general property tax has not been used for state purposes since 1932, and now is exclusively assigned to county and local units. The "sales tax" of 2 per cent adopted in 1933 when other tax receipts were reduced and relief needs were made acute by the depression, is now the principal source of state revenue; in 1962 it amounted to 47.8 per cent of the total. Strictly described, the tax is a retailers' occupation tax—a tax on the privilege of selling personal property at retail—passed on to the customer; lowered in 1940 to 2 per cent, as postwar expenditures mounted the state levy was increased in 1955 to 2½ per cent, with city governments allowed to impose another ½ of 1 per cent without referendum, and again in 1961 to 3½ per cent for the state plus the ½ per cent city-county levy. Loopholes which permitted buying in states where no such tax was levied were stopped by the adoption of the "use tax" in 1955, and by broadening the base in 1961 to include items previously untaxed, such as books, records, custom-made goods, and special order materials sold to contractors for construction and remodeling. A tax was levied also on a combined service occupation and use (drugs to a pharmacist, etc.). The rate was levied at a uniform 3½ per cent, provision being made against a double levy of the tax. In addition to sales taxes, motor fuel taxes, motor vehicle license fees, taxes on public utilities, cigarettes, beverages and liquors, and inheritances provide the state revenue in that order.

Approval by the voters of bond issues for carrying out large-scale projects still provides an important source of funds. In the 1960 election two such proposals authorized an issue of $145 million for state university expansion and $50 million for the construction and improvement of mental hospitals.

There seems a strong likelihood that Illinois, in common

OLD STATEHOUSE, SPRINGFIELD (1837–76), IN WHICH LINCOLN RECEIVED THE
NEWS OF HIS ELECTION TO THE PRESIDENCY

Courtesy of Illinois State Historical Library

ILLINOIS STATEHOUSE

with other states, will face a crisis in financing the state which will call for an overhauling of the tax structure. The burden of the property tax on certain taxpayers in a state where local taxes are a relatively high proportion of state-local taxation is leading various groups to go on record as favoring a state income tax. The Commission on Revenue, created by the General Assembly in 1961 to study and make recommendations for improving the state's tax structure, in 1963 published an exhaustive report on which to base future legislation.

The federal government has increasingly been the source of funds for a long list of state expenditures—about one-fifth of the total in the fiscal year 1962, by far the largest sum being assigned to road building. The public assistance programs set up by the Social Security Act—old-age assistance, aid to dependent children, to the blind, the disabled, and the medically indigent aged, financed jointly by federal and state governments, receive the next largest block of federal funds. Airport and hospital construction, various health services, school lunch programs, and vocational education also receive grants. The 1963 Federal Higher Education Facilities Act will provide new grants for expanded classrooms for colleges, junior colleges, and technical institutions; this grant is similar in terms to the College Housing Act of 1950. The Illinois Board of Higher Education will be the administration agency within the state.

Action looking to the decennial legislative reapportionment now required by the 1954 amendment was begun early in 1963 by the Seventy-third General Assembly where Republicans had a majority of 3 in the House (90 to 87) and 12 in the Senate (35 to 23). Based on the 1960 census, a remapping would take account of a loss of population in southern Illinois, and a great increase in the metropolitan area around Chicago; however, Chicago itself had lost 1.9 per cent in population since 1950; the suburban areas of Cook County had correspondingly gained. Republicans and Democrats both proposed bills, the Republican bill giving 21 districts to Chicago and 9 to Cook County suburbs, instead of 23 and 7 as in 1955, which the Democratic bill retained. Both bills took two districts from southern Illinois so as to give an additional district each to DuPage and Lake Counties. Following a southern Illinois protest at losing two districts, the Republican bill restored one district thereby withdrawing the extra district from Lake County. This bill was passed on June 21. On July 1 Governor Kerner vetoed the bill, citing the failure to give Lake County a second district, and population disparities in the southern districts. The governor's right to veto a reapportionment bill duly passed by the General Assembly was later upheld by the Sangamon County Circuit Court and the Illinois Supreme Court.

The bipartisan commission of 10 members as provided by the 1954 constitutional amendment was duly appointed by the governor, and for four months until a legal deadline on December 14 the Democrats held the line against Republican demands for 21 districts for Chicago and 9 for the suburbs. The end was a stalemate. The Supreme Court acting promptly on suits filed as a result, ruled that the old 1955 districts could not be restored; also those persons running for election to the Senate would run from their respective districts, and not "at large."

Following the Illinois Supreme Court decision of January 4, 1964, Governor Kerner called a special session of the legislature to provide measures to nominate and elect the House of Representatives of the Seventy-fourth General Assembly on an at-large basis. The at-large election plan adopted and signed by the governor on January 29 provided for the choice of no more than 118 candidates by state Democratic and Republican conventions to be held June 1 in Springfield, the figure 118 representing two-thirds control if one party should win all 118 members. Delegates to the convention were to be chosen in the regular April primary, two each from the old 1955 House of

Representative districts, delegates to have a weighted vote equal to half the vote cast for the party's candidates for representative in the 1962 election. Cumulative voting was to be abandoned for primary and fall elections. These arrangements were upheld by the Illinois Supreme Court on April 21.

Democratic and Republican conventions were held simultaneously in Springfield June 1 following the April 14 primary. Of the 118 candidates chosen by the Republicans, 70 were incumbents (30 from Cook County, 40 downstate); six incumbents seeking re-election, also serving as delegates, were dropped under fire of a threatening third-party ticket if these men were nominated. A "blue-ribbon" list of 22 non-political candidates who agreed not to run for a second term if elected was included among the non-incumbents. Democrats met briefly and named a 21-man executive committee to name their slate; on June 20 at a state convention the nominating list of 69 incumbents and 49 new candidates was adopted (47 from Chicago, 14 from Cook County, and 57 from downstate).

Although state senators were to be elected from their own districts in the election of 1964, the status of senatorial apportionment based on areas in Illinois as elsewhere was being seriously challenged. The U.S. Supreme Court in February, 1962, (in *Baker* v. *Carr*) announced that the federal courts had jurisdiction over the districting of state legislatures, and cases protesting existing apportionments were filed in thirty-nine states by the end of 1963. The Seventh Circuit Court of Appeals in Chicago, in July, 1963, dismissed a suit brought by the officials of the Steelworkers' Union and other Chicagoans, claiming the state senate should be based on population, not area. The case was appealed to the U.S. Supreme Court. In June, 1964, dealing with the cases involving six states, the Supreme Court held that in both houses of state legislatures members must represent substantially the same number of people. Next day the Illinois case, with those involving eight other states, was remanded to the lower courts for action in accordance with the general ruling. Members of Congress in both houses at once brought in bills to nullify or delay the court's decision. A proposal by Senator Dirksen was made a rider to the Foreign Aid Appropriation Bill. A compromise proposal ended weeks of debate, but perished in joint committee. Nevertheless Congress indicated that it wished federal and state judges to proceed slowly with the enforcement of upper house reapportionment.

With candidates for the State House of Representatives to be elected at large, Illinois endured in the 1964 election an experience which the constitutional amendment of 1954 had tried to forestall. In each county the special long orange ballots were sent from the election districts to special tallying points. A week later the first tabulation of a few rural counties was published. In Cook County officials refused to announce the tally until after the official canvass, and final results were withheld until December 4. The Democratic party won a two-thirds majority in the House by the election of 118 candidates. In the State Senate, filled by election from the old districts, the Republicans retained a majority.

On the national scene Lyndon B. Johnson, who had succeeded to office on the death of President Kennedy in November, 1963, headed the Democratic ticket. In a national Democratic landslide, President Johnson led Republican candidate Barry Goldwater by 890,887 votes. The margin was closer for state officials, and Governor Kerner led Republican Charles Percy by only 179,299 votes; all Democratic candidates for state office, including university trustees, were elected. In the State's congressional delegation the former balance of 12 to 12 became 13 Democrats, 11 Republicans. Two proposed amendments to the state constitution were defeated. These would have provided annual sessions of the General Assembly and conferred upon it emergency powers in event of nuclear attack.

The 1964 election marked another innovation in Illinois—the first judicial elections to the reorganized state courts. The judiciary was completely revolutionized by means of an amendment adopted by the voters in November, 1962. The new comprehensive system of three tiers of courts resembles a model system set up in 1914 by the American Judicature Society then organizing in Chicago; in January, 1964, the society celebrated its fiftieth anniversary along with the success of its goal. Organized efforts to remodel the court system were undertaken immediately after the adoption of the Gateway amendment in 1950. Proposed amendments failed in the legislature in 1953 and 1955; in 1957 a judicial amendment was adopted which was rejected in the 1958 election. A somewhat revised proposal was adopted by the legislature in 1961, and accepted by the voters in November, 1962, the new judiciary to be effective January 1, 1964.

The new system which operates through the three levels of the Supreme Court, Appellate Court, and Circuit Courts, was designed to simplify and modernize court procedures, to effect a reduction in costs and delays in litigation, and to assure greater independence to the judiciary. The Supreme Court comprising seven judges which administers the whole system, numbers three from Cook County (the new First District), one each from the new second to fifth districts. The Appellate Court has twenty-four judges, twelve from Cook County, four each from the other three same districts. Judges of the Supreme Court and the Appellate Court serve ten-year terms. The Circuit Court of Cook County under a chief judge has two departments, County and Municipal. On the trial level in each of the twenty-one circuit districts (Cook County and twenty downstate) there is to be a single circuit court replacing all county and probate courts, superior and criminal courts of

Cook County, municipal, city, village, and town courts, as well as police magistrate and justice of the peace courts. All the court officials under the old system will be absorbed until the end of the terms for which they were elected. Judges will initially be named by party choice and elected in November instead of at special judicial elections; thereafter each will run on his own record without opposition and party designation.

The circuit courts have unlimited jurisdiction. Each will have a circuit court judge as before, associate judges, and magistrates; each county has at least one branch of the court, with an associate judge in residence, and such other branches with general or special functions as are needed. Positions of court officials are fulltime occupations; all functionaries are barred from private practice or all private occupation, as well as from political appointments. Salaries are paid by the state, although some supplements will be paid in Cook County and elsewhere. There will be no fee officers. Preparations for changeover on January 1, 1964, demanded great efforts throughout 1963, especially on the part of the circuit judges. Judges of each circuit elected one of their colleagues as acting chief judge who held work sessions in Springfield to plan details of reorganization under the Supreme Court administrator, an office of recent origin which is continued as that of administrative director. Details of handling traffic violations, minor offenses, and such cases as would arise immediately on the changeover (New Year's Eve) were anticipated; the transition appeared to have been accomplished smoothly.

Law enforcement agencies as well as others have been expanded and reorganized to serve a highly populated, urbanized, industrialized state. The Illinois Department of Public Safety is responsible for the administration of the state's law enforcement agencies and penal institutions; since its organization in 1941 the areas of its work have included crime detection, programs of crime prevention, supervision of paroles, as well as traffic safety and fire prevention programs. Pardons and paroles are granted by a board appointed by the governor. The Illinois state police, now some twelve hundred officers under the merit system, have state-wide authority similar to that of a county sheriff. To set up a program to prevent juvenile delinquency and deal with young offenders committed by the courts, the Youth Commission was created in 1953 by the General Assembly, taking over services performed since 1939 by the Department of Public Welfare. A Division of Community Services of the Youth Commission sponsors state-wide local organizations which operate recreational centers and help to find jobs for out-of-school juveniles. On the local level there are many evidences of a positive approach to the problem: counseling services are offered in the schools, volunteer organizations offer tutoring and study facilities to prevent school drop outs, and police departments in many communities are operating their own youth projects.

The investigation of crime syndicate activities of all kinds—infiltration into legitimate business, business frauds, gambling, as well as specific acts of violence—has been made the responsibility of the Illinois Crime Commission created in 1963 by the General Assembly. A director and staff of ten was appointed in late 1963; the director has power to issue subpoenas for witnesses and the commission may file recommendations for prosecution before any state's attorney, and may initiate crime fighting legislation. Hearings were begun in early 1964, and a report will be made to the General Assembly.

For the recreation and enjoyment of its citizens and an increasing number of visitors, the state of Illinois maintains some eighty parks, conservation areas, and memorial sites. These commemorate all phases of the state's history from the time of prehistoric Indians to the present, the most numerous being fifteen sites associated with Abraham Lincoln, including the restored village of New Salem where he lived as a young man. There are no national parks in the state but the federal government owns some two hundred sixteen thousand acres of forest land in southern Illinois, most of which lies within the Shawnee National Forest. The state owns ten thousand acres of forest, and nine counties have forest preserves. The Cook County Forest Preserve has secured the remaining bits of woodland in the Calumet and Des Plaines valleys and on the hills above them. Illinois, however, is considered deficient in recreational park acreage, having the lowest per capita holdings of any state. Two new dams projected on the Kaskaskia River, one near Shelbyville, another at Carlyle, will supply water resources, flood control, and greatly enlarged recreational facilities, which will be increased by lakes under construction in many counties. The Department of Conservation, which maintains the state's parks, stocks the lakes with fish, and maintains a game propagation program with the co-operation of the Illinois Natural History Survey, an agency continuously engaged in wildlife research.

The extent to which Illinois citizens are participating in the creative arts and various cultural pursuits is currently being studied by the Governor's Arts Council appointed in July, 1963. Quincy is an example of the type of community whose activities are now being surveyed by the commission. As a parent organization the Quincy Society of Fine Arts, organized in 1948, now has fourteen member organizations devoted to art, music, the theater, photography, and a youth development organization. It has a symphony orchestra, as do various other Illinois cities. In 1964 the Council received foundation grants which partially financed some out-of-town performances of the Chicago Symphony Orchestra. In Chicago the Mayor's Committee on Economic and Cultural Development is aiming at creating a cultural center and repertory theater in Chicago; it also began the publication of a quarterly magazine *Chicago* in July, 1964. Instruction in music and art is offered at all levels in the schools, and is supplemented by extension programs carried out by various educational institutions. The University of Illinois offers such programs in numerous communities and on the campus at Urbana. Art extension courses were offered in nineteen communities in the summer of 1963. In 1964, its sixteenth season, the summer youth music program enrolled 1,316 students in three two-week programs; and since 1951 students from 154 high schools have participated in the summer youth theater. Similar groups are held in forensics. School of Music organizations give many performances off-campus every year; in 1964 the symphony orchestra made a concert tour of Central and South America.

Illinois' centennial in 1918 fell in a year significant perhaps as the end of an era. Participation in a world war had so increased federal activities within the state that it would no longer possess a unique social and economic entity. Events in the succeeding years have multiplied the federal agencies which affect Illinoisans directly, and indirectly through services performed jointly with state and local governments. Inter-state activities too are increasingly important. Reciprocal laws, inter-state compacts, conferences of governors, legislators, county officials, and others deal with problems on a wide horizontal basis. But the state which emerged from the vast area known as the Illinois Country nearly one hundred and fifty years ago has always played out its story on a broad canvas, and so it will continue.

APPENDIX

Population of Illinois by Census Years 1790–1960

1790	
1800	
1810	12,282
1820	55,162
1830	157,445
1840	476,183
1850	851,470
1860	1,711,951
1870	2,539,891
1880	3,077,871
1890	3,826,351
1900	4,821,550
1910	5,638,591
1920	6,485,280
1930	7,630,654
1940	7,897,241
1950	8,712,176
1960	10,081,158

Selected Bibliography

BIBLIOGRAPHIES AND GUIDES

ANGLE, PAUL M., and BEYER, RICHARD L. *A Handbook of Illinois History*. Springfield, 1943. Reprinted from Illinois State Historical Society *Papers in Illinois History*. Springfield, 1941.

BUCK, SOLON J. *Travel and Description*. ("Illinois Historical Collections," Vol. 9.) Springfield, 1914. In addition to works on travel and description, this volume lists county histories, atlases, biographical collections, and publications of territorial and state laws.

GOVE, SAMUEL (ed.). *State and Local Government in Illinois: A Bibliography*. Urbana: University of Illinois, December, 1953; Institute of Government and Public Affairs. *1958 Supplement to State and Local Government in Illinois: A Bibliography* (with Alvin D. Sokolow). Includes a complete listing of reports, periodicals, and other publications of Illinois governmental agencies.

HOWARD, VIVIAN H.; LUNSDEN, ALMA; and SHAY, AGATHA (compilers). *Illinois: A Bibliography*. *Illinois Libraries*, October, 1948. Revised and printed as a separate, March, 1952. Revised and printed in *Illinois Libraries*, September, 1960. Lists publications issued by state agencies.

SCOTT, FRANKLIN W. *Newspapers and Periodicals of Illinois, 1814–1879*. ("Illinois Historical Collections," Vol. 6.) Springfield, 1910.

Selected Bibliography. Illinois, Chicago and Its Environs. ("American Guide Series.") Federal Writers Project. Chicago, 1937.

GENERAL REFERENCES

BATEMAN, NEWTON, and SELBY, PAUL (eds.). *Historical Encyclopedia of Illinois*. Chicago: Munsell Pub. Co., 1899. Reissued in combination with some 34 county histories and biographical collections, 1899-1913. *Historical Encyclopedia with Commemorative Biographies* (with J. Seymour Currey and others). 3 vols. Chicago 1926–43. (A still later issue.)

Illinois: A Descriptive and Historical Guide. ("American Guide Series.") Federal Writers Project. Chicago: A. C. McClurg & Co., 1939; rev. ed., 1947. Guides were also published for the following cities: Cairo, 1938; Galena, 1937; Hillsboro, 1940; Nauvoo, n.d.; Princeton, 1939; Rockford, 1941.

"Illinois Historical Collections." 31 vols. Springfield: Illinois Historical Library, 1907–50. These volumes have long historical introductions and contain documents for various periods of Illinois history. Issued in series as follows: French, British, Virginia, Executive, Lincoln, Law, Statistical, Bibliographical. Separate volumes listed below.

Illinois History. Successor to the *Junior Historian,* a magazine for young readers. 1946 to date. Illinois State Historical Society.

Inventory of the County Archives of Illinois. Historical Records Survey. This series was started under the Federal Writers Project and from 1939 was sponsored by the State of Illinois. Surveys were published for 34 counties; each contains a history of the county.

Journal of the Illinois State Historical Society. 1908 to date.

MOSES, JOHN. *Illinois Historical and Statistical.* 2 vols. Chicago: Fergus Printing Co., 1889–92.

Publications of the Illinois State Historical Society, 1905–42. These were successively *Bulletins, Transactions,* and *Papers in Illinois History.*

THE LAND AND THE PEOPLE

Bulletins 1–4, 1959–63. Urbana: Illinois Archaeological Survey. Periodic reports of current archaeological projects, particularly in areas scheduled for bulldozing.

GARLAND, JOHN H. *The North American Midwest: A Regional Geography.* New York: Wiley, 1955.

GRAY, JAMES. *The Illinois.* ("The Rivers of America") New York: Farrar & Rinehart, 1940.

HANSEN, HARRY. *The Chicago.* ("The Rivers of America.") New York: Farrar & Rinehart, 1942.

MASTERS, EDGAR LEE. *The Sangamon.* ("The Rivers of America.") New York: Farrar & Rinehart, 1942.

PAGE, JOHN L. *Climate of Illinois.* Urbana: University of Illinois Agricultural Experiment Station *Bulletin* 532, 1949.

PEASE, THEODORE C., and WERNER, RAYMOND C. *The French Foundations. 1680–1693.* ("Illinois Historical Collections," Vol. 23.) Springfield, 1934. The "Degannes Memoir," pages 302–96, is the best early description of Illinois and its Indians.

Poggi, Edith Muriel. *The Prairie Province of Illinois.* Urbana: University of Illinois Studies in the Social Sciences, 1934.

Prehistoric People of Illinois. Chicago Natural History Museum, 1963.

Smith, Harriet. *Indians of Early Chicago.* Chicago Natural History Museum, 1957.

Story of Illinois Booklets, Numbers 1–13, covering anthropology, art, botany, geology, history, zoölogy. Springfield: Illinois State Museum, 1954–63.

Tucker, Sarah Jones. *Indian Villages of the Illinois Country: Atlas.* ("Illinois State Museum Scientific Papers," Vol. 2, Part 1.) Springfield, 1942.

THE FRENCH REGIME, 1673–1763

Alvord, Clarence W. *The Illinois Country, 1673–1818.* ("The Centennial History of Illinois," Vol. 1.) Chicago: A. C. McClurg & Co., 1918–20.

Belting, Natalia M. *Kaskaskia under the French Regime.* Urbana: University of Illinois Press, 1948.

Breese, Sidney. *The Early History of Illinois from its discovery by the French in 1673 until its cession to Great Britain in 1763, including the narrative of Marquette's Discovery of the Mississippi.* Chicago: E. B. Myers & Co., 1884.

Caldwell, Norman. *The French in the Mississippi Valley.* Urbana: University of Illinois Press, 1941.

DeLanglez, Jean. *Life and Voyages of Louis Jolliet, 1645–1700.* Chicago: Institute of Jesuit History, 1948.

Knight, Robert, and Zeuch, Lucius H. *The Location of the Chicago Portage of the Seventeenth Century.* Chicago: University of Chicago Press, 1920.

Palm, Sister Mary Borgias. *The Jesuit Missions of the Illinois Country, 1673–1763.* Cleveland: The Sisters of Notre Dame, 1933.

Parkman, Francis. *LaSalle and the Discovery of the Great West.* Boston: Little, Brown & Co., 1926.

Pease, Theodore C. *Anglo-French Boundary Disputes in the West.* ("Illinois Historical Collections," Vol. 27.) Springfield, 1936.

Pease, Theodore C., and Jenison, Ernestine. *Illinois on the Eve of the Seven Years' War.* ("Illinois Historical Collections," Vol. 29.) Springfield, 1940.

Quaife, Milo M. *Checagou, 1673–1835.* Chicago: University of Chicago Press, 1933.

THE BRITISH REGIME, 1763–78

ALVORD, CLARENCE W. *The Mississippi Valley in British Politics.* 2 vols. Cleveland: Arthur H. Clark Co., 1917.

ALVORD, CLARENCE W., and CARTER, CLARENCE E. *The Critical Period, 1763–1765; The New Regime, 1765–1767; Trade and Politics, 1767–1769.* ("Illinois Historical Collections," Vols. 10, 11, and 16.) Springfield, 1915, 1916, 1921.

CARTER, CLARENCE E. *Great Britain and the Illinois Country, 1763–1774.* Washington: American Historical Association, 1910.

MASON, EDWARD (ed.). "British Illinois" and "Rocheblave Papers," *Early Chicago and Illinois.* ("Chicago Historical Society's Collection," Vol. 4.) 1890.

MOSES, JOHN (ed.). "Court of Enquiry at Fort Chartres, 1770," *Early Chicago and Illinois.* ("Chicago Historical Society's Collection," Vol. 4.) 1890.

PECKHAM, HOWARD. *Pontiac and the Indian Uprising.* Princeton: Princeton University Press, 1947.

SAVELLE, MAX. *George Morgan, Colony Builder.* New York: Columbia University Press, 1932.

SCHUYLER, ROBERT L. *The Transition in Illinois from British to American Government.* New York: Columbia University Press, 1909.

TRANSITION TO STATEHOOD, 1778–1818

ALVORD, CLARENCE W. (ed.). *Cahokia Records, 1778–90; Kaskaskia Records, 1778–90.* ("Illinois Historical Collections," Vols. 2 and 5.) Springfield, 1907, 1910.

JAMES, JAMES ALTON (ed.). *George Rogers Clark Papers, 1771–1781* and *1781–1783.* ("Illinois Historical Collections," Vols. 8 and 19.) Springfield, 1912, 1926.

———. *The Life of George Rogers Clark.* Chicago: University of Chicago Press, 1928.

MASON, EDWARD (ed.). "John Todd," "John Todd's Letter Book," "Lists of Early Illinois Citizens," *Early Chicago and Illinois.* ("Chicago Historical Society's Collection," Vol. 4.) 1890.

PEASE, THEODORE C. (ed.). *Laws of the Northwest Territory, 1788–1800.* ("Illinois Historical Collections," Vol. 17.) Springfield, 1925.

PEASE, THEODORE C. and MARGUERITE J. *George Rogers Clark and the Revolution in Illinois, 1763–1787*. Springfield: Illinois State Historical Library, 1929.

PHILBRICK, FRANCIS S. (ed.). *Laws of Indiana Territory, 1801–1809; Laws of Illinois Territory, 1809–1818*. ("Illinois Historical Collections," Vols. 21 and 25.) Springfield, 1930, 1950.

THE FRONTIER STATE, 1818–48

BIRKBECK, MORRIS. *Letters from Illinois*. London: Printed for Taylor and Messey, 1818.

BOGGESS, ARTHUR C. *The Settlement of Illinois, 1778–1830*. ("Chicago Historical Society's Collection," Vol. 5.) 1908.

BUCK, SOLON J. *Illinois in 1818*. (Introductory volume of "The Centennial History of Illinois.") Springfield: The Illinois Centennial Commission, 1917.

CARLSON, THEODORE L. *The Illinois Military Tract: A Study of Land Occupation, Utilization and Tenure*. Urbana: University of Illinois Press, 1951.

CARTWRIGHT, PETER. *Autobiography of Peter Cartwright, the Backwoods Preacher*. Edited by W. P. Strickland. Cincinnati: L. Swormstedt & A. Poe, 1856.

CAVANAUGH, HELEN. *Funk of Funk's Grove: Farmer Legislator and Cattle King of the Old Northwest, 1797–1865*. Bloomington, Ill., 1952.

COLE, ARTHUR C. (ed.). *Constitutional Debates of 1847*. ("Illinois Historical Collections," Vol. 14.) Springfield, 1919.

DAVIS, INEZ SMITH. *The Story of the Church: Reorganized Church of Jesus Christ of Latter Day Saints*. Independence, Mo.: Herald Pub. House, 1948.

DOWRIE, GEORGE W. *The Development of Banking in Illinois, 1817–1863*. Urbana: University of Illinois Studies in the Social Sciences, 1913.

EDWARDS, NINIAN. *History of Illinois from 1778 to 1863; and Life and Times of Ninian Edwards*. Springfield: Illinois State Journal Co., 1870.

FLOWER, GEORGE. *History of the English Settlement in Edwards County, Illinois, Founded in 1817 and 1818 by Morris Birkbeck and George Flower*. ("Chicago Historical Society's Collection," Vol. 1.) 1882.

GREENE, E. B., and ALVORD C. W. (eds.). *Governor's Letterbooks, 1818–1834*. E. B. GREENE and C. M. THOMPSON, *Governor's Letterbooks, 1840–1853*. ("Illinois Historical Collections," Vols. 4 and 7.) Springfield, 1909, 1911.

JACKSON, DONALD (ed.). *Black Hawk: An Autobiography*. Urbana: University of Illinois Press, 1955.

KRENKEL, JOHN. *Illinois Internal Improvements, 1818–1848*. Cedar Rapids, Iowa: Torch Press, 1958.

NORTON, MARGARET CROSS (ed.). *Illinois Census Returns, 1810, 1818; Illinois Census Returns, 1820*. ("Illinois Historical Collections," Vols. 24 and 26.) Springfield, 1934, 1935.

O'DEA, THOMAS F. *The Mormons*. Chicago: University of Chicago Press, 1957.

PEASE, THEODORE C. *The Frontier State, 1818–1848* ("The Centennial History of Illinois," Vol. II.) Springfield: Illinois Centennial Commission, 1918.

PECK, JOHN MASON. *A Gazetter of Illinois, in Three Parts*. Jacksonville: R. Goudy, 1834.

———. *Memoir of John Mason Peck*. Edited from his Journals and Correspondence by Rufus Babcock. Philadelphia, 1864.

PIERCE, BESSIE LOUISE. *A History of Chicago. 1673–1848*, Vol. I. New York: A. A. Knopf, 1937.

PUTNAM, JAMES W. *Illinois and Michigan Canal: A Study in Economic History*. ("Chicago Historical Society's Collection," Vol. 10.) 1917.

REYNOLDS, JOHN. *My Own Times, Embracing also the History of My Life*. Belleville: B. H. Perryman and H. L. Davison, 1855.

———. *The Pioneer History of Illinois*. Chicago: Fergus Printing Co., 1887.

ROSS, HARVEY LEE. *The Early Pioneers and Pioneer Events of the State of Illinois* (Including personal recollections of the author; of Abraham Lincoln, Andrew Jackson and Peter Cartwright.) Chicago: Eastman Brothers, 1899.

SCOTT-THOMSON, GADYS. *A Pioneer Family: The Birkbecks in Illinois*. London, 1953. Letters written to English relatives.

THE ERA OF THE CIVIL WAR, 1848–70

ACKERMAN, WILLIAM K. *Early Illinois Railroads*. ("Fergus Historical Series," No. 23.) Chicago, 1884.

Bibliography 307

BROWN, D. A. *The Grierson Raid*. Urbana: University of Illinois Press, 1954.

CARRIEL, MARY TURNER. *The Life of Jonathan Baldwin Turner*. Urbana: University of Illinois Press, 1961.

CATTON, BRUCE. *Grant Moves South*. Boston: Little, Brown, 1960.

COLE, ARTHUR C. *The Era of the Civil War, 1848–1870*. ("The Centennial History of Illinois," Vol. 3.) Chicago: A. C. McClurg & Co., 1918–20.

DICKERSON, OLIVER M. *The Illinois Constitutional Convention of 1862*. Urbana: University of Illinois Press, 1905.

DILLON, MERTON L. *Elijah P. Lovejoy, Abolitionist Editor*. Urbana: University of Illinois Press, 1961.

GATES, PAUL W. *The Illinois Central Railroad and Its Colonization Work*. Cambridge: Harvard University Press, 1934.

GILL, JOHN. *Tide without Turning: Elijah P. Lovejoy and Freedom of the Press*. Boston: Starr King Press, 1958.

HARRIS, NORMAN D. *History of Negro Slavery in Illinois and of the Slavery Agitation in that State*. Chicago, 1906.

JOHNSON, ALLEN. *Stephen A. Douglas: A Study in American Politics*. New York: Macmillan Co., 1908.

JOHANNSEN, ROBERT. *The Letters of Stephen A. Douglas*. Urbana: University of Illinois Press, 1961.

KING, WILLARD. *Lincoln's Manager, David Davis*. Cambridge: Harvard University Press, 1960.

LEE, JUDSON FISKE. "Transportation: A Factor in the Development of Northern Illinois Previous to 1860." *Journal of the Illinois State Historical Society*, April, 1917, pp. 17–85.

LEWIS, LLOYD. *Captain Sam Grant*. Boston: Little, Brown, 1950.

MILTON, GEORGE FORT. *The Eve of Conflict: Stephen A. Douglas and the Needless War*. Boston: Houghton Mifflin Co., 1934.

PEASE, THEODORE C. and RANDALL, JAMES G. (eds.). *The Diary of Orville Hickman Browning, 1830–1881*. ("Illinois Historical Collections," Vols. 20 and 22.) Springfield, 1927, 1933.

PIERCE, BESSIE L. *A History of Chicago, 1848–1871*. Vol. II. New York: A. A. Knopf, 1937.

RANDALL, JAMES G. *Lincoln the President*. 4 vols. New York: Dodd, Mead, 1945–55. (Richard N. Current is co-author of Volume 4.)

RANDALL, JAMES G., and DONALD, DAVID. *The Divided Union*. Boston: D. C. Heath and Co., 1937. (Based on James G. Randall's *The Civil War and Reconstruction*, published in 1937.)

Report, 1861–1866. 9 vols. Adjutant General of Illinois. Springfield, 1900–1902. Contains histories and rosters of all military units organized in Illinois during the Civil War; volume 9 contains rosters for units for the Black Hawk, Mexican, and Spanish-American wars.

SPARKS, E. E. (ed.). *The Lincoln-Douglas Debates of 1858.* ("Illinois Historical Collections," Vol. 3.) Springfield, 1908.

THOMAS, BENJAMIN. *Abraham Lincoln, a Biography.* New York: Knopf, 1952.

GROWTH AND DEVELOPMENT, 1870–1914

ADDAMS, JANE. *Twenty Years at Hull House.* New York: Macmillan Co., 1910.

ANTHONY, ELLIOT. *Constitutional History of Illinois.* Chicago: Chicago Legal News Print, 1891.

BARNARD, HARRY. *"Eagle Forgotten": the Life of John Peter Altgeld.* Indianapolis, 1938.

BECKNER, EARL R. *A History of Labor Legislation in Illinois.* Chicago, 1929.

BOGART, ERNEST L., and MATHEWS, JOHN M. *The Modern Commonwealth, 1893–1918.* ("Centennial History of Illinois," Vol. 5.) Springfield: Illinois Centennial Commission, 1920.

BOGART, ERNEST L., and THOMPSON, CHARLES M. *The Industrial State, 1870–1893.* ("Centennial History of Illinois," Vol. 4.) Springfield: Illinois Centennial Commission, 1920.

BOGUE, MARGARET BEATTIE. *Patterns from the Sod.* ("Collections of the Illinois State Historical Library," Vol. 34.) Springfield: 1959.

BUCK, SOLON J. *The Granger Movement: A Study in Agricultural Organization.* Lincoln: University of Nebraska, 1963.

———. *Agrarian Crusade, a Chronicle of the Farmer in Politics.* New Haven: Yale University Press, 1920.

CAVANAUGH, HELEN. *Seed, Soil and Science: The Story of Eugene D. Funk.* Chicago: Lakeside Press, 1959.

COOK, JOHN WILLISTON. *Educational History of Illinois.* Chicago: Henry O. Shepherd Co., 1912.

DAVID, HENRY. *The History of the Haymarket Affair.* New York: Farrar & Rinehart, 1936.

Debates and Proceedings of the Constitutional Convention of the State of Illinois, convened at the city of Springfield, Tuesday, Dec. 13, 1869. 2 vols. Illinois Constitutional Convention. Springfield: E. L. Merritt & Brothers, 1870.

GOODSPEED, THOMAS WAKEFIELD. *Story of the University of Chicago.* Chicago: University of Chicago Press, 1925.

HUTCHINSON, WILLIAM T. *Cyrus Hall McCormick.* 2 vols. New York: Century Co., 1930–35.

LINDSEY, ALMONT. *The Pullman Strike.* Chicago: University of Chicago Press, 1942.

LINN, JAMES WEBER. *Jane Addams: A Biography.* New York: D. Appleton-Century Co., 1935.

MANNING, THOMAS G. (ed.). *The Chicago Strike of 1894: Industrial Labor in the Nineteenth Century.* New York: Holt, 1960.

NEVINS, ALLAN. *Illinois.* ("American College and University Series.") New York: Oxford University Press, 1917.

NEWCOMB, REXFORD. *Architecture of the Old Northwest Territory.* Chicago: University of Chicago Press, 1950.

PALMER, GEORGE T. *A Conscientious Turncoat: The Story of John M. Palmer, 1817–1900.* New Haven: Yale University Press, 1917.

PIERCE, BESSIE L. *History of Chicago, 1871–1893.* Vol. III, New York, 1957.

SCOTT, ROY V. *The Agrarian Movement in Illinois, 1880–1896.* Urbana: University of Illinois Press, 1962.

STALEY, ALVAH EUGENE. *History of Illinois State Federation of Labor.* Chicago: University of Chicago Press, 1930.

TALLMADGE, THOMAS E. *Architecture in Old Chicago.* Chicago: University of Chicago Press, 1941.

WARD, ESTELLE FRANCES. *Story of Northwestern University.* New York: Dodd, Mead and Co., 1924.

WHITE, HORACE. *The Life of Lyman Trumbull.* Boston: Houghton Mifflin Co., 1913.

THE FIRST WORLD WAR

Blue Book of Illinois 1919–1920. Contains articles on the State's war participation by Adjutant General Frank S. Dickson, "Military Achievements of Illinois in the World War," and others.

The Centennial of the State of Illinois: Report of the Centennial Commission. Illinois Centennial Commission. Springfield, 1920.

Final Report of the Illinois State Council of Defense, 1917–1918–1919. Illinois State Council of Defense. Chicago, 1919.

Final Report, 1917–1919. Woman's Committee, Illinois State Council of Defense. Chicago, 1919.

HUIDEKOPER, FREDERICK L. *History of the Thirty-third Division. A.E.F.* 3 vols. and a portfolio of maps. *Illinois in the World War.* Ed. by T. C. PEASE. Vols. 1–4. Springfield: Illinois State Historical Library, 1921.

HUTCHINSON, WILLIAM T. *Lowden of Illinois: The Life of Governor Frank O. Lowden.* 2 vols. Chicago: University of Chicago Press, 1957.

Illinois: First Administrative Report of the Director of Departments under the Civil Administrative Code, Together with the Adjutant General's Report. July 1, 1917, to June 30, 1918. Springfield, 1918.

JENISON, MARGUERITE E. *The War-Time Organization of Illinois: Illinois in the World War.* Vol. 5. Springfield: Illinois State Historical Library, 1923. Contains a full bibliography.

THE DEPRESSION, WORLD WAR II, AND THE KOREAN WAR

GLICK, FRANK G. *The Illinois Emergency Relief Commission.* Chicago: University of Chicago Press, 1940.

HAVIGHURST R. J., and MORGAN, H. G. *The Social History of a War-Boom Community.* New York: Longmans, Green, 1951.

Historical Lineage, Illinois National Guard, Illinois Naval Militia. Illinois Military and Naval Department. July 1, 1953.

Illinois War Council, 1941–1945; Organization, Procedure and Recommendations: Final Report of the Executive Director. Illinois War Council. June 22, 1945.

KLEBER, VICTOR. *Selective Service in Illinois, 1940–1947.* Chicago: Printed by authority of the State of Illinois, 1949.

Monthly Bulletin. Illinois Emergency Relief Commission, later Illinois Public Aid Commission. Chicago, 1933–41.

NEWELL, BARBARA W. *Chicago and the Labor Movement. Metropolitan Unionism in the 1930's.* Urbana: University of Illinois Press, 1961.

WATTERS, MARY. *Illinois in the Second World War.* 2 vols. Springfield: Illinois State Historical Library, 1951–52.

SOCIAL AND ECONOMIC DEVELOPMENT

ALDRICH, S. R. *Illinois Field Crops and Soils.* Urbana: University of Illinois; Agricultural Extension Service *Circular* 901. January, 1965.

ANGLE, PAUL. *Bloody Williamson: A Chapter in American Lawlessness.* New York: Knopf. 1952.

Architectural Forum. Chicago issue, May, 1962.

Basic Policies for the Comprehensive Plan of Chicago. Chicago Department of City of Planning. August, 1964.

BELL, A. H., *et al. Petroleum Industry in Illinois in 1962.* Urbana: Illinois State Geological Survey. ("Illinois Petroleum Series," No. 77.) 1963.

BROWN, MALCOLM, and WEBB, JOHN N. *Seven Stranded Coal Towns.* Washington: U.S. Government Printing Office, 1941.

BUSCH, W. L. *Mineral Production in Illinois in 1963. Circular 374.* Urbana: Illinois State Geological Survey, 1964.

COLBY, CHARLES C. *Pilot Study of Southern Illinois.* Carbondale: Southern Illinois University Press, 1956.

CONDIT, CARL W. *The Chicago School of Architecture: A History of Commercial and Public Buildings in the Chicago Area, 1875–1925.* Chicago: University of Chicago Press, 1964.

Current Economic Comment (name changed from *Opinion and Comment,* 1949). Quarterly Publication of Bureau of Economic and Business Research, College of Commerce. University of Illinois. Discontinued November, 1960.

DUFFEY, BERNARD I. *Chicago Renaissance in American Letters: A Critical History.* East Lansing: Michigan State University Press, 1957.

DUNBAR, OLIVIA HOWARD. *A House in Chicago.* Chicago: University of Chicago Press, 1947.

FOLSE, C. L. *Changes in Illinois Population by Counties through Natural Increase and Migration, 1940 to 1950.* Urbana: University of Illinois; Department of Agricultural Economics, College of Agriculture; August, 1955.

———. *Illinois Population Highlights from 1960 Census.* Urbana: University of Illinois; Department of Agricultural Economics, College of Agriculture; January 1, 1962.

Illinois Business Review. A monthly review of business conditions for Illinois. Bureau of Economic and Business Research. Urbana: University of Illinois, 1955–64.

Illinois Division of Industrial Planning and Development and other state agencies. *Atlas of Illinois Resources,* Sections 1 to 6: 1. *Water Resources and Climate,* November, 1958; 2. *Mineral Resources,* June, 1959; 3. *Forest, Wildlife and Recreational Resources,* January, 1960; 4. *Transportation,* June, 1960; 5. *Manpower,* May, 1963; 6. *Agriculture in the Illinois Economy,* November, 1962.

LEIGHTON, M. M. *Illinois Resources—an Atlas.* Illinois Post-War Planning Commission. March, 1946.

LEWIS, LLOYD, and SMITH, HENRY JUSTIN. *Chicago: The History of Its Reputation.* New York: Harcourt, Brace and Co., 1929.

MAYER, HAROLD M. *The Port of Chicago and the St. Lawrence Seaway.* Chicago: University of Chicago Press, 1957.

A Provisional Master Plan. Springfield: Illinois Board of Higher Education, 1964.

Report. Springfield: Governor's Committee on Unemployment. January, 1963.

Reports. Nos. 1–6. Springfield: Illinois School Problems Commission. 1951–61.

ROSS, R. C., and CASE, H. C. M. *Types of Farming in Illinois: An Analysis of Differences by Areas.* Urbana: University of Illinois Agricultural Extension Service *Bulletin* 601. April, 1956.

SCAMEHORN, HOWARD L. *Balloons to Jets: A Century of Aeronautics in Illinois, 1855–1955.* Chicago: H. Regnery Co., 1957.

The St. Lawrence Seaway: Its Impact by 1965 upon Industry of Metropolitan Illinois—Illinois Waterways Associated Areas. 2 vols. Chicago: Association of Commerce and Industry.

Southern Illinois: Resources and Potentials of the Sixteen Southernmost Counties. Executive Committee of Southern Illinois. Urbana: University of Illinois Press, 1949.

UNITED STATES BUREAU OF THE CENSUS, DEPARTMENT OF COMMERCE. *Census of Agriculture,* 1959; *Census of Housing,* 1960; *Census of Manufactures,* 1958; *Annual Survey of Manufactures,* 1942; *Census of Population,* Vol. 1, Part 1; *Characteristics of Population; Part 15, Illinois; Congressional District Data Book* (Eighty-eighth Congress), 1963.

WAGENKNECHT, EDWARD. *Chicago*. Norman: University of Oklahoma Press, 1964.

WAKELY, ROY E. (1) *Population Changes and Prospects in Southern Illinois*. (2) *Growth and Decline of Towns and Cities in Southern Illinois*. (3) *Types of Rural and Urban Community Centers in Southern Illinois*. Carbondale: Southern Illinois University.

Where Two Great Waterways Meet: First Biennial Report. Chicago Regional Port District Board. February, 1953.

WILLOUGHBY, WILLIAM R. *The St. Lawrence Waterway*. Madison: University of Wisconsin Press, 1961.

ADMINISTRATION AND POLITICS

The Book of the States. 1964–1965. Chicago: Council of State Governments and the American Legislators' Association, 1964.

Counties of Illinois: Their Origin and Evolution. With 23 maps showing the original and present boundary lines of each county of the state. Numerous printings since inaugurated by James Rose in 1906. Springfield: Illinois Secretary of State.

DUE, JOHN. *State Sales Tax Administration*. Chicago: Public Administration Service, 1963.

FISHER, GLENN W. *Financing Illinois State Government: A Report of the Institute of Government and Public Affairs*. Urbana: University of Illinois Press, 1960.

GARVEY, NEIL F. *The Government and Administration of Illinois*. New York: Crowell, 1958.

Illinois Blue Book. Published biennially by the Secretary of State of Illinois. A one-volume (1,005 pages) source of information on Illinois state and local government. (1963–64.)

Illinois Government. Urbana: University of Illinois; Institute of Government and Public Affairs, Nos. 1–20, 1959–64.

LOHMANN, KARL. *Cities and Towns of Illinois—a Handbook of Community Facts*. Urbana: University of Illinois Press, 1951.

MERRIAM, CHARLES E. *Chicago: A More Intimate View of Urban Politics*. New York: Macmillan Co., 1929.

MONYPENNY, PHILLIP. *The Impact of Federal Grants in Illinois*. Urbana: University of Illinois Institute of Government and Public Affairs, 1958.

Organization and Functioning of the State Government: Report to the General Assembly. Springfield: Illinois Commission to Study State Government, 1950.

Report. Springfield: Illinois Efficiency and Economy Committee, 1916.

Report of the Commission on Revenue of the State of Illinois. Springfield: Illinois Commission on Revenue, 1963.

SNIDER, CLYDE F., and HOWARDS, IRVING. *County Government in Illinois.* Carbondale: Southern Illinois University Press, 1960.

STEINER, GILBERT Y., and GOVE, SAMUEL K. *Legislative Politics in Illinois.* Urbana: University of Illinois Press, 1960.

VERLIE, E. J. (ed.). *Illinois Constitutions.* ("Illinois Historical Collections," Vol. 13.) Springfield, 1919.

ZEIGLER, MRS. GEORGE B. (ed.). *Illinois Voters' Handbook, 1962.* Chicago: League of Women Voters of Illinois, 1962.

Index